Directing Youth Sports Programs

Rainer Martens

American Sport Education Program

Human Kinetics

Library of Congress Cataloging-in-Publication Data

Martens, Rainer, 1942-
    Directing youth sports programs / Rainer Martens.
        p. cm.
    ISBN 0-7360-3696-2
        1. Sports for children--Coaching.   I. Title.
    GV709.24 .M37   2001
    796'.06'9--dc21

                                                            2001024447

ISBN-10: 0-7360-3696-2
ISBN-13: 978-0-7360-3696-2

Acquisitions Editor: Karen Decker; **Managing Editor**: Wendy McLaughlin; **Assistant Editor**: John Wentworth; **Copyeditor**: Jackie Blakely; **Proofreader**: Sue Fetters; **Permission Manager**: Toni Harte; **Graphic Designer**: Nancy Rasmus; **Graphic Artist**: Sandra Meier; **Photo Manager**: Gayle Garrison; **Cover Designer**: Jack W. Davis; **Photographer (cover)**: Tom Roberts; **Photographer (interior)**: pages 33, 170 © Karen Decker; page 148 © Kari Cornelius; all other photos by Tom Roberts, unless otherwise noted; **Printer**: United Graphics

Copies of this book are available at special discounts for bulk purchase for sales promotions, premiums, fund-raising, or educational use. Special editions or book excerpts can also be created to specifications. For details, contact the Special Sales Manager at Human Kinetics.

Printed in the United States of America   20   19   18   17   16   15   14   13   12

The paper in this book is certified under a sustainable forestry program.

Human Kinetics
Website: www.HumanKinetics.com

United States: Human Kinetics, P.O. Box 5076, Champaign, IL 61825-5076
800-747-4457
email: humank@hkusa.com

Canada: Human Kinetics, 475 Devonshire Road Unit 100, Windsor, ON N8Y 2L5
800-465-7301 (in Canada only)
email: info@hkcanada.com

Europe: Human Kinetics, 107 Bradford Road, Stanningley, Leeds LS28 6 AT, United Kingdom
+44 (0) 113 255 5665
email: hk@hkeurope.com

Australia: Human Kinetics, 57A Price Avenue, Lower Mitcham, South Australia 5062
08 8372 0999
e-mail: info@hkaustralia.com

New Zealand: Human Kinetics, P.O. Box 80, Torrens Park, South Australia 5062
0800 222 062
e-mail: info@hknewzealand.com

contents

preface

Most youth sport program directors receive little formal preparation for fulfilling the duties of their position, and what formal education they do receive is often quite general. Few youth sports administrators have the opportunity to systematically think through a program philosophy and develop policies that articulate that philosophy.

Directing Youth Sports Programs not only will help you as a sport administrator to develop a sound program philosophy and compatible policies, it contains a wealth of other practical information. This book will help you develop a comprehensive system for recruiting, selecting, educating, and evaluating coaches. It gives you a step-by-step plan for involving parents using American Sport Education Program's (ASEP) SportParent program, which will help you make youth sport a *family affair.*

Directing Youth Sports Programs also addresses the issue of risk management with a straightforward, functional approach. You will be guided through the process of evaluating the risk in your program and offered recommendations on how to reduce or eliminate these risks. You will also learn what your insurance needs really are.

This text helps with your financial management responsibilities. You will learn how to increase your program income through special event fundraising and commercial sponsorships. And you will find practical help with setting up a budget and financial recordkeeping.

Directing Youth Sports Programs's last chapter, Managing Events, begins by having you evaluate your own management skills, because the key to good management is *you*—the manager. Then you will discover a very useful Sport Event Planner, an indispensable tool that will guide you through the process of planning youth sport events.

Directing Youth Sports Programs is not an A to Z compendium on how to be a youth sport director. I've selected key topics that youth sport administrators have told me they would like more information about. Throughout the book you will find a series of practical exercises and forms to help you with your administrative work. I invite you to copy and use the forms, a copy of which you'll find at the end of each respective chapter.

This text is the resource for the American Sport Education Program's Sport Administrators Course within the Volunteer Education Program. ASEP has spent more than 20 years developing resources and educational programs to help youth sport administrators offer quality sport experiences to our youth. I hope you find that *Directing Youth Sports Programs* fulfills that objective. I invite you to write ASEP with your advice on how I can improve this guide for future editions.

I would like to thank Karen Decker for her assistance in preparing the second edition of this text.

Rainer Martens
2001

Your Program Philosophy

Every day, you make numerous decisions about your youth sport program based on principles that you value. These principles, or beliefs, are derived from your life experience, and they form the pillars of your program philosophy. You may be quite aware of these principles, or they may be more subconscious. In chapter 1, we have three objectives:

1. To help you refine your program philosophy and, if it operates more subconsciously, bring it to a conscious level so that you can better examine it
2. To examine your leadership style and help you determine whether it is compatible with your program philosophy
3. To provide you an opportunity to use your program philosophy to develop specific program policies

Importance of Your Program Philosophy

Don't worry—this chapter is not a bunch of mumbo-jumbo irrelevant to the day-to-day administration of a youth sport program. On the contrary, we hope to show you that a well-developed program philosophy will be your best companion in administering an outstanding youth sport program.

Philosophy Defined

Philosophy refers to the pursuit of wisdom. Your philosophy is the system of principles that gives you direction in answering questions about what, why, and how. These principles represent what you value.

We all have philosophies about many things. Your most important philosophy concerns your beliefs about what you value in life and what type of person you strive to be. When you played a sport, you had a philosophy about playing that sport; when you coached, you had a philosophy about coaching. And now, as a director of a youth sport program, you have a philosophy about your program.

As we proceed in this chapter, we'll challenge you to think about your program philosophy. Remember that each person has a right to his own philosophy, as long as its principles are in accord with the legal and moral codes of our society.

Program Philosophy

Your program philosophy consists of principles that serve as your guide to administering the program, helping you make daily decisions. Some of your principles are likely to be well-developed convictions, whereas others are less defined.

As you administer your program, these formative principles will be tested when you confront situations in which you are uncertain about the best way to respond. When you do respond, you will evaluate the consequences of your actions against your principles. If your self-evaluation is favorable, it will strengthen your principles. If the evaluation is unfavorable, and repeatedly so, you will likely modify your principles.

Developing a Program Philosophy

Developing a program philosophy involves three major tasks:

1. Determining the objectives you and the leaders of your organization would like to achieve with your youth sport program
2. Establishing the principles you want to use to guide you and your staff in managing your program
3. Using these principles to form a set of coherent policies

As you can appreciate, your program philosophy is not solely yours. It needs to be the philosophy of the organization for which you administer the youth sport program. Your organization may or may not have a well-developed program philosophy. If it does, then your challenge is to implement policies based on this philosophy. (We'll look at the challenge of doing this later in this chapter.) If your organization does not have a well-developed program philosophy, you need to help create one.

To develop a program philosophy for your organization, bring together the organization's

As you develop your program's philosophy, consider every member and element as a single unit working toward the same goals.

leaders and jointly develop the objectives and principles you want to follow. The content of this chapter will help you do this. We'll begin by considering the objectives you would like to achieve with your program.

Objectives of Youth Sport Programs

What do you and your organization expect the sport experience to do for young people? Do you know? Have the objectives of your youth sport program been written down? Have you discussed the objectives with the leaders of your organization, or are the objectives implicit?

Perhaps you feel that the objectives of youth sport programs are obvious. Everyone knows what they are, so they don't need to be stated. You may think the objectives could be summed up this way: "We offer youth sport programs to young people to have fun, to learn the sports of our culture, and to become physically fit."

Yet often there is greater consensus about the spoken objectives than the practiced objectives. Almost all youth sport directors agree that

sport programs ought to help young people develop physically, psychologically, and socially. They also agree that sport participation should help prepare young people to become responsible, independent, contributing members of society. Unfortunately, these spoken objectives are not always the ones pursued in the day-to-day operation of a program.

The discrepancy between what is said and what is actually done in a program most often occurs because the program's objectives are vague and the program director does not develop policies or, in daily operations, make the kind of decisions that lead to meeting the program's objectives. Even when administrators do have clear objectives they sometimes do not develop and enforce policies that are consistent with them. For example, administrators may claim to be committed to an "everybody plays" principle, but they fail both to develop the necessary program policies and to educate coaches about the value of such a principle and how to implement it.

Our first exercise allows you to take a close look at how you view your program's objectives.

Establishing Your Program's Objectives

Exercise 1.1 includes an extensive list of commonly recognized objectives for youth sport programs. Rate each objective by circling the number that best corresponds to your opinion about how important this objective is to you.

We are looking here for your personal opinion, not necessarily that of your organization. As you rate the importance of these objectives, keep in mind your position on the issues presented in exercise 1.1. We'll come back to them in exercise 1.4.

	Not important at all		Somewhat important		Highly important
1. To develop physical skills such as coordination, speed, and balance in young people.	1	2	3	4	5
2. To develop leadership skills in young people.	1	2	3	4	5
3. To improve physical fitness through sport participation.	1	2	3	4	5
4. To help children develop positive self-concepts.	1	2	3	4	5
5. To entertain the parents of the participants.	1	2	3	4	5
6. To encourage lifetime participation in sports by teaching the basic skills early and providing a positive experience.	1	2	3	4	5
7. To provide an opportunity for the entire family to be involved.	1	2	3	4	5
8. To provide the better youth athletes an opportunity to move on to higher levels of sport.	1	2	3	4	5
9. To provide safe, enjoyable recreation for young people.	1	2	3	4	5
10. To develop self-responsibility in young athletes.	1	2	3	4	5
11. To achieve by winning games.	1	2	3	4	5
12. To learn sportsmanship so young people develop morally.	1	2	3	4	5
13. To teach children the sports of our culture.	1	2	3	4	5
14. To teach children how to compete and cooperate.	1	2	3	4	5
15. To develop a young person's motive to achieve and the desire to strive for excellence.	1	2	3	4	5

In the spaces below, list any other objectives you want to consider and indicate how important each is to you.

16. _____	1	2	3	4	5
17. _____	1	2	3	4	5
18. _____	1	2	3	4	5

If you are like most youth sport administrators, you've rated many of the objectives in exercise 1.1 as Highly Important or Somewhat Important. It is, of course, difficult to give all these objectives equal emphasis in your program. So let's continue to examine your program philosophy and see which of the objectives are your priorities.

Exercise 1.2 revisits the program objectives listed in exercise 1.1 and asks you to prioritize their importance to you. Completing this exercise will give you a clearer perspective on which program objectives you feel are the most important for you to achieve.

Now look at the rankings in exercise 1.2 and think about your current youth sport program. Is your program organized and operated to achieve the objectives that you've ranked as more important?

Active vs. Passive Objectives

Let's look at these objectives again in a different light. How many of them do you actively pursue? How many are passive outcomes that you hope for but do not actively pursue? To "actively pursue" means that you take specific planned action in your program to see that this objective is met. Complete exercise 1.3 to determine which objectives you actively pursue.

Youth sport administrators recognize that many of their objectives are outcomes for which they do not actively program. Although some of your program participants might be meeting

Exercise 1.2 Prioritizing Your Program's Objectives

Below there are 15 objectives listed in exercise 1.1 with space for you to include up to three other objectives if you added any. Go through the list and rank the objectives in priority of importance to you. Ask yourself: If I could achieve only one objective, which would it be? Put a "1" on the line next to that objective. Then put a "2" next to the objective you consider the second most important and so on.

_____ Develop physical skills

_____ Develop leadership skills

_____ Develop physical fitness

_____ Develop self-concept

_____ Entertain parents

_____ Encourage lifetime participation

_____ Opportunity for family involvement

_____ Provide a feeder system

_____ Provide safe, enjoyable recreation

_____ Develop self-responsibility

_____ Win games

_____ Learn sportsmanship

_____ Teach sports of our culture

_____ Learn how to compete and cooperate

_____ Develop motive to achieve

_____ _____

_____ _____

_____ _____

Exercise 1.3	Pursuing Your Program's Objectives

For each of the 15 objectives listed in exercise 1.2, circle **Active** if you actively pursue this objective in your program and **Passive** if this is an objective that you hope occurs but for which you do not actively program. If you added any objectives to exercise 1.2, there is space for them at the end of this exercise.

Active   Passive   Develop physical skills

Active   Passive   Develop leadership skills

Active   Passive   Develop physical fitness

Active   Passive   Develop self-concept

Active   Passive   Entertain parents

Active   Passive   Encourage lifetime participation

Active   Passive   Opportunity for family involvement

Active   Passive   Provide a feeder system

Active   Passive   Provide safe, enjoyable recreation

Active   Passive   Develop self-responsibility

Active   Passive   Win games

Active   Passive   Learn sportsmanship

Active   Passive   Teach sports of our culture

Active   Passive   Learn how to complete and cooperate

Active   Passive   Develop motive to achieve

Active   Passive   _____

Active   Passive   _____

Active   Passive   _____

these passive objectives as a result of their participation, ask yourself this: If this objective is important, can I do more to see that it is being consistently reached?

For example, if learning sportsmanship is an important objective of your program philosophy, do you

• offer training to coaches to provide them with specific ways to teach sportsmanship?

• have parent orientation programs that ask parents to be models of good sportsmanship and define what these behaviors are?

• help officials understand how to interpret the rules and provide guidance to athletes as to what is appropriate behavior?

Or do you hope good sportsmanship just happens? If it's the latter, you shouldn't expect to achieve much. If you do the former, learning sportsmanship is an objective of your program philosophy that you actively seek—and you deserve to be applauded for it!

Short-Term vs. Long-Term Objectives

Consider another perspective on these objectives. Some are short term and others are long term. The preeminent short-term objective of sport is to win. The prominent long-term objective is to help young athletes develop physically, psychologically, and socially. The short-term objective of winning is an objective of the contest, whereas helping athletes develop physically, psychologically, and socially is an objective of participation in sport.

We point out this difference because all too often coaches, parents, and athletes focus so much on the short-term objectives that they lose sight of the long-term objectives. It's easy to do, but don't let it happen to you. It's essential that you maintain perspective about the short-term goals of the contest and the long-term goals of participation. A strong program philosophy will help you do that.

Ask yourself this: How much emphasis are you giving in your program to achieving each of these types of objectives? Do you spend almost all of your time planning the program to achieve the short-term objectives, and then hope the long-term participation objectives just happen? Or do you develop program policies that strive to provide balance in achieving both short-term and long-term objectives? It's not an easy task.

Identifying Your Program Principles

Now you are clearer about the objectives you are pursuing with your youth sport program. Next we'll consider those broad principles you'll use to guide you in managing your program according to your objectives. In exercise 1.4 we'll examine several major issues in youth sport, most of which you probably have a position on. This position, whether well developed or vaguely formulated, is the basis of a philosophical principle. Remember, principles are predetermined modes of action or rules concerning how you'll make judgments that become policies, and policies are plans or courses of action adopted by you or your organization.

Setting solid policies is important for the safety of everyone participating in your program.

Identifying the Principles of Your Program's Philosophy

The purpose of exercise 1.4 is to have you think about and articulate your position on nine key issues of vital importance to youth sport programs. We briefly describe each issue and then offer two positions at the opposite ends of the continuum for your comparison. Read the two views, and then decide what your position is. In the space provided, write out your own position that fits your program.

Issue #1: Athlete-Centered vs. Adult-Centered

The extent to which decisions are made about the program to meet the needs of young athletes versus those of the adults involved (you, your staff, coaches, and parents).

Position 1: The program is designed and run for young people. Every decision is made based on careful consideration of the needs of the athletes and without considering the needs of the adults involved.

Position 2: Although the program is for young people, it is made possible by the adults who organize and guide it. Thus, the program must meet the needs of the adults who have the maturity and experience to best plan the youth sport experience.

Your position:

_____

_____

_____

Issue #2: Recreations vs. Competition

The extent to which the program emphasizes playing sports primarily as recreation and with fun as a major objective versus an emphasis on competition to compare the physical skills of the participants in that particular sport.

Position 1: The program is primarily recreational, with competition de-emphasized. Fun, social interaction, and cooperation are more important than the development of excellent physical skills.

Position 2: The program emphasizes wholesome competition among children of similar abilities. Competition among children is viewed as positive, encouraging them to strive for excellence by making a commitment to master the challenges and physical skills of the sport.

Your position:

_____

_____

_____

Issue #3: Learning vs. Performing

The extent to which the program emphasizes the learning of skills through developmentally appropriate instruction versus an emphasis on the performance of these skills in competitive contests.

Position 1: The learning of sports skills in developmentally appropriate progressions is considered more important than performing theses skills in contests. Practices and contests are both viewed as learning opportunities.

Position 2: The program emphasizes children performing previously learned skills. Practices provide opportunities to learn skills for the purpose of performing these skills in contests.

Your position:

_____

_____

_____

Issue #4: Winning vs. Participation

The extent to which the program rewards the winning of contests and the benefits thereby derived versus rewarding participation in the sport and the associated benefits.

Position 1: Teaching young people to win—to pursue excellence—by committing themselves to mastering the skills of a sport is a unique contribution the program can make. The program wants to recognize those young people who demonstrate their mastery through winning.

Position 2: Whether athletes win or lose is far less important than their participation in the sport. Through participation they will not only have fun but will learn many valuable lessons that will benefit them throughout their lives. The program recognizes all young people who participate regardless of how much they win or lose.

Your position:

_____

_____

_____

Issue #5: Child-Only vs. Parent Involvement

The extent to which the program encourages parent involvement in the program versus discouraging parents from being involved.

Position 1: Parents are encouraged to be involved by helping to conduct the program. Too many forces already separate the family; youth sport programs should help bring the family together.

Position 2: Parents are discouraged from being actively involved because they are too emotional and tend to overemphasize winning. The program can provide children with a better sport experience without parent involvement.

Your position:

_____

_____

_____

Issue #6: Quantity vs. Quality

The extent to which the program emphasizes involving as many young people as possible in as many sports as the resources permit versus involving fewer young people in a smaller group of sports with greater emphasis on the quality of the participants' sport experience.

(continued)

Position 1: The program is committed to offering as many sport programs for different age groups, genders, and abilities as the resources permit. The more children involved in the program, the more successful the program.

Position 2: The program emphasizes ensuring that those involved have the best experience possible. The program would rather have fewer participants who gain more from sport than more participants who gain less from sport.

Your position:

_____

_____

_____

Issue #7: Ends vs. Means

The extent to which participation in the sport program by young athletes is viewed as an end in itself versus the view that such participation is a means for young people to develop physically, psychologically, and socially.

Position 1: Playing sport just to play the sport, for whatever reason the youngster wants to play, is the primary purpose for offering the program.

Position 2: Sport is an important institution for socializing young people to become productive members of society. The sport program is committed to teaching physical, psychological, and social skills through sport participation.

Your position:

_____

_____

_____

Issue #8: Shared Decision Making vs. Centralized Decision Making

The extent to which the other adults (coaches, parents, officials) involved in the program have input into formulating the program principles and policies versus these principles and policies being determined solely by the organization's leadership and program administrator.

Position 1: The program is offered for the participants and their families, and it should meet their needs. Involving them in developing program principles and policies will lead them to take greater ownership of the program and thus ensure that it meets their needs.

Position 2: Because the program administrator is given the responsibility to direct the program based on his or her qualifications, the principles and policies of the program will be set by the administrator along with the organization's leadership.

Your position:

_____

_____

_____

Issue #9: Sports for All vs. Sport for the Gifted

The extent to which the program should provide opportunities for children of different age levels, genders, and abilities versus a program to provide opportunities to those who are physically gifted or striving to be so.

Position 1: The program is designed to involve as many children as possible by offering the widest range of sports possible. Teams and contests are organized by age level or by ability and gender.

Position 2: The program is for those young people who want to develop their sports skills to the fullest. Just as schools have educational tracks for the mentally gifted, this program offers opportunities for the physically gifted.

Your position:

_____

_____

_____

What other issues do you think are important to establish principles for? Below we have provided space for you to add two issues of your own.

Issue:

_____

_____

_____

Description:

_____

_____

_____

Your position:

_____

_____

_____

Issue:

_____

_____

_____

(continued)

Description:

_____

_____

_____

Your position:

_____

_____

_____

The purpose of exercise 1.4 is to help you think through broad issues pertaining to the design and operation of your youth sport program. As you can see, these are tough issues, but determining your position on them is vital to your program philosophy. Continue to think about the issues in this exercise—to discuss them with fellow administrators, to read the professional literature addressing them, and, most important, to have your organization's leaders join you in formulating a set of principles you can all agree on.

Leadership Style

As a youth sport administrator, you not only influence the program objectives for your organization, you also play a vital role in determining how those objectives are achieved. These are issues that pertain to leadership, and in this section we look at your leadership style to see whether it is compatible with the principles and objectives you've indicated are important to you.

Leadership Defined

Leadership is knowing how to chart a course to give others direction by having a vision of what can be—and then developing the social and psychological environment to achieve the goals you have charted. _Leadership style_ refers to the way you typically approach the administration of your youth sport program. Administrators obviously differ in personality characteristics, such as optimism and pessimism, assertiveness and passiveness, cautiousness and boldness,

and rigidity and flexibility. Disposition has a strong influence on leadership style.

Autocratic and Democratic Styles

You're likely to be familiar with the two most widely recognized leadership styles—the _autocratic_ style and the _democratic_ style. The differences in these two styles as they pertain to youth sport administration are shown in table 1.1.

These two styles are typically considered dichotomous; you are either one or the other. But that's not necessarily the case. Most people possess qualities in degrees, rather than having all of one and none of the other. For example, even if you are autocratic, you are not necessarily also task-oriented. Thus, in exercise 1.5, an adaptation of Robert Blake and Anne Adams McCanse's well-known managerial grid, shows more realistic leadership styles that integrate both the autocratic and democratic styles.

This exercise will help you discover the strengths and weaknesses of your leadership style and focus on the areas that need improvement.

Table 1.1 Characteristics of Autocratic and Democratic Leadership Styles

Autocratic style	Democratic style
Outcome-centered	Athlete-centered
Command	Cooperative
Task-oriented	People-oriented

Evaluating Your Leadership Style

The purpose of exercise 1.5 is to help you evaluate your leadership style when administering your youth sport program. Begin by studying the leadership style grid below. The horizontal dimension evaluates how task-oriented you are, and the vertical dimension considers how people-oriented you are. The various types of managerial styles are numbered, with the degree of task orientation being the first number and the degree of people orientation being the second number. As you can see, a manager can be high in both orientations (9,9), low in both (1,1), high in one and low in another [(9,1) or (1,9)], or a mix of the two (5,5).

Now follow the three steps on page 14 as you study the grid.

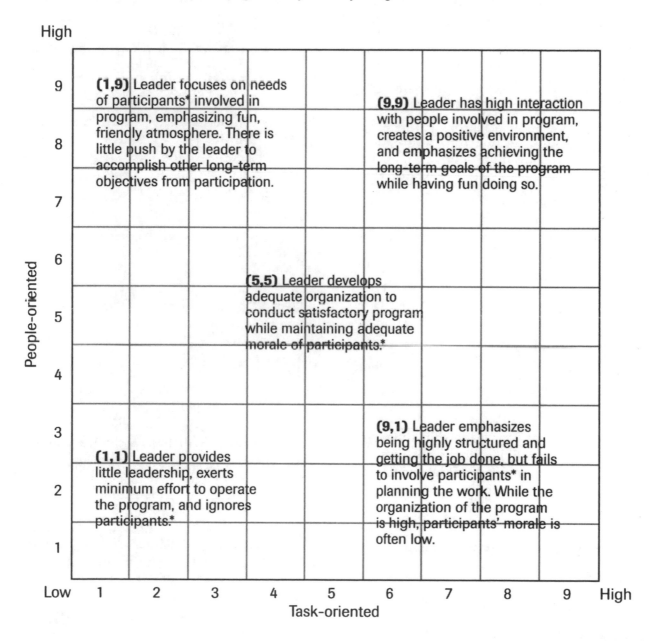

High

(1,9) Leader focuses on needs of participants* involved in program, emphasizing fun, friendly atmosphere. There is little push by the leader to accomplish other long-term objectives from participation.

(9,9) Leader has high interaction with people involved in program, creates a positive environment, and emphasizes achieving the long-term goals of the program while having fun doing so.

(5,5) Leader develops adequate organization to conduct satisfactory program while maintaining adequate morale of participants.*

(9,1) Leader emphasizes being highly structured and getting the job done, but fails to involve participants* in planning the work. While the organization of the program is high, participants' morale is often low.

(1,1) Leader provides little leadership, exerts minimum effort to operate the program, and ignores participants.*

People-oriented

Low   1   2   3   4   5   6   7   8   9   High

Task-oriented

Participants refers to the children, coaches, parents, and other adults involved in the program.

(continued)

1. Read the descriptions for each type of director. Then put your initials on the grid in the space that best represents your leadership style on these two dimensions.

2. Would your supervisor agree with your rating of yourself? Put an "S" where you think your supervisor would rate you.

3. How would the adults you supervise in your program rate you? Put an "A" in the grid that represents what you think they perceive your style to be.

Evaluating Your Leadership Style

The (9,9) leader is the ideal—a person with a flexible leadership style. This style is neither autocratic nor democratic, but a blend of the two that employs democratic or autocratic methods according to the particular situation. This style calls for both directing (even forcefully, when the situation demands it) and empowering staff and volunteers with responsibilities for achieving program objectives. The challenge for the (9,9) leader is to know when to use a more autocratic approach and when to use a more democratic approach. An essential ingredient for knowing which approach to use is a well-developed program philosophy.

Unfortunately, some administrators who have strong convictions about what objectives ought to be sought and how they ought to be obtained alienate the very people they are trying to serve because of their high task orientation and consequent disregard for the program participants. These are (9,1) leaders. They tend to think the program belongs to them and forget the participants.

Now think about whether your leadership style for administering your youth sport program is compatible with your objectives. Do you see some discrepancies? What can you do to make your leadership style and program objectives more compatible?

Personal Objectives

In this section we want you to consider your personal objectives as a youth sport administrator. So far you've been evaluating the program objectives, but what do you want to achieve personally by administering this program? Exercise 1.6 will help you evaluate your personal objectives and gain insight about why you perform at the level you do.

All these personal objectives are worthwhile as long as none becomes overly dominant. If gaining recognition becomes more important to you than achieving the program objectives, you're likely to make decisions that put you ahead of the young athletes for whom the program is intended. If pleasing your supervisor is more important than feeling intrinsically satisfied with the job being done, you're not likely to be happy in this job.

Thus, as you refine your program philosophy, keep in mind your own personal reasons for performing this job. If these reasons are incompatible with the program philosophy, either you will be miserable doing the job or the program will be short-changed.

The ASEP Program Philosophy

The ASEP coaching philosophy is well known. It is succinctly expressed through the ASEP motto: *Athletes First, Winning Second*.

This motto means that every action adults take should be based first on what is best for young athletes, and second on what may improve the athletes' or team's chances of winning. It does *not* mean that winning—or, more accurately, striving to win—is unimportant. It simply means that winning should take a back seat to what is in the best interests of the young participants. Stated another way, the short-term objective of the contest—winning—should never override the long-term participation objectives of helping athletes develop physically, psychologically, and socially.

We urge you to adopt the ASEP philosophy as the cornerstone of your program philosophy. In this section, we'll interpret the philosophy further as it pertains to the administration of your youth sport program. Then we'll express our position on the nine issues in

Exercise 1.6   Evaluating Personal Objectives

Following are some common objectives that youth sport administrators have. Evaluate the importance of each objective by rating it on a 5-point scale as shown. Circle the number that corresponds best to your opinion about how important each objective is to you. Use the space at the end to list and rate any additional objectives.

1	2	3	4	5
Not at all important		Somewhat important		Highly important

	1	2	3	4	5
1. To satisfy my supervisor	1	2	3	4	5
2. To be promoted	1	2	3	4	5
3. To satisfy the staff and volunteers	1	2	3	4	5
4. To achieve the program objectives	1	2	3	4	5
5. To increase my salary	1	2	3	4	5
6. To feel intrinsically satisfied	1	2	3	4	5
7. To gain recognition in the community	1	2	3	4	5
8. _____	1	2	3	4	5
9. _____	1	2	3	4	5
10. _____	1	2	3	4	5

exercise 1.4 before concluding by considering the Bill of Rights for Young Athletes.

ASEP Philosophy Interpreted

The ASEP philosophy encourages the pursuit of both short- and long-term program objectives. Designing the program to help athletes learn sports skills to maximize their opportunity to win is a worthwhile goal. It is well established that young people obtain many benefits by making a commitment to try to win—to strive for excellence—as long as this pursuit is kept in its proper perspective. Coaches should know as much as possible about teaching the skills and strategies of the sport. They should be skillful at organizing practices and contests that enable their athletes to compete at their highest potential level.

But sport should do much more than just help athletes win and have fun. Sport is one of

society's significant institutions for helping young people become better human beings—for helping them develop physically, psychologically, and socially. If, as a program administrator, you subscribe to this program philosophy, it is your task to see that these objectives are sought actively rather than passively. It is your task to engineer the program to obtain these participation objectives.

ASEP's Position on Key Program Principles

In exercise 1.4 we identified nine key issues of a program philosophy and provided you with examples of two differing positions on these issues. You were then asked to determine your own position. Earlier in this chapter, you examined your program objectives in exercise 1.1; then, in exercises 1.5 and 1.6, you evaluated your leadership style and personal objectives as steps toward further development of your program philosophy. Now we would like to share with you our response to the nine key issues in exercise 1.4 so that you may compare our position with yours.

Issue #1: Athlete-Centered vs. Adult-Centered

Youth sport programs should be designed and operated foremost for the purpose of meeting the needs of the athletes. Programs must guard against adult-imposed objectives that put the needs and wishes of adults ahead of the needs of children. However, adults (especially coaches and parents) play a vital role in helping to achieve the program objectives. Thus, a successful program must meet the needs and wishes of the participating adults without subjugating the best interests of the children.

Issue #2: Recreation vs. Competition

Children play sports for many reasons. Some play primarily for fun and to socialize with their friends; others find challenge in mastering the skills of sport and thrive on the competition. Thus, a well-balanced program should offer opportunities to meet the needs of both recreation-oriented and competition-oriented young athletes.

Issue #3: Learning vs. Performing

Many programs for young children provide too little opportunity to learn sports skills and then overemphasize performing these skills in contests. The learning of sports skills in developmentally appropriate progressions should be given priority over performing these skills in contests. For most children, contests should be approached as learning opportunities rather than as evaluations that reflect the self-worth of the child. However, as children mature and move into advanced skill programs, a greater emphasis on performance is appropriate.

Issue #4: Winning vs. Participation

Participation goals should always take priority over winning. Nevertheless, striving to win—not winning itself—should be encouraged as long as the pursuit of winning remains second-

ary to the participation objectives. Through the commitment to and pursuit of excellence, which is fueled by the motivation to win, your program can attain some of the long-term participation objectives.

Issue #5: Child-Only vs. Parent Involvement

We highly encourage parental involvement (Position 1 on page 9). It is a failure of the program when parental interference disrupts the program to the point that parents are denied the opportunity to share the youth sport experience with their children. Parent involvement is essential for maximizing the benefits of youth sport programs.

Issue #6: Quantity vs. Quality

The quantity–quality tradeoff is always a tough decision and is often best determined by the mandates of your specific organization. Consider not only your own organization's objectives, but those of the other programs available to children in your community. In general, ASEP's position is that it is better to offer the program to fewer participants and ensure that each has a safe and beneficial experience than to offer programs to more young people but sacrifice quality. Remember that mere participation in a sport program does not ensure that children will obtain the program's intended benefits; in fact, a poorly conducted program may harm them.

Issue #7: Ends vs. Means

Youth sport programs should have room for children who want nothing else from sport than to play for fun. Not every participant should be expected to pursue sport to become a gifted athlete or to make winning the highest priority. On the other hand, good youth sport programs should be designed to achieve other objectives as well. Youth sport programs are known to be important institutions for helping prepare young people to become responsible adults. Thus, youth sport programs should be an end for those children who wish nothing more, and at the same time be a means for helping children develop physically, psychologically, and socially.

Issue #8: Shared Decision Making vs. Centralized Decision Making

In making decisions about the conduct of the program, program administrators should involve parents, coaches, officials, and the young participants. In accord with the (9,9) leadership style (see page 14), the administrator needs to know when and how to involve others in the decision-making process. For some issues it is vital to solicit input and perhaps even obtain consensus from the participants in the program. Other situations call for decisions to be made by the leader alone.

Issue #9: Sport for All vs. Sport for the Gifted

Every community should provide the broadest range of sport programs possible for all members of the community in accordance with available resources. The objective of your program on this issue should be determined by the mandate of your organization and the other programs offered in your community. If your program is a community parks and recreation organization funded largely by tax dollars, then you should provide sport programs for as many children of diverse ability, age, and gender as your resources allow. On the other hand, if you are a private club in a community where other programs are primarily recreational, then the offering of sport programs for the gifted is applauded.

Bill of Rights for Young Athletes

In the late 1970s, a task force of the American Alliance for Health, Physical Education, Recreation and Dance developed the Bill of Rights for Young Athletes. This Bill of Rights, founded on the ASEP philosophy of Athletes First, Winning Second, is presented on page 18.

We hope you will do more than just read these rights. We encourage you to think about how you can help ensure that each athlete in your program retains them. As a youth sport administrator, you are a member of the helping professions, and your ultimate success as an administrator is measured by how much your program helps the children who participate.

From Principle to Policy

So far you've evaluated which objectives are important to you and given thought to the key principles that will guide you in managing your youth sport program. You've also considered your leadership style and how compatible it is with your objectives and principles. The next step in building your program philosophy is to develop specific policies for operating your program based on your objectives and principles. Remember, policies are specific plans, rules, or courses of action.

Using the structure of this chapter as your guide, develop a program policy manual divided into three parts:

- Program objectives
- Program principles
- Program policies

Before you begin developing your program policies, you'll need the leaders of your organization to agree on the program's objectives and principles. You will have your own views on what these objectives and principles should be, but it is essential that the program philosophy be the philosophy for the program, and not just for you. Take the initiative in developing a consensus among the leaders of your organization regarding the program philosophy. In the next section, we describe two approaches, either of which you may follow in helping your organization reach agreement on your program's objectives and principles.

Approach 1

With the appropriate people, follow a similar approach to the one you have taken in completing this chapter. These are the recommended steps:

1. Call a meeting of your organization's leaders and include members of the community, such as parents, coaches, and officials.
2. Discuss the need for a program philosophy with clearly stated objectives, principles, and policies.

BILL OF RIGHTS
FOR YOUNG ATHLETES

I Right to participate in sports

II Right to participate at a level commensurate with each child's maturity and ability

III Right to have qualified adult leadership

IV Right to play as a child and not as an adult

V Right of children to share in the leadership and decision making of their sport participation

VI Right to participate in safe and healthy environment

VII Right to proper preparation for participation in sports

VIII Right to an equal opportunity to strive for success

IX Right to be treated with dignity

X Right to have fun in sports

Figure 1.1 Bill of Rights for Young Athletes.

From Guidelines for Children's Sports by R. Martens and V. Seefeldt (Eds.), 1979, Reston, VA: AAHPERD. (D 1979 by AAHPERD. Reprinted by permission of the American Alliance for Health, Physical Education, Recreation and Dance, 1900 Association Dr., Reston, VA 22091.

3. Duplicate this chapter and ask each person to complete the exercises as a self-study activity. (You have permission to duplicate the chapter for this purpose.)

4. Call a second meeting. Using the structure and content of this chapter, agree on the program objectives and principles. (If your organization has not developed a well-established position on its objectives and the principles it will follow to achieve them, this step may take a while.)

5. Write down the program objectives and principles you've agreed on and share them with your organization's leaders.

Approach 2

If you think Approach 1 may be too time consuming or lead to disagreements that may not be easily resolved, you may want to use Approach 2, which provides more guidance. These are the steps:

1. Based on your study of this chapter, write down your recommended list of program objectives and principles. Use and adapt the content of this chapter as you deem appropriate.

2. At a meeting of the organization's leaders, present your program philosophy, including the objectives and principles. Ask them to review it.

3. After your organization's leaders have had adequate time to review the content of your program philosophy, call a special meeting of the group to discuss each item. Guide the group to accept, reject, or modify each of your objectives and principles. Also, give them an opportunity to add any objectives and principles. (Because this is your program philosophy, you may want someone else to guide the discussion so that you are in a better position to discuss the issues raised in your written program philosophy.)

4. Revise your program objectives and principles based on the decisions made by the group. Submit the final version to the organization's leaders.

Moving your program's principles into policies is the final step in creating and implementing a comprehensive youth sport program philosophy. Now that you have your organization's program philosophy in writing, you have the mandate you need to develop your program policies. Exercise 1.7 will help you develop these program policies.

Exercise 1.7   Developing Your Organization's Program Policies

The purpose of this exercise is to help you develop a coherent set of program policies that is consistent with your program objectives and principles. Your policies, of course, need to be specific to your situation. Thus, our approach will not be to state recommended policies but to outline key topics to provide a structure and to ask questions that should prompt you in formulating your policies. If we have overlooked any topic, feel free to add it to our list. Your goal is to develop a comprehensive and functional set of program policies.

Remember that your policies should be consistent with your objectives and principles. You should also ask yourself for each contemplated policy whether or not you need a program policy on this matter. For some issues you may decide it is best to let the coaches, parents, or officials decide on a case-by-case basis.

Your program policy document should be viewed as a "living" document. Do not view it as set in stone, never to be changed. Review your program philosophy and policies at least annually. You may see policies that are not working well and need to be changed. You may encounter events during the course of the year that make it clear a policy is needed.

(continued)

Program Policies Outline

I. Program Content

You will want policies on the types of sports to be included in your program as well as on the process for deciding which sports to include.

1. Which sports best meet your program objectives?

_____

2. Which sports, if any, are contrary to your objectives?

_____

3. Are boxing and kickboxing acceptable sports for your program?

_____

4. Are there other high-risk sports that you wish either to exclude or restrict?

_____

5. What are your policies regarding offering sports programs for different age groups, skill levels, disabilities, and genders?

_____

6. What is the process for considering requests to include or exclude various sports in your program?

_____

II. Athlete Participation Guidelines

Every program needs clear policies on who may and may not participate. Review your policies by considering these questions to see whether you've addressed all these issues.

1. How old do youngsters need to be to participate in each sport? What are the minimum and maximum ages for each sport and each level of play? Are school grade levels a better way than age to determine participant eligibility?

_____

2. Must athletes live in a particular area (such as a city or county) to be eligible to participate?

_____

3. Are boys and girls permitted to participate together in each sport and at each level of play?

_____

4. Should the size (weight and/or height) of the youngster determine eligibility to participate in a sport and the level of play?

_____

5. Should the skill level of the athlete determine eligibility to participate in a sport and the level of play?

_____

6. If a player is an early- or late-maturing child, do you have a policy for assigning him or her to a level of participation that is an exception to the age, gender, grade, or size eligibility requirements?

_____

7. Will you permit youths to participate on two teams within your program? Will you permit them to participate on a team within your program and one in some other organization's program?

_____

8. Will you permit youngsters to participate in two sports at the same time within your program? Will you permit them to participate in two sports at the same time, one within your program and one in another program?

_____

9. What are the fees, if any, to participate in each sport offered?

_____

10. What is your policy if the parents cannot afford to pay the participation fee?

_____

11. Should you have a policy regarding athletes' participation for those who are underachieving in school? If so, what is your policy?

_____

12. Do youngsters need a medical examination or medical clearance to participate?

_____

13. Should you have a policy on the medical conditions that disqualify children from participation? (The American Academy of Pediatrics' recommendations on such medical conditions appear in appendix A.) Should you adopt these recommendations as an eligibility policy?

_____

14. Are players with HIV-positive or other blood-borne pathogens eligible to participate? (See the American Academy of Pediatrics' recommendation in Appendix B.) How are your coaches prepared to work with these youngsters?

_____

15. Are youths with various disabilities eligible to participate in each of the sports you offer? When developing your policy you'll need to consider the Americans With Disabilities Act.

_____

III. Coach Eligibility

Just as you have policies on who is eligible to participate, you should also have policies on who is eligible to coach. No other single factor is as important as the quality of the coaches you select to ensure the achievement of your program objectives. We'll address the issue of coaching qualifications and education in much greater depth in chapter 2.

1. What is the minimum age to be eligible to coach?

_____

(continued)

2. What experiences, if any, are required to be eligible to coach? Do potential coaches need to be former players in that sport?

_____

3. Do you require potential coaches to go through any screening process, such as completing an application form or checking references, criminal records, and child and family service records for potential child abusers?

_____

4. Do you require potential coaches to complete an education program such as the one offered by ASEP?

_____

5. Will you permit or encourage a parent to coach his or her own child on a team?

_____

6. Will you permit or encourage adults of either gender to coach boys only, girls only, and mixed teams?

_____

7. Are the eligibility requirements for head coaches different from those for assistant coaches? For example, must head coaches have a year or two of experience as an assistant coach under a mentor coach?

_____

8. Are the eligibility requirements different for coaches at different levels of play?

_____

IV. Referee/Official Eligibility

Many of the same questions asked for coach eligibility apply to referees. Consider these issues as you form your policies.

1. What is the minimum age to be eligible to officiate?

_____

2. What experiences, if any, are required to be eligible to officiate?

_____

3. Do you require potential officials to go through any screening process, such as completing an application form or checking references, criminal records, and child and family service records for potential child abusers?

_____

4. Do you require potential officials to be certified by an official's association and/or to complete a training program that you offer?

_____

5. Will you permit a parent to officiate a contest in which his or her own child is participating?

6. Will you permit or encourage adults of either gender to officiate contests played by boys only, girls only, and mixed teams?

7. Are the eligibility requirements different for officials at different levels of play?

V. Player Selection

You've developed your policies for athlete eligibility. In this section we'll consider policies pertaining to how participants should be selected to a team and matched for safe and equitable competition. Keep in mind your program objectives and principles as you evaluate your existing policies and consider adding new ones.

1. How will individuals be assigned to teams? Will a lottery or draft system be used? Should teams be formed by geographical region or neighborhood?

2. Do you permit coaches to recruit youngsters for a team?

3. Do you consider skill or ability level in assigning youths to teams?

4. May athletes be "cut" or eliminated from the team based on skill or ability?

5. May participants request reassignment to a different team? If so, under what conditions will such reassignment be made?

6. Are there other policies needed to match players to teams in order to have safe and equitable competition?

7. How many athletes may each team select?

VI. Equipment Policies

Policies about equipment will help you manage the costs of the program and contain risks associated with improper or defective equipment. Consider the following issues when establishing equipment policies.

1. Who provides the equipment for the program: you or the participants?

(continued)

2. How is the equipment purchased?

_____

3. What equipment is needed to ensure participant safety and minimize risk to your program?

_____

4. Will minimum safety standards be established? How will these standards be ensured? Will a list of acceptable equipment be provided from which your staff, coaches, or parents must purchase?

_____

5. Who is responsible for checking equipment at the beginning of the season and periodically throughout the season?

_____

6. When equipment needs to be repaired, who is responsible for the repair and for determining that the repair meets minimum safety standards?

_____

7. If equipment is checked out on a free or rental basis to coaches or participants, what are the responsibilities of the coaches or players for this equipment?

_____

8. If equipment is provided by your program, what are the policies for returning it? What are the policies if equipment is lost, stolen, or damaged beyond normal wear and tear?

_____

VII.   Facility Policies

Facility management requires a comprehensive set of policies. Your program may have its own facilities, or you may rent or use another organization's facilities. Either way, policies are needed to provide for clear use and the safety of participants and to manage the legal risk to your program.

1. If the facilities are owned by your program, what are your policies for coaches, officials, participants, and parents on how these facilities may be used? Consider all these as facilities: locker rooms, practice sites, game fields, courts, bleachers, training rooms, weight rooms, classrooms, concession stands, parking lots, rest rooms, and access ways to each of these areas.

_____

_____

2. If the facilities are rented, leased, or used by your program, what are your policies for coaches, officials, and parents on how these facilities are to be used in accordance with the owner's requirements?

_____

_____

3. Will liability insurance be provided to protect and minimize the risk to the organization and its participants? Who provides this insurance?

_____

_____

4. Who is responsible for checking the risks or hazards at each facility? What can be done to remove or minimize these hazards?

_____

_____

5. How frequently are the facilities inspected for hazards?

_____

6. Who is responsible for the maintenance of each facility?

_____

7. Who is responsible for the supervision of events at these facilities? What are the supervisor's specific duties? What is the supervisor to do when such events as accidents, thefts, vandalism, severe weather, and other incidents occur?

_____

_____

8. How is each facility controlled? Who opens and closes the facility? Who turns the lights on and off? Who controls the temperature?

_____

_____

9. Who determines whether an event must be canceled or postponed due to bad weather or because the site is unsafe? How is this information communicated to the coaches, participants, parents, and officials?

_____

_____

VIII.   Practice Policies

Consider the need for policies pertaining to practices to ensure that participation in sport is a safe and balanced part of a child's development. Communicating these policies and the reasons for them to all who are involved is essential in managing a successful program.

1. At what point in the year will teams be allowed to begin practicing?

_____

2. Are there any limitations on the number of practices before the competitive season? During the competitive season?

_____

(continued)

3. At what time during the day can practices take place? Where will practices be held? Will your organization establish practice schedules for leagues, or are these left to the coaches to plan?

_____

_____

4. Should there be an upper limit on the number of minutes any one practice can last?

_____

5. Should your practice policies be adjusted by sport and level of play?

_____

6. Do you need a policy with regard to who will supervise practices? Must the head coach be present or is it enough for only an assistant coach to be there? May anyone fill in to supervise in the absence of the head and/or assistant coach?

_____

_____

7. Is a policy needed for how practices are canceled?

_____

IX. Contest Policies

Policies pertaining to contests are needed for the same reasons policies are needed for practices. Consider these questions in formulating contest policies.

1. Do you need a policy on the number of contests that athletes can participate in, or is this managed by the way you schedule contests?

_____

2. At what time during the day can contests take place? Where will contests be held?

_____

3. Do you need policies for limiting the length of contests or the extent of participation in competitive events? For example, you may need policies on the number of innings played, minutes played, and distances run.

_____

4. How should these contest policies be adjusted by sport and level of play?

_____

5. Do you need a policy regarding who will supervise contests? Must the head coach be present or is it sufficient for only an assistant coach to be there? May anyone fill in to supervise in the absence of the head and/or assistant coach?

_____

_____

6. Who decides when contests should be canceled or discontinued due to bad weather or other conditions that may endanger the participants?

_____

7. Do you need policies for discontinuing contests when the score is extremely lopsided?

_____

8. Do you need policies to mandate that every player gets to play? The extent to which each player gets to play?

_____

9. What policies do you have for forfeits because of insufficient participants on one team?

_____

X. Participant Behavior Policies

Should your organization set minimum or optimal guidelines for acceptable behavior for the youngsters who participate, or should this be left for the coaches to determine? If your philosophy is to set policies for participant behavior, then consider these questions.

1. What types of behavior are unacceptable? Cheating, violence, drug and alcohol use, harassment, smoking, swearing, and use of derogatory language and gestures are some of the behaviors to consider.

_____

_____

2. How should unacceptable behavior be handled in practices? In contests?

_____

3. What types of discipline may coaches administer to misbehaving youngsters? What types of discipline will your organization take for various types of misbehaviors?

_____

_____

4. Should certain unacceptable behavior outside of the athlete's sport participation be punished by banning them from participation?

_____

5. How will your organization involve parents when disciplining or handing out penalties for misbehavior?

_____

6. What policies can you set to encourage and recognize good sportsmanship?

_____

(continued)

XI. Adult Participant Behavior Policies

Coaches, officials, and other volunteers who help conduct your youth sport programs should be held accountable to certain standards of behavior, just as the young athletes are. The following questions will help you set policies for these adults.

1. What types of behavior are unacceptable? Cheating, violence, drug and alcohol use, harassment, smoking, swearing, and use of derogatory language and gestures are some of the behaviors to consider.

   _____

   _____

2. How should unacceptable behavior be handled in practices? In contests?

   _____

3. What discipline will your organization invoke for various types of misbehaviors? When is it appropriate to press criminal charges?

   _____

   _____

4. What unacceptable behaviors that occur outside of the adult's involvement in your program should be punished by banning the adult from further involvement?

   _____

5. What is the procedure for parents or participants to lodge complaints about coaches, officials, or other volunteers?

   _____

6. What policies can you set to encourage and recognize good sportsmanship?

   _____

7. Should you have a policy regarding team prayers or other expressions of religious beliefs by coaches or other adults associated with the team?

   _____

XII. Parent Behavior Policies

Many parents are vitally interested in their child's sport participation, some too much so. When problems occur with parents it is usually because their expectations are not met by coaches, officials, or your administration. To manage parents effectively, consider these questions in developing policies.

1. Are parents permitted and encouraged to attend practices? Contests?

   _____

2. What types of behavior are unacceptable at practices and contests? Drug and alcohol use, harassment, smoking, swearing, and using derogatory language and gestures are some of the behaviors to consider.

   _____

   _____

3. How should unacceptable behavior be treated in practices? In contests?

_____

4. What discipline will your organization invoke for various types of misbehaviors? When is it appropriate to press criminal charges?

_____

5. What is the procedure for coaches, officials, and participants to lodge complaints against parents?

_____

6. What policies can you set to encourage and recognize good sportsmanship? Should you establish guidelines for appropriate behavior at practices and contests?

_____

XIII. Awards and Recognition Policies

Controversy about the giving of awards and other types of recognition in youth sport programs has existed for years. Some believe that these awards are appropriate for recognizing superior achievement, while others feel these awards deliver messages of failure to those who do not receive them. Consider these questions in developing your policies about awards.

1. Will you conduct tournaments to identify the best athletes or teams?

_____

2. Will your program select all-star teams and most valuable players? If so, how will these teams and athletes be selected?

_____

_____

3. Will your program encourage teams and individuals to receive publicity through the media?

_____

4. Will your program provide trophies, medals, and other forms of recognition to teams and individuals for certain achievements? If so, what are the criteria for selecting teams and players to receive these awards?

_____

_____

XIV. Health and Safety Policies

Many of the issues already mentioned pertain to safeguarding the participants involved in your program. Here are some additional questions to consider as you complete your policies.

1. What are your policies for proper attire to ensure the safety of the participants? Must helmets and other protective equipment be worn? What type of eyewear is required, if any? May rings, earrings, and other jewelry be worn?

_____

_____

(continued)

2. What is your policy about dealing with drug and alcohol use by youngsters? By coaches and other volunteers? By parents?

_____

_____

3. What are your policies for transporting participants to and from practices and contests? What about transportation policies for out-of-town contests?

_____

_____

4. What is your policy on coaches and officials knowing first aid? On having a first-aid kit present at every practice and contest?

_____

_____

5. Do you have a plan in place for dealing with medical emergencies? Do all coaches and officials know how to follow this plan?

_____

6. Do you need a policy for deciding when children who have been injured or ill can return to practice and competition?

_____

Now that you have drafted your policies, review them carefully to see that each is consistent with your program objectives and principles. Then have your supervisor and other members of the staff review them for completeness and consistency with the program philosophy.

Summary

A well-developed program philosophy is the cornerstone of a quality youth sport program. In this chapter you have worked on shaping your program philosophy by

a. establishing your program's objectives,
b. prioritizing your program's objectives,
c. pursuing your program's objectives,
d. identifying the principles of your program's philosophy,
e. evaluating your leadership style, and
f. evaluating your personal objectives.

Having formulated your program philosophy, you then tackled the development of your organization's program policies. With a sound philosophy and sound policies as your program's foundation, you now have the base for an outstanding youth sport program.

Managing Coaches

The days of taking just any "warm bodies" and letting them coach the youth of our nation are rapidly disappearing. Responsible youth sport directors can no longer place the health and well-being of youth in the hands of well-intentioned volunteers who are not prepared for the important position of coach.

The purpose of this chapter is to help you effectively manage your coaches, who are vital resources for achieving your program objectives. Youth sport directors who indiscriminately recruit adult volunteers, hand them the equipment bag, and wish them good luck are irresponsible. Directors who follow this approach are likely to see inconsistency in the quality of coaching, as well as high turnover of dissatisfied coaches.

Successful adults—the type of volunteers you want—do not like to fail. Without training and support, coaches are more likely to fail and have problems with parents, athletes, and fellow coaches, such as the following:

- More injuries to participants (because coaches lack training to prevent injuries)
- More lawsuits (because of poor management)
- Recurring criticism from parents and fellow directors

In this chapter you will learn how to

- recruit the best talent pool of potential coaches,
- select people who will coach to achieve your program objectives,
- offer a quality education program to your volunteer coaches,
- supervise and evaluate your coaches, and
- recognize and reward your coaches for their contributions.

Before we look at these goals, let's reflect on the importance of the coach.

Importance of the Coach

Experienced youth sport directors know that the most important element of a successful youth sport program is quality coaching.

There Are Little Eyes Upon You

There are little eyes upon you

And they're watching night and day;

There are little ears that quickly

Take in every word you say;

There are little hands all eager

To do anything you do;

And a little boy or girl who's dreaming

Of the day he'll be like you.

You're the little fellow's idol;

You're the wisest of the wise,

In his little mind about you,

No suspicions ever rise;

He believes in you devoutly,

Holds that all you can do,

He will say and do, in your way

When he's grown-up like you.

There's a wide-eyed little fellow,

Who believes you're always right,

And his ears are always open,

And he watches day and night;

You are setting an example,

Every day in all you do,

For the little boy who's waiting

To grow up to be like you.

Source: Unknown

Many other elements are necessary and important, but the coach makes or breaks the program.

The value of sport for each child in your program depends so much on the values of that child's coach. The *coach* in our society is a powerful, influential role model to many young people who place great importance on playing sports. The coach controls access to these young people's opportunities to play and can help or hinder their potential to play well. Often the coach is the first significant adult in the child's life besides his parents. The importance of the coach is captured eloquently in the poem on the previous page.

Our society subscribes to several myths that have impeded our progress in providing better volunteer coaches. For example:

"If you've played the sport, you can coach it."

Teaching sport skills requires knowledge above and beyond having played the sport. And a coach must know not only the techniques and tactics of the sport, but also how the bodies and minds of young people work.

Coaching young athletes is rewarding and challenging.

"The better you played the sport, the more qualified you are to coach."

A prevailing myth is that if you were skilled as a player and had a winning record, you are more qualified to coach. There is no evidence to corroborate this belief. The qualifications for being a good coach are simply not the same as the qualifications for being a good athlete.

"The best coaches are needed at the highest level of sport."

Each level of sport places different demands on coaches, and all levels of sport require competent coaches. The case can certainly be made that coaching children in their formative years is as challenging as coaching at other levels, if not more so.

"A successful coach is a winning coach."

Our society continues to define *success* as synonymous with *winning*. This belief was once restricted to high school, college, and professional sports, but today it is prevalent in children's sports as well. One of the great challenges for any youth sport director is to redefine what a successful coach is for those adults who occupy this important position in your program.

A successful coach is foremost a person who helps children become better human beings—physically, psychologically, socially—and does so while striving for victory within an environment of fun and mutual respect. Stated more simply, a successful coach places Athletes First, Winning Second. This is the new definition of a successful coach. Winning is a by-product of successful coaching. Coaches who are successful in helping athletes develop physically, psychologically, and socially, who maintain an environment of fun and respect, are much more likely to win than coaches who emphasize winning.

"Volunteer coaches can't be fired."

Just one bad coach can really hurt the integrity of your program—to say nothing of the potential damage done to the children being coached by this person. So don't feel that your hands are tied when it comes to "releasing" a coach who isn't doing the job. Allowing a coach who is guilty of a major violation (abuse of drugs or alcohol, or physical or psychological abuse) to continue coaching in your program is a breach of your responsibility. Have a written policy and procedure regarding the firing of coaches that is endorsed and supported by your organization and follow these procedures in the event of a dismissal.

On the other hand, if you're having a minor problem with one of your coaches—for example, a lack of technical ability or motivation—firing the coach is probably not the best solution. Instead, consider moving this volunteer to a position for which he or she is better suited, such as official scorekeeper or groundskeeper.

In Praise of Coaches

The United States has one of the most extensive amateur sports programs in the world. Most of these programs are possible only because adults volunteer to become coaches and officials. If communities relied entirely on paid professionals to coach, millions of young people would not get to play because the programs would be too expensive. In our quest to improve the quality of children's sports programs we should not forget the generosity of these adult volunteers.

As the saying goes, a few bad apples can spoil the barrel. It takes only a few bad coaches, and the attention that they attract, to defile the image of a thousand good coaches. It does not nullify, of course, the good work of those coaches, but it certainly taints their image. This is unfortunate, for bad coaches likely make it harder for youth sport directors to attract capable adults into coaching. How many good coaches quit because they refuse to hassle with the one "bad apple"?

The vast majority of coaches deserve the accolades of the community. We read and hear so much criticism of coaches that we are led to believe that the bad coaches dominate the profession. But this is not so. Most coaches have the well-being of athletes as their primary interest. Certainly coaches make mistakes—just as parents and teachers make mistakes. And sometimes the coach does the right thing, and the kids are at fault. The intent and effort of most coaches are positive. What is needed is a means for culling out the bad apples and helping the coaches with good intentions do the best coaching they possibly can. That is the purpose of this chapter.

Coaching Director

In the remainder of this chapter we will refer to the *coaching director* of your youth sport program. In small programs this may be your responsibility as the youth sport director, but you may want to consider appointing a volunteer as coaching director to help you out. In larger programs you may have the resources to pay a full- or part-time person to serve as the coaching director. The duties of the coaching director will be clarified in the sections to follow.

In addition, consider forming a coaching committee to help you carry out the important responsibilities of managing your coaches. This committee of volunteers is likely to comprise three to six people who are experienced coaches, professionals trained in physical education or sport administration, or highly experienced sports officials. Your committee will help you recruit, select, educate, supervise, evaluate, and recognize your coaches, all of which will make your job more manageable and increase volunteer participation in your program.

Recruiting Coaches

Recruiting volunteer coaches is a challenge for many youth sport directors, but current statistics indicate that there are more willing volunteers out there than ever before. The challenge is getting these volunteers to commit to your program. An increasing number of organizations are requesting volunteers, so you need an effective plan to attract and keep good ones.

A survey of youth sport programs revealed that better programs make the recruitment of coaches a systematic, year-long effort. To do this you need a plan that identifies the number of coaches you will need for each sport in your program, the activities you will initiate to recruit coaches, the time of year that you will initiate each recruiting activity, and the cost associated with each.

In this section you'll learn how to develop such a plan. The first step is to determine what your needs are.

Needs Assessment

Form 2.1 on page 62 will help you determine your needs for a particular sport for up to five leagues. We have completed form 2.1 in form 2.2 (see page 63) as an example for you to follow.

Complete form 2.1 now to become familiar with it, estimating your coaching needs as best you can. Then, later, complete this form again after carefully consulting your records.

You will complete one form for each sport you supervise and later consolidate this information into a summary form. If you have more than five leagues in one sport, then simply complete two or more forms and add up the totals.

If you administer a one-sport program, then form 2.1 provides you the information needed. If you administer a multiple-sport program, you will need to complete form 2.1 for each sport. After doing so, you'll want to summarize your coaching needs for all sports on form 2.3 (see page 64).

Now you are ready to determine the qualifications required to coach at each level within each sport. As you examine your coaching needs, consider the following to help you identify the qualifications coaches will need.

- **The extent of knowledge required about the sport to coach children safely.** For example, the requirements to coach basketball or soccer safely are quite different from those to safely coach swimming or gymnastics.

- **The age range of the participants.** You may want coaches to have more experience in competitive sports when coaching older participants.

- **The gender of the participants.** You will need to consider whether the coach's gender will influence his ability to supervise the participants.

Next, you need to prepare a job description for each type of coach you need. Usually this includes a job description for head coaches and assistant coaches in each sport.

Job Descriptions

Just as in business or government, it's essential to have a detailed description of the requisite qualifications and duties for the position of coach. We've outlined the elements of a job description and provided a sample job description for a head coach in the next section. Modify these job descriptions to meet your needs.

Elements of a Coaching Job Description

1. **Position title:** Name the position by identifying it as the head or assistant coaching position, naming the sport to be coached, and indicating the level of coaching by giving the age level, grade, or name of the league.

2. **Position description:** Provide a brief description of the position without getting into the position's specific duties. Include the following items:

   • Whether the position is a paid or volunteer

   • Reference to the role associated with head or assistant coach

   • League within which the person will coach, or the specific team, if known (if not mentioned in the position title)

   • Age, sex, and skill level of players

   • Number of players to be coached

   • Time commitment in weeks, days, and hours

3. **Activities and responsibilities:** Describe all activities the coach is expected to perform routinely. These may include the following:

   • Finding a sponsor

   • Purchasing and distributing equipment

   • Meeting with parents

   • Conducting practices

   • Scheduling and supervising contests

   • Obtaining officials or officiating contests

   • Preparing the playing site

   • Transporting athletes

   • Recordkeeping

   • Attending meetings

This is also a good place to briefly comment on the coach's responsibilities to the participants, such as providing for their safety, teaching skills correctly, maximizing participation, imparting values, and helping parents to keep the contest in perspective.

4. **Qualifications:** Describe the required or desired experiences, and the level of education required or to be obtained.

This is not the place to list the personal attributes you desire in a coach. Everyone who applies to coach will think he is a responsible, ethical, and capable teacher, so you will not screen anyone out by listing these characteristics as qualifications. Instead, determine whether individual applicants possess these qualities through the selection process we will describe in the next section.

5. **Benefits:** Describe the tangible and intangible benefits to be obtained from serving as a coach, including the following:

   • Compensation (if any)

   • Other tangible benefits

   • Any recognition associated with the position

   • Other intangible benefits

6. **Supervisor:** List the name, address, and telephone number of the youth sport director.

Now it's your turn to create a job description for any coaching position in your program. Remember to make it specific to your particular needs by modifying our examples. Use the outline in form 2.4 (see page 65) to prepare your job description.

Publicizing Your Need for Coaches

Now you know how many coaches you will need, what their duties will be, and the type of person you want to recruit. Next, you are ready to let your community know of your needs by publicizing the availability of these positions. Remember that you want to recruit more coaches than you are likely to need because not all who volunteer to coach are likely to meet your selection criteria.

Recruiting coaches is a communication process involving the delivery of a message to a target audience via an appropriate medium to solicit interest in coaching in your program.

Message

What do you want to communicate to recruit coaches? Keep in mind that a good recruiting

Sample Coaching Job Description

Position title

Head basketball coach for 9- to 10-year-olds

Position description

Volunteer head coach for girls aged 9 to 10 in the Fastbreak League of the Westwood Park District. The head coach is responsible for all aspects of directing the team's practice and play in games and will supervise one assistant coach. Most of the girls participating will have previous experience playing in the Dribblers League, but others will be playing their first organized basketball. The team will have about 10 players. League games are played each Saturday morning between 9 o'clock and noon in the Duncan Recreation Center. The season begins January 5 and continues for 10 weeks through March 12. Coaches are requested to hold one or two practices of no more than one hour each week during the season and the 4 weeks before the season.

Activities and responsibilities

1. Teach basketball skills through effectively planned practices at a level appropriate for each member of the team.
2. Organize the players to participate in games and coach them during games.
3. Conduct a preseason parent orientation program and a postseason meeting with the players' parents.
4. Encourage parent involvement and coordinate their assistance.
5. Supervise the players before, during, and immediately after practices and games.
6. Provide a safe and enjoyable environment for all players, giving each child an equal opportunity to participate.
7. Follow the Westwood Park District medical emergency plan when a player is injured, and complete the Medical Emergency Record form after the emergency.
8. Communicate with the coaching director on all matters of policy.
9. Serve as a positive role model for the players, parents, officials, and fellow coaches by following all rules, demonstrating good sportsmanship, and coaching consistently with the Westwood Park District's philosophy.

Qualifications

- Must have one year of experience as an assistant coach in the Westwood Park District, or one year of head coaching experience, or two years of assistant coaching experience in another comparable youth sport organization.
- Must complete the ASEP Level One Coaches Course or one of ASEP's more advanced courses.
- Must be of sound mind and good character without a criminal record or criminal action pending.

(continued)

Benefits

The position is without compensation. The Westwood Park District provides liability and medical insurance for coaches when engaged in coaching for the park district. Coaches receive a Westwood Park District knit shirt and whistle. Coaches are recognized at the annual coaching banquet, with special recognition given to the Coach of the Year based on demonstrated sportsmanship.

Coaches also have the opportunity to be of service to the community by providing guidance and leadership to our youth. The positive impact that coaches can have on the lives of young people is an intangible reward impossible to value.

Dates of service

December 1 to March 12

Supervisor

Lori Thomas, Westwood Park District

---

campaign is a public relations program; it should present your program in its best light. It is a mistake to campaign for coaches by indicating you are so desperate that you will gladly accept anyone. Thus, the content of the message should include the following:

- A clear statement of your need for coaches of certain sports at specified times of the year
- The duties and time demands of the position
- The qualifications and expectations of the position, including any training offered
- The importance of the position and its contribution to the community
- The benefits of volunteering to coach
- Information about your youth sport program and your organization

Audience

Whom do you want to target to receive your initial message to recruit coaches? Where are you likely to find the people who have the interest and qualifications to serve as quality coaches? Consider the following possible target audiences, and select those most likely to suit your needs.

- Parents of the participants
- Businesspeople
- Professionals such as doctors, lawyers, bankers, and accountants
- College students and faculty, especially those in physical education
- Adult members of churches
- Military personnel living in the community
- Members of service clubs (Rotary, Lions, Optimists, Kiwanis, Moose, Elks, Civitans, and so on)
- Senior citizens groups
- Teachers in local elementary and secondary schools
- Members of parent-teacher associations
- Local fitness club members
- Members of your organization
- Members of labor unions
- Adults who participate in local sport programs

Medium

The medium is the means of delivering your message to your audience. Most of these sources are obvious, although we have been surprised at how many youth sport directors use only one or two of them rather than a more diversified approach. Media for you to consider include the following:

- **Local newspapers.** Direct your news releases to a specific member of the newspaper staff—the sports director is the likely choice. Format your releases to make it easy for a reporter to prepare the information for insertion into the newspaper.
- **Newsletters to members of certain groups.** Such groups might include businesses, religious groups, service clubs, schools, or PTAs. Send the same news releases you give to the newspaper to the editors of newsletters in your community, selecting those newsletters whose readers are likely prospects to become coaches.
- **Web site.** If you have not already had a web site designed for your program, find a designer to create a page that relates all the crucial information about the program. Create circulation to the web page by including the URL on all ads and fliers. Search the web for sites at which you might add a link to your web page.
- **Printed brochures.** A youth sport program brochure is an excellent public relations tool for recruiting coaches. Form 2.5 (page 66) shows a sample brochure that you may modify to meet your specific needs.
- **Posters.** Find a local graphic designer who will volunteer to develop an attractive poster containing your message. Perhaps you can get a local print shop to print copies for free as a public service gesture. Display the posters in prominent locations in your community.
- **Public service announcements (PSAs).** These announcements are a traditional and effective way of using radio or television to spread the word about your program and your need for coaches. Consider having a former athlete in the program who is now a prominent member of the community deliver your message. Plan to have your PSA aired well in advance of your needs.
- **Media appearances.** Seek interviews on local radio and television talk shows. When you or a representative of your program is on the air, provide brief responses to the questions to inform those listening about your program. Have a method planned for interested listeners to get more information.
- **Public access cable television.** This newer medium is ideally designed for you to

let your community know about your youth sport program. Make frequent use of this medium if it is available to you.
- **Personal presentations.** Seek opportunities to speak before local civic, religious, and professional groups in the community to promote your program and recruit coaches.
- **Video presentations.** Making an informative video about your youth sport program is not that difficult or expensive. A video can be useful for supplementing personal presentations, airing on public access cable TV, showing in your lobby, and giving to your coaches to show at their parent orientation program meetings.
- **Telephone solicitation.** Use the telephone to follow up any leads generated by your advertisement efforts. Though time consuming, phone contact is an effective way to complete the recruitment of these potential volunteer coaches. We all like to be asked personally for our help.

Making the Pitch

The amount of information to communicate is substantial. Obviously, in attempting to find potential coaches through such media as the newspaper, radio, and television, you are unable to deliver all this information economically. Thus, just as in most advertising programs, your initial effort is to entice quality potential candidates to inquire about coaching in your program. Once they've made the inquiry, you need to provide them with all the relevant information.

Publicity (free announcements through the media) is the primary means youth sport directors use to obtain leads on potential candidates for coaching positions. Once you have these leads, you then need to "make the pitch," which is the point in the recruitment process where youth sport directors often fail. One recommended solution is to develop a brochure that contains the information described in the previous section.

Recruiting Plans

You are now ready to develop specific recruiting plans by bringing the three elements of the recruiting communication process together. Each specific recruiting activity identifies a target audience, prepares a specific message to be delivered, and delivers it through a particular medium. At the end of this section you'll be asked to develop your specific recruiting plans; to help you get started, consider the following ideas.

1. Personal contact with individuals in any of your target audiences is an effective way to recruit coaches. Throughout the year, you and your staff should inform those adults you come in contact with of your upcoming needs for coaches.

2. Write, call, or meet with the coaches now in the program who are returning next season and ask them to identify friends who may qualify as coaches. Be sure to contact the coaches in sports other than the sport for which you are currently recruiting. They may be able to help you find coaches, or they may wish to begin coaching another sport. Once a person is referred to you, follow up with a phone call to invite her to apply.

3. Write high school and college coaches in your area who may know of local residents interested in coaching. Enclose your program brochure and a form for listing names, addresses, and telephone numbers of prospective coaches.

4. Speak with the parents of the participants at a preseason SportParent Course, inviting them to coach.

5. Publicize your need for coaches by sending a public service announcement to local radio and television stations.

6. Participate in local information fairs and community gatherings where it is appropriate to set up a display about your youth sport program. Explain the program to those who visit your display, share the program brochure, and invite visitors to apply for coaching positions.

7. Arrange to have announcements made over the public address system at community sporting events.

8. Contact the nearest college or university to recruit students from physical education departments. Speak with the instructors of coaching courses to suggest an arrangement by which students can receive course credit and obtain experience by coaching. It may also be useful to speak directly with students to encourage them to volunteer as coaches.

9. Contact adult athletes in your community who participate in their sports at times that don't conflict with your program.

10. Speak at local service clubs and professional society meetings to explain your program and the need for coaches. Invite members to apply.

11. If your community has athletic booster clubs, contact them to recruit coaches.

12. Contact local senior citizen organizations and speak with the members about your coaching needs.

13. Initiate ASEP's Volunteer Level One Courses Clinic in continuing or adult education classes through the local schools or community college. People who take this course make up an excellent group of potential coaches, because they will have already completed the coaching education requirements you should establish.

14. Contact large employers in your community to find out the best way to invite employees to apply to coach. For example, you may be able to speak at a company meeting, post announcements on bulletin boards, or include an article in the company newsletter.

One of the most important ingredients in recruiting, as many college coaches can tell you, is the image that the public has of your program. People are more inclined to become a part of a quality youth sport program than one that has a shabby image. So throughout the year take every opportunity to let your public know what your program is doing.

You are now prepared to develop a comprehensive plan to recruit more coaches than you will need, giving you the opportunity to select those most qualified. Exercise 2.1 gives you the chance to complete a recruiting plan for your youth sport program. Before completing the exercise, however, review the sample plan we've devised for a multisport park and recreation department that follows.

| **Exercise 2.1** | **Your Year-Long Coaching Recruiting Plan** |

"Failing to plan is planning to fail!" So the adage goes. But this is especially true as you work to recruit volunteer coaches. In this exercise, we ask you to develop a plan for your own youth sport program. Form 2.6 provides a template for your use (see page 69). Briefly describe each activity you will undertake. Three activities fit on each page. Duplicate the form as many times as you need to describe each of the activities you will undertake.

Begin by considering what you have done in the past that has worked and then consider any additional ideas mentioned in this section. Review your needs assessment for coaches and target audiences you want to reach to recruit, the media you want to use to reach them, and the message you want to deliver.

When completing form 2.6, enter a brief title where it says "Activity." Give the date on which you plan to initiate this activity. In the "Objective" space, describe what you want to accomplish through this recruiting activity; be specific, indicating who your target audience is, the medium you'll use, and the outcome you hope for. Then briefly summarize the message you want to deliver to this audience. Finally, compile the list of activities in chronological order to form a systematic plan.

Selecting Coaches

Your recruiting program was so successful that you now have the enviable challenge of selecting the most qualified coaches from numerous candidates. To have a quality program, you must be selective—or at least be sure that those you choose to be coaches meet the minimum qualifications.

Face it: Some people simply do not have the skills, knowledge, or attitude to coach young people. Some adults enter coaching not to help young people learn sport skills and have fun, but to relive their past athletic careers or enact their dreams of athletic glory. These adults coach for personal aggrandizement; they emphasize winning at all costs, which jeopardizes the well-being of the young people who play for them.

Unfortunately, many members of our society are unfit to lead children in sport or any other activity. It is your responsibility to ensure that the coaches in your program are not criminals, chemical abusers, or child sex offenders. It is your responsibility to ensure that the coaches in your program are emotionally stable and know how to coach the sport safely, effectively, and consistently with your program philosophy.

To meet your responsibility, follow a selection process consisting of the following two parts:

1. A three-step screening process
2. A two-step self-selection process

These steps do involve additional work, but failure to take them increases both the risk to your participants and the legal risk to your organization. Let's discuss how to execute these steps as efficiently as possible.

The Screening Process

The recommended three-step process for screening and selecting coaches includes the following:

1. A review of the applicants' completed coaching application forms
2. A brief interview
3. A reference check

Your coaching committee, under your or your coaching director's guidance, should complete the screening process. Begin by having all applicants fill out a coaching application form (such as form 2.7 on page 70) at the time they express interest in coaching for your organization. The coaching committee then reviews all applications, screening out those who do not meet the minimum qualifications as stated in the sample coaching job description on pages 37 to 38.

Sample Year-Long Coaching Recruiting Plan

Organization	T.J. Hill Family YMCA		
Coaching director	Joe Miller		
Date	September 1	**League/sport**	Basketball
Season dates	January-March		

Activity	Fall program brochure article	**Date to initiate**	September 1
Objective	To promote the youth basketball program and create awareness of the need for volunteer coaches		
Message	Moms and dads, friends and family, and other interested adults are asked to apply to become volunteer youth sport coaches.		
Contact	Publicity manager	**Estimated cost**	$0

Activity	Service group presentations	**Date to initiate**	Monthly
Objective	To arrange presentations at local service club meetings to promote the program and the need for interested adults to serve as youth sport coaches		
Message	Give an open invitation to service group members along with program brochures and application forms, making the application process as attractive as possible.		
Contact	Presidents of local service clubs	**Estimated cost**	$0

Activity	School program flyer	**Date to initiate**	November 1
Objective	To invite children to participate in the youth basketball program and to promote the need for volunteer coaches		
Message	Give specifics of program-registration dates, practice and game dates, program costs and coach training dates.		
Contact	Grade school principal	**Estimated cost**	$25

Activity	Letter to former coaches	**Date to initiate**	November 7
Objective	To invite coaches who have volunteered in the past to be involved in this year's program		
Message	Focus attention on their past generosity and how important it is that such generosity continue to help the participants of this year s program.		
Contact	Former coaches	**Estimated cost**	$10 in postage

Activity	Space ads in local paper	**Date to initiate**	November 15
Objective	To highlight the youth basketball program; allow space to promote the need for adult volunteer coaches		
Message	Provide program specifics and objectives that focus on the need for adult volunteers as coaches for the program.		
Contact	Newspaper advertising department	**Estimated cost**	$30-$100

Activity	Posters	**Date to initiate**	November 15
Objective	To highlight the program and the need for adult volunteers through posters hung at local businesses and churches		
Message	Stress the need for interested adults to apply for volunteer coaching positions, emphasizing the benefits of the position and the results of their involvement in the program.		
Contact	Business managers/pastors	**Estimated cost**	$20 in materials

Activity	Telemarketing to volunteers	**Date to initiate**	November 15
Objective	To contact former volunteers, inviting them to apply for volunteer coaching positions		
Message	Invite volunteers to apply and/or confirm their interest in working as a volunteer youth sport coach for the youth basketball program.		
Contact	Internal staff	**Estimated cost**	Staff hours

Activity	Registration	**Date to initiate**	November 16 & 18
Objective	To ask parents and other adults at registration to apply as volunteer coaches		
Message	The registration form would include a line asking for parents to volunteer to coach. The YSA may also recruit in person during the registration.		
Contact	Self	**Estimated cost**	$0

Activity	Training recognition	**Date to initiate**	December 8
Objective	To promote the coaches' training program, reward the volunteers, and show the community the emphasis you place on educating volunteers so they can have success in your program		
Message	Thank the current volunteers, educate adults in the community about the availability of training within your program and the important role it plays in assuring the success of the volunteer.		
Contact	Local media	**Estimated cost**	$0

(continued)

Activity	Human interest story	**Date to initiate**	January 20
Objective	To bring awareness to the position of volunteer youth sport coach and the importance this person plays in the overall success of the program and the life of the young athlete		
Message	Get quotes from the local coaches; what they like about their role and how they feel about making a positive contribution to the community. Focus on the positive attributes of being a volunteer youth sport coach.		
Contact	Newspaper editor	**Estimated cost**	$0
Activity	Coaches' letter	**Date to initiate**	March 5
Objective	To invite coaches to the awards banquet, thank them for their involvement with the program, and ask them to volunteer for future coaching positions		
Message	Special letter of thanks will include a schedule of upcoming programs and your continued need for quality volunteers.		
Contact	Self	**Estimated cost**	Postage
Activity	Coaches' awards	**Date to initiate**	March 12
Objective	To thank the volunteers who worked in the program and to reiterate the value that the organization and the community place on these individuals		
Message	A special thank you along with an appreciation award will be given to each volunteer. Local media to report on the awards banquet.		
Contact	Local media	**Estimated cost**	Awards

Next, interview those candidates who meet the minimum qualifications. We recognize that in a large youth sport program, interviewing can take substantial time, but because the coach's role is so important, there really is no other way to responsibly select coaches. If your program is small, the coaching committee can meet as a group to interview each candidate. If your program is large, each member of the committee may be assigned to interview a certain number of coaches alone and then later report back to the coaching committee.

The interview need not be extensive; usually 15 minutes is sufficient to help you evaluate the candidate. During the interview, ask questions that will give you insight into the person's

- motives for volunteering as a coach,
- knowledge of the sport,
- knowledge of how to work with young people, and
- character and emotional stability.

To help you conduct the interview efficiently, use form 2.8 (see pages 72-73), which contains questions to solicit information about these qualifications and space for you to comment about their responses to each. You should also ask questions that follow up on any concerns you have about information presented in the coaching application form. Exercise 2.2 will help you evaluate an interview.

Exercise 2.2　Evaluating an Interview

The interview process can be an effective means of selecting the volunteers you want and need for your youth sport program. In this exercise, evaluate the responses noted by an interviewer in this sample and help decide whether the applicant should be hired.

Coaching Interview Form

Interviewer's name I.B. Boss   Applicant's name Allen Becker

Date 3/20   Position Baseball coach

Motives for Volunteering to Coach

Why do you wish to coach? Enjoys working w/kids. Has a boy of his own. Thought it would be fun!

What do you hope to gain personally from coaching? Better understanding of the game. Give his boy an opportunity to have a better coach than last year.

How much time will you be able to commit to coaching? Works 9-5 at the glue factory— occasional overtime and a Saturday every now & then.

Knowledge of the Sport

How would you conduct a typical practice? Stretching, drills, game-type situation. No formal training, no experience. Allen will need help here!

How familiar are you with the rules of this sport? Played the sport as a kid. No high school/ college experience. Watches a lot of sports on T.V.

What do you think would be helpful to learn about the sport to improve your ability to coach it? Pitching—thinks pitching is key to the game. Also need to learn how to work w/12 to 15 kids at one time—has only 1 child.

Knowledge of How to Work With Young People

How would you describe your coaching philosophy? Kids should have fun, but it is sports—they'll have to meet some expectations—making practices, staying in shape, etc.

(continued)

What do you consider the important differences in coaching this age group compared to adults?
No experience—didn't have enough knowledge to express differences.

Have you had other experience teaching or directing young people? _Was a volunteer for a canoe trip_
last summer, enjoyed the experience—but really didn't do too much w/the kids.

Character and Emotional Stability

On what basis will you judge yourself to have been a successful or unsuccessful coach? _Winning_
isn't everything, but want to do better than the coach did last year. Would like to see his own kid hit
.300 for the season.

How long have you held your present position of employment? _3 years—laid off once during that time._

What behaviors in other people irritate you? _People who always think they're right annoy Allen._

Other Questions Based on Coaching Application

After the interview we recommend that you call at least two references for all candidates you select for further consideration. When calling, ask specific questions to verify the information you obtained from the Coaching Application Form (form 2.7) and interview. Also ask specific questions about aspects of the person's qualifications you are concerned about.

Call references as the third step of your screening process. It's true that reference letters are often requested to be submitted with the initial application for a position, but these letters are almost always positive and often quite general. They seldom tell you much about the person. Thus, talking to references by telephone tends to be more helpful (after you have learned enough about the applicant to ask specific questions).

The next step is to consider all the information gathered and rate the qualifications of the coach. Form 2.9 is a straightforward evaluation form you can use for this purpose.

After the interviews and references are obtained, the coaching committee convenes to make the final selection decisions. Those selected to be coaches should be contacted, preferably by telephone, to be notified of their appointments. At any stage of the process that individuals are rejected for further consideration, they should promptly be written a courteous letter notifying them that they did not qualify.

Self-Selection Process

The second part of the selection process involves asking coaches, as a condition of receiving the position, to agree to the following:

1. To successfully pass the ASEP Level One coaching education course. We believe that

responsible youth sport directors can no longer simply assign any willing volunteer to the position of coach unless this person has some minimum education to fulfill the position satisfactorily. ASEP courses, described in the next section, are effective in helping you educate prospective coaches. Table 2.1 shows the results of a coaching education survey conducted by the National Youth Sports Research and Development Center. Their findings support

One of the most important parts of coaching is the ability to communicate well with players.

Table 2.1   Coaching Education Survey
67%   Paying a fee would not be discouraging
72%   Mandatory coaching education encouraged them to continue
85%   Prefer a league that requires training
85%   Believe that training increases skill and confidence
86%   Would attend training even if not required

Data from the National Youth Sports Research and Development Center.

ASEP's position on the value of coaching education.

2. To read and agree to the conditions of a coaching contract. A sample contract is shown in form 2.10 on page 75. Please feel free to use this form as is or to modify it to meet your preferences. Distribute this contract to applicants when you give them the Coaching Application Form. This will give them time to read it and consider its contents. Coaches are asked to sign two copies: one that you retain and another that both of you sign for the coach to keep. This simple procedure is helpful in obtaining a minimum commitment to your program objectives.

Coaches who are unwilling to fulfill these two requirements eliminate themselves from further consideration for your coaching position.

Educating Coaches

The single most important way you can ensure that the young people who participate in your sport program have a beneficial experience is to provide a quality education program for your coaches. More than anything else, poorly qualified coaches limit young people's opportunities to derive the full benefits from sport participation. In fact, such coaches can cause physical and psychological harm. Consequently, responsible youth sport directors must do more than merely recruit and select quality people to serve as coaches—they must offer

these volunteers at least a minimum education to prepare them for the important responsibilities of coaching. In this section you'll learn how you can implement ASEP's Volunteer Coach Education program with minimal time and at a very reasonable cost. Before describing the program in detail, let's first examine the need for coaching education and review a brief history of ASEP.

Need for Coaching Education

Over 20 million children are coached by 2.0 to 2.5 million volunteer adults in youth sport programs across the U.S. each year. These generally well-intentioned coaches make sport programs possible for young people. They constitute one of the largest volunteer groups in the country, and they are often underappreciated. Although most volunteer coaches succeed reasonably well without any formal training, most would benefit substantially from such training. Veteran coaches, sport scientists, and coaching educators have learned much about how to coach more effectively, yet the vast majority of coaches do not have access to this information.

Among youth volunteer coaches, two types of coaching problems prevail. The first occurs among coaches who lack training and therefore make errors simply because they do not have adequate knowledge. The second occurs among coaches who are so caught up with winning that they disregard the well-being of the kids in pursuit of personal recognition by winning games. Education programs can help both types of coaches, but coaches of the latter type are often more difficult to reach because they usually do not perceive that they need training. If they are receptive to any training, the only information they are likely to be interested in is that which will help them win. This is why it is so important that a good coaching education program convey the values, or program philosophy, to all coaches.

When suddenly thrust into the role of coach, novices do the obvious: They coach as they were coached or as they see others coach. Novice coaches are particularly likely to imitate the style of some winning college or professional coach because such coaches receive considerable publicity for their success. Such coaching practices may be appropriate for achieving the goals of professional adult sports, but seldom are they suitable for obtaining the long-term goals of children's sports. The tragedy is that some novice coaches fail to recognize the difference. For 25 years we've known that depriving athletes of water during intensive competition or practice is foolish, yet coaches continue to do it today. Coaches still teach situps incorrectly, organize practices inefficiently, misunderstand the principles of physical conditioning, give poor or incorrect nutritional advice, and use sarcasm as a substitute for positive instruction. Why? Because their coaches did it with them and no one has shown them a better way!

Many believe that coaching is something you learn by doing. This suggests that they believe that consequences of coaches' actions are benign and that inexperienced coaches do not have the potential to harm those they coach while they gain experience. Such thinking may have been acceptable for coaching in the past, but not today. We now know how important coaches can be in influencing the lives of young people, and we know so much more about what coaches need to know to be competent. Regardless of whether coaches are coaching eight-year-olds in a community recreational soccer program, high school varsity basketball players, or elite-level Olympic swimmers, they can benefit from formal training.

The American public today is recognizing the need for better-qualified coaches. Parents of children participating in sport are refusing to accept incompetent teaching of sport skills, disorganized practices, psychological abuse of players, improper training techniques, and malpractice in injury treatment. The media seize every opportunity to expose ineptness in coaching practices. And the courts are ruling against coaches and directors who fail to provide the standard of coaching offered by the most qualified coaches. So, for many reasons—but ultimately for the youth of our nation—now is the time for you as a youth sport director to introduce a quality coaching education program.

The two most common reasons that youth sport directors do not offer education programs to their coaches is lack of time and money. By using the American Sport Education Program's widely used Volunteer Education Program, we'll show you how little time education can take and how inexpensive it is. When the benefits are weighed against the costs, you'll see why more and more youth sport organizations are offering ASEP courses.

What Should a Good Coaching Education Program Do?

You want your coaching education program to

- convey your program philosophy;
- teach the fundamental principles of coaching, including the psychological, mechanical, physical, and teaching principles essential for every coach to know;
- teach the basic techniques and tactics of the sport;
- show coaches how to prevent injuries and provide proper first aid when injuries occur; and
- teach the specific procedures to be followed in your organization regarding equipment use, facility use, league rules, game modifications, and so on.

The American Sport Education Program

ASEP, or the American Sport Education Program (formerly ACEP—the American Coaching Effectiveness Program), is a multi-level educational program that has provided courses, printed resources, and videos for over one million coaches since 1981. Now ASEP has expanded its offerings to provide education for officials, sport administrators and parents. ASEP courses are offered through community youth sport programs, junior and senior high school, colleges and universities, national governing bodies, and sport associations. ASEP's curriculum is built on the philosophical foundation of Athletes First, Winning Second.

ASEP's coaching curriculum is organized into educational training for volunteer and professional coaches. The Volunteer Education Program is geared toward adults who work with children's sports (young people under the age of 14), many of whom are volunteers.

The Professional Education Program is for coaches, parents, and directors involved with interscholastic or club sports. The coaches training at this level is designed especially for school coaches, for those who have completed the Volunteer Education Program and want to learn more, and for those with coaching experience but no formal training to coach. The coaching curriculum consists of three levels: Bronze, Silver, and Gold. The National Federation of State High School Associations (NFHS) and over 34 state high school activity associations have adopted the ASEP Bronze level certification as their coaching education program.

The courses in the Volunteer and Professional programs are offered both in classroom format and, soon, as online courses. The classroom format has been the foundation of coaching training for many years, and instructors and coaches are able to delve into the various challenges of working with players of all ages and skill levels.

The online format allows coaches to enroll online and take the entire course, including the test, through their computer. The online courses will offer sport administrators a convenient method of training coaches who are unable to attend classroom courses.

Volunteer Coach Education Program

This program is for educating volunteer coaches who will be coaching children and youth up to the age of 14 and who have little or no formal education to serve as coaches. The program is especially designed for community-based youth sports programs offered by park and recreation departments, local chapters of national youth sports organizations such as Little League Baseball, YMCA, Boys and Girls Clubs, and nonaffiliated local sports clubs.

The Volunteer Coach Education Program has two levels. Each level has a series of sport-specific courses:

The **Level One** course covers the coaching principles that volunteer coaches need to be successful, as well as the basic techniques and tactics of their particular sport. Increasing numbers of youth sport organizations are making these courses mandatory for every coach in their program, be they head coaches

or assistants. Resources for the Level One course include the *Coaching Basics video series*, a set of three 20-minute videos that cover the general principles of coaching young athletes. The three videos contain:

- Tape 1: *Being a C.O.A.C.H.* Coaches' roles, philosophy, psychology, communication, and sportsmanship.
- Tape 2: *Coaching Safety.* Safety, conditioning, and injury treatment.
- Tape 3: *Preparing for Game Day.* Games approach, teaching principles, practice, and game planning.

The *Level One: Coaching Education Facilitator Guide* on CD-ROM, which contains the Facilitator Guide for both the coaching principles and tactics and techniques. The outline of the classroom course and active learning exercises engage the coaches and encourage classroom discussion, adding to the learning experience.

The *Coaching Youth* books and videos, ASEP's sport-specific resources for beginning coaches. The books explore coaching principles and the basic techniques and tactics for each sport. Chapters on the *games approach* to teaching sport skills and game-day coaching provide valuable information for beginning coaches. Our *Coaching Youth* books are endorsed by several national governing bodies and set the standard for volunteer coach education. These videos contain the essential tactics and techniques needed to become a successful coach. The books and videos are packaged together so that each coach attending the classroom or online course will have these resources to review again and again.

After the clinic, a review of the material using a *Coaching Youth* book and video, coaches complete a 25-item self-study test. They return their tests to the course administrator, who grades them using an answer key provided in the Level One: Coaching Education Facilitator Guide.

Using the facilitator guide, you or members of your coaching committee can easily teach the Level One Program. The course is easy to teach and the cost of offering it is very low. The teaching materials—the video series and CD-

ROM instructor guide—are a one-time purchase. The books and videos for each coach are sport-specific and will aid the coach for seasons to come.

Level Two courses are being developed for coaches who have mastered the Level One and want to learn more. These courses teach the more advanced method of coaching called the *games approach*, whereby coaches teach the tactics and skills of the sport through a series of carefully designed games. Sport specific videos offer information and examples of practice ready games that coaches can use to drill the tactics and techniques of the sport.

ASEP's Volunteer Education Program curriculum offers information and educational resources on education for officials, parents, and administrators. Sports administrators that have lots to do and little budget to work with will be interested in receiving information about the **Premiere Classroom Course Package**. If you train 100 coaches over a three year period for a fee per coach, much of the educational recourses necessary for the courses will be provide free of charge. For more information concerning these resources and programs, call ASEP and ask to talk with a volunteer implementation specialist. Our staff will be happy to help you get started. Just call 800-747-5698, or visit our website at **http://www.asep.com**.

Professional Coach Education

ASEP's Professional Coach Education program is for educating school, club, and college coaches, as well as college students who are preparing to become coaches. Coaches at these levels are expected to be more professional in their coaching. Thus, the curriculum is more extensive in both what is covered and how extensively it is covered than the Volunteer program.

The Professional Coach Education program has three levels, with the Bronze level being recommended for all coaches.

The **Bronze level** consists of three courses that should be required of all coaches, grounding them in coaching principles, the fundamentals of being a capable first responder to injuries, and coaching their sport successfully. Coaches will be required to successfully complete ASEP 301 Coaching Principles, ASEP 302 Sport First Aid, and a sport-specific course from ASEP 320-358, based on the successful sports series *Coaching Successfully*. Coaches completing all three Silver-level courses will be prepared to coach at the school level. Since 1990, ASEP and the National Federation of State High School Associations (NFHS) have provided practical, convenient, and economical coaches education for high school coaches. ASEP's coach education courses are required for high school coaches in 34 states and the numbers are growing! Coaching Principles and Sport First Aid are the foundation courses of ASEP's coach education programs.

The **Gold level** is the next step for coaches, including sport-specific courses in advanced techniques and tactics as well as courses in sport physiology, sport psychology, mechanics of sport, and teaching sport skills. These latter four courses are not sport-specific; they apply the knowledge of each sport science to the practice of coaching.

The **Platinum level** consists of five courses—three are general (sport nutrition, sport risk management, and social issues in sport), and two are sport-specific (advanced conditioning and advanced practice and season planning).

If you have any questions about the Professional Education Program, call ASEP at 800-747-5698 and ask to talk with a professional implementation specialist, or visit our website at **http://www.asep.com**. See table 2.2, page 52.

Supervision and Evaluation

You've done a great job of recruiting, selecting, and educating your coaches. Now you can sit back, relax, and let the coaches go to work—right? Not quite. You've taken three important steps toward assuring quality coaching in your program, but now you need to take one more step—to supervise and evaluate. As a major part of supervising, we'll emphasize formally evaluating your coaches using the ASEP Coaching Appraisal Form.

Many youth sport directors never supervise or evaluate their coaches. Are you one of them? Do you throw the coaches the ball and say "good luck" without offering any further help?

Table 2.2 ASEP Youth Sport Programs

	Volunteer education program	Professional education program
Coach education	Level One certification Level Two certification	Bronze-level certification Silver-level certification Gold-level certification
Administrator education	Directing Community Sports Programs course Sport Director Software, YMCA Edition	Professional Sport Administrator resources Sport Director: NFHS Edition software
Official education	Youth Sport Officiating course	Principles of Sports Officiating course
Parent education	SportParent Orientation Kit	Parenting a High School Athlete

If so, please consider what is recommended in this section.

Yes, we know that it takes a lot of time to supervise coaches, especially if you have a large program. But you can do it efficiently and cost-effectively by implementing the plan described here using your coaching committee.

Supervision of your coaches is your legal responsibility as a youth sport program director. You are responsible to direct and inspect the performance of your coaches—to oversee their coaching. Evaluation is a component of this supervisory responsibility; it is your duty to appraise the performance of your coaches.

Some youth sport directors view supervision as a policing function, but try to think of it more as a means of providing support: you're coaching your coaches. When supervising, you'll see how your entire program is working. You'll have the opportunity to provide positive feedback to coaches who perform well, and you'll be able to offer constructive guidelines for improving coaching methods to those who are not coaching consistently with your program principles and policies.

You may worry that coaches will resent being supervised. Those who do probably lack confidence in their coaching or recognize they are not coaching in accordance with your program principles. However, most coaches want to do well and will appreciate the support and

help that comes from supervisors who approach this responsibility in a constructive way. And knowing that someone will observe them in action from time to time says that you as the program director care about the program, are interested in them, and expect them to do well.

Your Plan to Supervise and Evaluate Coaches

If you have hundreds of coaches, you can hardly supervise and evaluate them all by yourself. Your coaching committee should be assigned this responsibility, and you need to have enough qualified individuals on this committee to do the job properly. Your task as program director is to manage this process, and that begins with a supervision and evaluation plan. In this section we'll provide you with guidelines and steps to help develop your plan, and offer you useful tools to conduct your evaluations.

In most youth sport programs it is not possible to supervise all coaches at all sites at all times. On the other hand, it is irresponsible not to supervise your coaches at all. Thus, you must do what you can by making optimal use of the resources available to you. Here are nine guidelines to keep in mind as you develop your plan for supervising and evaluating your coaches.

- Supervise and evaluate all coaches, not just those you hear are having problems.
- Supervise as much as possible, given the limits of staff and volunteer time.
- Supervise and evaluate coaches in contests and practices.
- Use supervisors who have demonstrated competency as coaches and have credibility with the coaches being supervised.
- Supervise and evaluate coaches throughout the season.
- Evaluate coaches unannounced.
- Evaluate coaches early in the practice season and early in the competitive season so that you can provide any useful feedback for their continued coaching.
- Evaluate coaches by looking not only for weaknesses, but strengths as well.
- Provide feedback to coaches as soon after the evaluation as possible.

Before preparing your supervision and evaluation plan you may find it helpful to review the following sample plan.

Developing Your Plan for Supervising Coaches

Following are seven steps to follow in developing your plan for supervising and evaluating coaches. This plan is not for general supervision of the program or a facility, but specifically for supervising and evaluating coaches. When implementing this plan in your program, you may want to incorporate the supervision and evaluation of coaches along with other supervisory duties; but for this exercise, focus on the supervision and evaluation of coaches exclusively.

1. To help you determine how you will supervise and evaluate your coaches, first compile information regarding the scope of your program, including

- number of leagues and teams,
- number of head coaches and assistant coaches,
- dates of practices and contests, and

- locations where practices and contests are held.

2. Identify who will supervise and evaluate. Only you? A volunteer coaching director and your coaching committee? Someone else?

3. Describe the specific duties of the supervisors when they are only to supervise. What are they to observe and record? What actions are they authorized to take when certain events occur?

4. Describe the specific duties of the supervisors when they are to evaluate the coaches. Consider using the ASEP Coaching Appraisal Form (form 2.11, page 76) for conducting these evaluations.

5. Determine how frequently and how long head coaches and assistant coaches will be supervised. Determine how frequently and how long they will be evaluated.

6. Describe in detail how the supervisory staff will be assigned to sites, leagues, and teams to conduct the supervision and evaluation.

7. Describe what feedback you will give coaches when they have been evaluated. What form will this feedback take? When will it be given?

Coaching Appraisals

The ASEP Coaching Appraisal Form (form 2.11, see page 76) can be used as is or modified to meet your needs. To use the ASEP Coaching Appraisal Form as part of your coaching supervision and evaluation plan, follow these steps:

1. Become thoroughly familiar with the form and be able to further define the criteria for rating coaches.

2. Condu æ......ct a training session for your appraisers. Review the form and show them how to use it in evaluating coaches. Have all appraisers join you in evaluating one or two coaches at the same time. Then discuss the differences and similarities in the ratings, developing guidelines to help all appraisers use the ASEP Coaching Appraisal Form consistently.

Sample Plan for Supervising and Evaluating Coaches

Rockford Park and Recreation Fall Soccer Program

Step 1: Scope of Program

Number of leagues and teams

11 leagues with 8 teams in each league. Ages of participants range from 7 years through 14 years, with boys', girls', and coed leagues.

Coaches

Each team has a head coach. Many have one assistant coach, and a few have two assistant coaches. The total number of coaches is 216—88 head coaches and 128 assistant coaches.

Practices and games

Leagues A, B, C, and D practice once per week and play one game per week for 8 weeks. Practices begin August 24 for 3 weeks before the season, during which time teams may conduct two practices. All practices are held between 5 and 7 P.M. on weekdays; all games are played on Saturday mornings.

All other leagues may practice up to twice per week and play one game per week for 10 weeks. Practices begin August 24 for 3 weeks before the season begins. Each team may practice up to three times per week. All practices are held between 5 and 7 P.M. on weekdays; all games are played on Saturdays and Sundays.

Practice and game locations

Leagues A and B play at Bond Park; Leagues C, D, and E play at Washington Grade School; Leagues F, G, H, and I play at Webster Park; and Leagues J and K play at Centennial Junior High School.

Step 2: Personnel to Supervise and Evaluate

Supervisors

One supervisor will be provided for each of the 11 leagues.

Evaluators

A team of evaluators will consist of the supervisor and two league evaluators selected and appointed by the program committee.

Step 3: Supervision Duties

Each supervisor is responsible for general supervision of all practices and games scheduled at the location of each of the leagues to ensure the safety and well-being of program participants and promote the objectives of the program.

Supervisors are responsible for completing all accident report forms, along with the biweekly summary of practices and games. In the event that a problem or incident occurs, supervisors are asked to complete the incident report form and contact the program director within 24 hours.

Step 4: Evaluation Duties

The evaluation team has the responsibility to conduct three evaluations of all head coaches and assistant coaches throughout the course of the season, as listed in step 5. Each evaluator will be responsible for four teams. The coaches' evaluation forms will be completed by the evaluator and shared with the league supervisor. The evaluation team will share the results of the evaluation with each of the coaches and provide feedback, as listed in step 7.

Step 5: Supervision and Evaluation Frequency and Time

General supervision on behalf of the league supervisor will take place daily. Supervisory reports are to be completed and filed biweekly.

Evaluations will be conducted by the evaluation team following the schedule below:

1. Third week of practice (September 6-12)
2. After the second week of games (September 20-25)
3. Final week of practices (week of October 25 for Leagues A, B, C, D, and E; week of November 9 for Leagues F, G, H, 1, J, and K)

Evaluations will be scheduled in advance and last no longer than 20 minutes.

Step 6: Personnel Assignments

Supervisors are responsible for the leagues they represent. The evaluation team, supervisor, and two evaluators will divide the responsibility of evaluating the coaches of the eight teams in the league using the following format:

Supervisor	Evaluator 1	Evaluator 2
Teams 1, 2	Teams 3, 4, 5	Teams 6, 7, 8

Responsibility for team evaluations will be rotated after each evaluation. Each member of the evaluation team will evaluate each team only once.

Step 7: Feedback From Evaluation

Immediate feedback during practice (or following practice, if safety risk exists) will be given for any general supervision. Feedback from evaluations will be done during a planned meeting established by the coach and the evaluation team, following a scheduled practice or game.

The supervision/evaluation form will be shared with the coach during this meeting.

Recommendations will be made by the evaluation team as a result of the evaluation following the guidelines listed in the evaluation guide.

If a coach is having problems or has been placed on probation due to a conduct violation, additional supervisor evaluations may be prescribed.

3. At the bottom of the form, define for the appraisers what type of recommendations you want to receive. Are they to recommend special recognition for outstanding coaching? Are they to suggest that remedial training be undertaken if they see problems with a coach? Should they ever recommend that a coach be placed on probation or terminated?

4. Have appraisers complete a separate form each time they evaluate a coach, be it in practice or a contest.

5. Follow your supervision and evaluation plans for giving coaches feedback (see pages 52-53 for recommendations).

6. Tell appraisers when forms are to be submitted to you.

7. Give appraisers their assignments for evaluating the coaches.

Guidelines for Providing Feedback

You will gain vital feedback and greatly improve your program by evaluating your coaches systematically. Equally, if you communicate correctly with your coaches, this feedback will help them improve their coaching skills. The result will be a higher-quality program that makes greater contributions to the youth of your community.

Exercise 2.3 will help you learn the effectiveness of your coaching appraisal system and how to respond to an appraisal after an evaluation of the coach is completed.

Exercise 2.3　Evaluating a Coaching Appraisal

Review the completed coach's appraisal form below and decide what your recommendations to the coaching director would be regarding the coach discussed in the form. Do you recommend praise, reward, reprimand, or dismissal? Explain what led you to your decision. Finally, consider the following questions as you review your program's appraisal system: How do you react to the appraisals completed for each of your coaches? Does your system reward and reprimand coaches fairly? Do you actively respond to the appraisals of your coaches or do you simply complete them to appease your boss?

ASEP Coaching Appraisal Form

Coach name _Allen Becker_　　　　　　　　　　Sport _Baseball_

Team _White Socks_　　　　　　　　　　League _Jr. Division_

Appraiser _I.B. Boss_　　　　　　　　　　Date _4/25_

Observation during:　(Practice)　　Competition

Minutes observed _45_

Circle only one response using the following rating system:

	Unsatisfactory	Needs improvement	Adequate	Good	Excellent
Knowledge					
Knowledge of the sport (rules, skills, strategies)	1	2	(3)	4	5
Teaching of skills	1	2	(3)	4	5
Correcting errors	1	(2)	3	4	5

	Unsatisfactory	Needs improvement	Adequate	Good	Excellent
Management					
Organization of activities	1	2	(3)	4	5
Use of time	1	2	(3)	4	5
Involvement of athletes	1	(2)	3	4	5
Communication					
Provides clear instructions	1	2	(3)	4	5
Listens to others	1	(2)	3	4	5
Uses appropriate language	1	2	3	(4)	5
Health					
Provides safe environment	1	2	3	(4)	5
Conditions athletes properly	1	2	(3)	4	5
Is sensitive to child's self-esteem and emotions	1	(2)	3	4	5
Self-control					
Physical appearance	1	2	3	(4)	5
Control of emotions	1	(2)	3	4	5
Use of tobacco, alcohol, or other drugs	1	2	3	(4)	5
Relationships					
With athletes	1	(2)	3	4	5
With parents	1	(2)	3	4	5
With other coaches	1	(2)	3	4	5
With officials and directors	1	(2)	3	4	5
Motivation					
Motivates athletes appropriately	1	(2)	3	4	5
Shows enthusiasm for coaching	1	2	(3)	4	5
Coaching philosophy					
Appropriate perspective about winning and losing	1	2	(3)	4	5
Coaching style	1	2	(3)	4	5
Coaches to make sport fun to play	1	(2)	3	4	5
Overall rating of coach	**1**	**(2)**	**3**	**4**	**5**

Recommendations to coaching director:

Remember that, unless the coach is very emotional or preoccupied with other matters, feedback is best when given immediately. Give your coaches a copy of the ASEP Coaching Appraisal Form completed by the appraiser (minus the recommendations to the coaching director) immediately after being evaluated, along with brief informal comments by the appraiser. During or after practice and games, however, is usually not a good time for appraisers to talk with coaches, because the coaches are busy with their coaching duties. Thus, at minimum, the appraiser should hand the coach a copy of the completed form with an invitation to call the appraiser to discuss any of the ratings.

In addition, you should provide a summary of coaching evaluations to coaches at midseason so that they have an opportunity to benefit from the feedback of the appraisers and receive positive reinforcement for their contributions to the program.

It's very challenging to provide people evaluations of their performance, especially when they're volunteering their time. Here are our Ten Commandments for Giving Feedback. Share these with your appraisers to help them handle this sensitive interaction better.

Coach Evaluation by Parents and Athletes

Direct observation of coaches by members of your coaching committee is an excellent way to evaluate coaches, but it is not the only way to get useful information. You may also find it worthwhile to have parents and athletes evaluate the coaches.

We have provided an ASEP Parent Evaluation of Coach Form (form 2.12, page 78) for you to give to parents to evaluate a coach. Ask parents to complete this form around mid-

Ten Commandments for Coaching Feedback

1. Establish that your feedback is designed to be constructive, that your purpose is to help the coach provide a better sport experience for the participants.

2. Be sincere in your remarks, conveying verbally and nonverbally that you wish to help. Show respect and understanding throughout the discussion.

3. Begin by complimenting the coach on what he has done well. Identify specific coaching behaviors that you observed.

4. Provide positive reinforcement for coaches' behaviors, not the outcomes of their behaviors. For example, praise the teaching of skills effectively rather than the winning of games.

5. Be direct in your comments; especially don't be wishy-washy when giving constructive criticism. Know what you want to say. Then point out what you saw that needs to be improved and recommend how to make the improvement.

6. Always recognize coaches for volunteering their time and for their positive intentions. Look to praise such intangibles as the demonstration of good judgment, self-control, and responsibility.

7. Give coaches an opportunity to share their thoughts about the evaluation and how to improve their coaching behaviors.

8. Use good judgment in selecting an appropriate time and place for providing constructive criticism. Do not provide constructive criticism when the coach is busy, emotional, or with other people.

9. Avoid providing feedback if you are angry, irritated, or emotional about a coach's behaviors. Delay the feedback until you have time to regain control and put things in perspective.

10. End the feedback session on a positive note. Refocus attention on what the coach did well and the value of her services as coach to the community.

season, as this allows parents enough opportunity to observe the coach, and affords coaches some time to consider the feedback and make any changes.

Use the ASEP Athlete Evaluation of Coach Form (form 2.13, page 79, at the end of the season for players 8 years of age or older. We do not recommend using the form during the season, because it may focus too much attention on judging coaches. For players 8 to 12 years old, ask their parents to read the questions to the children to help them complete the form. It is best if this form can be completed at a postseason gathering where its completion is supervised, rather than sending it home for return at a later time.

Coaches' Self-Evaluation

It is also valuable to ask coaches to evaluate themselves. The ASEP Coaching Appraisal Form is suitable for completion by your coaches. In fact, the process of having coaches evaluate themselves will draw their attention to their coaching behaviors and the criteria you are using to evaluate them. This step alone can be useful in improving some coaches' coaching behaviors.

Dealing With Problem Coaches

You'll likely encounter some in your program who are "problem coaches." These are coaches who are overly argumentative, cannot get along with parents or officials, overemphasize winning, are physically or psychologically abusive, are incompetent in teaching skills, expose children to needless risk of injury, fail to show up for practices and contests, and so on. As you discover these problems in your supervision, you'll need to determine how to address them.

Although each coach and each problem is unique, we offer these general guidelines for your consideration. Problems should be categorized as *major* or *minor*. For example, a coach arguing a call is a minor incident the first one or two times it happens, but if it happens repeatedly, it becomes a major problem. Slapping a player, yelling obscenities at a parent, and conducting a drill that is physically dangerous to the players are considered major problems. Of course criminal acts are major problems, and you should contact the appropriate authorities when these occur.

It is also useful to distinguish between what we call *technical* problems and *motivation* problems. Technical problems occur when coaches simply do not know how to do something correctly. The assumption is that if they had known better, they would have behaved differently. Motivation problems occur when coaches know how to do something correctly but choose not to or choose to achieve goals other than those your program values. For example, a coach may be more motivated to win games than to look after the welfare of his players. Or a coach may not care to put forth the effort to provide quality practices by not properly preparing, not coaching during practices but simply standing on the sidelines, or not showing up at all.

We have four types of coaching problems that warrant different strategies to solve. Each time the problem behavior occurs you should decide whether it is appropriate to take the next step in the recommended sequence. At every step, be sure to document all contact with problem coaches.

Coach A

Coach A has a minor technical coaching problem, such as not knowing how to teach a particular skill correctly or not knowing all the rules of the sport. She may not understand the sequence in teaching a skill or how to condition her athletes properly for the sport. Follow these steps in dealing with Coach A.

1. Provide constructive feedback.

2. Provide additional constructive feedback and suggestions for where to get more information.

3. Provide additional specific feedback and require the coach to repeat your coaching training program.

4. Provide additional specific feedback and reassign the coach to serve as an assistant under a competent head coach.

5. If the minor technical problems are cumulative and result in the coach being ineffective, do not reappoint this coach next season.

Coach B

This coach has a minor motivational problem. For example, he might often be late to practice, forget to bring the equipment, forget to make appropriate arrangements, fail to plan practices, or do very little actual coaching during practice. Each of these incidents alone is a minor problem, but put together they can quickly become a major problem. Follow these steps for dealing with Coach B.

1. Provide constructive feedback.

2. Discuss with the coach your concern about his motivation, presenting clear expectations of his coaching responsibilities and seeking his commitment to fulfill these expectations.

3. Provide specific feedback about the motivational problem and again seek commitment to fulfill his coaching responsibilities.

4. Provide specific feedback and reassign the coach to serve as an assistant under a competent head coach.

5. If the minor technical problems are cumulative and result in the coach being ineffective, do not reappoint this coach next season.

Coach C

This coach has a major technical problem, such as not knowing how to teach skills safely, which puts her athletes at increased and undue risk. Follow these steps in dealing with Coach C.

1. Provide immediate specific feedback to correct the problem. The coach should be permitted to continue coaching only under supervision until she has demonstrated knowledge of the correct technical skills.

2. If the same technical problem is repeated, either immediately reassign the coach to serve as an assistant under a competent head coach or dismiss her, depending on the circumstances. If it is a different technical problem, provide immediate feedback, permit the coach to continue only under supervision, and require that she complete a technique course in that sport.

3. If the same or another technical problem occurs again, either immediately reassign this coach to serve as an assistant under a competent head coach or dismiss her to protect the

well-being of your participants, depending on the circumstances.

Coach D

This coach exhibits major problems, displaying such behaviors as acting irresponsibly, flagrantly disregarding your policies, using alcohol or drugs, or being physically or psychologically abusive to the athletes. Take these steps in dealing with Coach D.

1. Depending on the nature of the offense, provide specific constructive feedback, a consultation on the responsibilities entrusted to coaches, and/or a warning that any further such incident will result in dismissal. The coach should be frequently supervised thereafter.

2. If another major motivational problem occurs, dismiss the coach immediately.

It's likely that a coach having problems in one of these categories is also having problems in one or more of the other categories. When this occurs, you need to use your judgment about the severity of the problems, the likelihood of the coach learning the correct technical coaching behaviors, and the likelihood of the coach rectifying the motivational problems. While you want to be fair to the coach, remember that your obligation is to protect the children participating in your program. However, if you think a problem coach would succeed in a different position in your program, explore that avenue as an alternative to releasing the coach.

Recognizing Coaches

Coaches are the lifeline of your program. They give hundreds of hours to the young athletes they coach, to your program, and to the community. Most volunteers look for the intrinsic rewards in coaching as their ultimate satisfaction in volunteering their time, but some extrinsic rewards are also appreciated. Following is a list of ideas for recognizing coaches.

1. Cover the coaches' cost of a comprehensive coaching education program (including resources).

2. Give them awards such as certificates, emblems, plaques, hats, jackets, and so on in recognition of their service.

3. Give awards based on the number of years coached (a small recognition for the first year, with increasing value in the awards as the number of years of service increase).

4. Recognize all coaches who complete the ASEP Level One Course with awards and/or other items that you think are appropriate, such as patches, caps, and so on.

5. Publicize the coaches' names in appropriate sources (list all the coaches on a wall in your organization's center or print their names in the newspaper, for example).

6. Host a picnic or some other function for all coaches and briefly recognize each one.

7. Recognize coaches at the start of each game, or at least at the first game of the season. This would be a good time to announce to the parents and players that the coach has completed the ASEP Volunteer Education Program.

8. Recognize assistant coaches who coach well by promoting them to head coaches.

9. Recognize head coaches who coach well by asking them to become members of the coaching committee to supervise other coaches.

10. Write a letter at the end of the season commending the coach and providing feedback about the coaching evaluation. Those who have coached well should be encouraged to return the next season.

11. Don't forget the significance of a personal thank-you from you and your staff.

Take the time to organize a good recognition system and you'll find that you have many more coaches returning next season. Doesn't it make sense to recruit back your experienced coaches—your best coaches—by taking a little time to properly thank them for their contributions?

Summary

The attrition rate among volunteer coaches in children's sport programs is reported to be between 40 and 60 percent a year. You can significantly reduce your attrition rate by investing more effort into your volunteer coaches by

- recruiting excellent people,
- selecting those best qualified,
- providing them with a quality education program,
- supervising, evaluating, and providing them with constructive feedback, and
- recognizing them appropriately.

As every supervisor eventually learns, every dollar spent on improving the quality of your help is an investment that yields big dividends.

Form 2.1 Coaching Needs Assessment Form

Organization name _____

Coaching director _____

Sport _____ Date _____

League name:	A league	B league	C league	D league	E league	Total
(1) Season dates (month to month)						
(2) Number of head coaches last season						
(3) Number of assistant coaches last season						
(4) Number of head coaches expected to return						
(5) Number of assistant coaches expected to return						
(6) Number of assistant coaches becoming head coaches						
(7) Number of head coaching positions needed this season						
(8) Number of assistant coaching positions needed this season						
(9) Estimated number of head coaches available (4) + (6)						
(10) Estimated number of assistant coaches available (5) − (6)						
(11) Number of new head coaches needed this season (7) − (9)						
(12) Number of new assistant coaches needed this season (8) − (10)						

Sample Coaching Needs Assessment Form

Organization name <u>We Wanna Play Youth Center</u>

Coaching director <u>Les B. Phair</u>

Sport <u>Basketball</u>   Date <u>Oct. 1</u>

League name:	A league	B league	C league	D league	E league	Total
(1) Season dates (month to month)	Dec. – Feb.	Dec. – Feb.	Jan. – Mar.	Jan. – Mar.		
(2) Number of head coaches last season	20	14	8	6		48
(3) Number of assistant coaches last season	26	14	5	9		54
(4) Number of head coaches expected to return	11	9	3	1		24
(5) Number of assistant coaches expected to return	8	11	3	1		23
(6) Number of assistant coaches becoming head coaches	3	5	1	1		10
(7) Number of head coaching positions needed this season	20	14	10	12		56
(8) Number of assistant coaching positions needed this season	30	14	10	12		66
(9) Estimated number of head coaches available (4) + (6)	14	14	4	2		34
(10) Estimated number of assistant coaches available (5) – (6)	5	6	2	0		13
(11) Number of new head coaches needed this season (7) – (9)	6	0	6	10		22
(12) Number of new assistant coaches needed this season (8) – (10)	25	8	8	12		53

Form 2.3 | Multiple-Sport Coaching Needs Assessment Summary

Organization name _____

Coaching director _____

Sport _____ Date _____

Sport	Number of head coaching positions (from F7)	Number of head coaches available (from F9)	Number of new head coaches needed (from F11)	Number of assistant coaching positions (from F8)	Number of assistant coaches available (from F10)	Number of new assistant coaches needed (from F12)	Months to recruit coaches

Position title:

Position description:

Activities and responsibilities:

1.

2.

3.

4.

5.

6.

7.

8.

Qualifications:

Benefits:

Dates of service:

Supervisor:

Make a difference . . .

	basketball photo
soccer photo	football or other sport photo
	softball/baseball photo

. . . become a Youth Sport Coach!

organization logo

Contact [name] of the [organization] at [phone number]

Why Become Involved?

The We Wanna Play Youth Center is a not-for-profit organization that offers sport programs to area youth. We want to provide kids opportunities to learn and develop sport skills in a safe, healthy, fun-filled environment.

We call on interested adults to coach. We provide our coaches the information and support they need and believe that this serves as a great opportunity for adults to positively influence young athletes.

Your Commitment

Each youth sport program operates on a 10-week schedule. The first 2 weeks coaches hold three 1-hour practices per week (two per week thereafter). Practices are held at the Center or at McRainer Field; we will work with you in setting this up.

During the third week (and from then on), one of your practices is replaced with a league game. Games are on Saturdays. (See back page for calendar of events.)

Administrative Support

We hold all our coaches in high regard; we don't just recruit coaches and let them go! If you are a first-year coach with us, we will train you through the American Sport Education Program (ASEP) Rookie Coaches Course. This involves a 3-hour clinic, study of a Rookie Coaches Guide, and a short open-book test. Our goal is to give you the information you need to be successful and enjoy your experience.

Coaches returning a second year will take the ASEP Coaching Young Athletes Course. The course operates similarly to the Rookie Coaches Course.

Through coaches' meetings and sport-specific clinics, we offer coaches further support. We're here to help you!

What's in It for You?

I've never been so rewarded as the time I saw Jimmy Edwards complete his first pass. You could see his grin a mile away. That's what coaching youth sports is all about.—Jack Smith, volunteer football coach.

I first started coaching when my daughter was 9 and wanted to play youth soccer. I figured I'd quit when she was through. She's 18 now and in college, but I loved the experience so much I'm still coaching! —Janice Sharkey, volunteer soccer coach

Becoming a volunteer coach for the We Wanna Play Youth Center helps children, and it also gives adults the chance to work with and learn from children. Our coaches receive excellent training through ASEP courses; our resources make it easy for coaches to enjoy the experience and be successful.

If you've never coached youth sport before, you may be in for a surprise! Making a difference in a child's life, being a role model, and teaching sport skills and fundamentals can be highly rewarding. Receiving smiles and thanks from your kids and seeing them return to the sport the next season are good measures of your success.

(continued)

Your Qualifications

So you haven't coached before? That's all right! You don't need a long list of coaching experiences. You need to care about kids, be patient, and be motivated to coach. A sense of humor can't hurt. Enthusiasm is a plus. Being organized and reliable also helps.

If you can bring these qualities to us, we'll provide the information you need to be a great coach! Our training program and support will carry you a long way.

Thanks for Your Interest

The We Wanna Play Youth Center thanks you for reading this brochure. We hope you understand our mission and goals. And we hope that if you feel you have the right qualifications (see above), you'll join us in offering our sport programs to kids.

To help us make a difference, see How to Apply.

How to Apply

It's easy! Come to the We Wanna Play Youth Center, 101 Hanlon Boulevard, and complete a short coaching application form. We'll give you a job description, set up an interview, and provide an orientation program schedule.

At the orientation program we'll give you more information on your responsibilities and duties. You and other prospective coaches will be able to ask us questions about our programs and what it takes to be a volunteer coach.

For More Information

Contact our youth sport program administrator at 555-2232 or come to the We Wanna Play Youth Center and ask for our coaching position description. You can also pick up additional information at the Center regarding facilities and program policies.

Calendar of Events

Sport	Program date	Coaches' orientation
Flag football	August-October	August 10
Floor hockey	October-December	October 13
Basketball	December-February	December 8
Soccer	March-May	March 10
T-ball/softball	May-July	May 12
Baseball	June-August	June 9

Form 2.6   Year-Long Coaching Recruiting Plan

Organization name _____

Coaching director _____

Date _____ League/sport _____

Season dates _____

Activity _____ Date to initiate _____

Objective _____

_____

_____

Message _____

_____

_____

Contact _____ Estimated cost _____

Activity _____ Date to initiate _____

Objective _____

_____

_____

Message _____

_____

_____

Contact _____ Estimated cost _____

Activity _____ Date to initiate _____

Objective _____

_____

_____

Message _____

_____

_____

Contact _____ Estimated cost _____

Form 2.7   Coaching Application Form

Name _____   Telephone: Home _____

Address _____   Business _____

_____   Sex: Male ❑   Female ❑

_____   Are you 18 years or older?   Yes   No

1. Circle the highest year you completed in school:

   Elementary   1,   2,   3,   4,   5,   6,   7,   8

   High school   1,   2,   3,   4

   College   1,   2,   3,   4,   5,   6,   7,   8

2. Work history (last 10 years)

Company	Position	Dates
_____	_____	_____
_____	_____	_____
_____	_____	_____

3. What is the sport for which you are applying to coach? _____

   Note: The sport you have written in here will be referred to as *this sport* in the remainder of the questionnaire.

4. Why do you want to coach this sport? (Be specific.) _____

   _____

   _____

   _____

Coaching Background

5. Have you played this sport?   Yes ❑   No ❑   Number of years _____

6. What other sports have you played?

Sport	Age level	Number of years played
_____	_____	_____
_____	_____	_____
_____	_____	_____

7. Have you *coached* this sport?   Yes ❑   No ❑   Number of years _____

8. What other sports have you coached?

Sport	Sponsoring agency	Age level	Years coached
_____	_____	_____	_____
_____	_____	_____	_____
_____	_____	_____	_____

9. Have you had any formal training as a coach?   Yes ☐   No ☐   If yes, please describe (for example, PE degree, coaching courses, or clinics).

_____

_____

_____

10. Describe any informal training that would help you coach (for example, reading books or watching sports). _____

_____

_____

11. Have you ever been convicted of a crime? If so, please explain. _____

_____

12. Do you have any medical conditions that may affect your ability to coach? Yes ☐   No ☐

13. Please rate your knowledge of the following topics with regard to this sport by circling the appropriate number.

1 = You know very little about it
2 = You have reasonably good knowledge about it
3 = You know a great deal about it

1 2 3 • Skills and strategies of the sport
1 2 3 • Rules of the sport
1 2 3 • Organizing practices
1 2 3 • Equipment needs and specifications
1 2 3 • Injury prevention and treatment
1 2 3 • Legal duties

1 2 3 • Developing sportsmanship
1 2 3 • Communication skills
1 2 3 • Warm-up and physical
1 2 3 • Working with parents
1 2 3 • Principles for teaching sport skills
1 2 3 • Managing time

14. Please list the name, address, and telephone number (if available) of two persons who can attest to your coaching potential. One should be your most recent supervisor.

Name	Address	Telephone
_____	_____	_____
_____	_____	_____
_____	_____	_____

Form 2.8   Coaching Interview Form

Consider the question in the four categories below when interviewing potential candidates for your coaching positions. Use these as introductory questions to get the candidate talking. Then listen carefully and ask appropriate follow-up questions. Modify the questions below based on information presented in the Coaching Application Form.

Interviewer's name _____ Applicant's name _____

Date _____ Position _____

Motives for Volunteering to Coach

Why do you wish to coach? _____

_____

_____

What do you hope to gain personally from coaching? _____

_____

_____

How much time can you commit to coaching? _____

_____

_____

Knowledge of the Sport

How would you conduct a typical practice? _____

_____

_____

How familiar are you with the rules of this sport? _____

_____

_____

What do you think would be helpful to learn about the sport to improve your ability to coach it?

_____

_____

Knowledge of How to Work With Young People

How would you describe your coaching philosophy? _____

_____

_____

What do you consider the important differences in coaching this age group compared to adults?

_____

_____

Have you had other experiences in teaching or directing young people? _____

_____

_____

Character and Emotional Stability

On what basis will you judge yourself to have been a successful or unsuccessful coach? _____

_____

_____

How long have you held your present position of employment? _____

_____

_____

What behaviors in other people irritate you? _____

_____

_____

Form 2.9   Coach Evaluation Form

Name of coach _____

Coaching position _____

Evaluator _____ Date _____

Coaching Qualifications

	Rating		
	Weak	**Moderate**	**High**
Positive motives for coaching	1	2	3
Knowledge of the sport	1	2	3
Previous experience as a coach	1	2	3
Knowledge of how to work with young people	1	2	3
Communication skills	1	2	3
Maturity	1	2	3
Emotional stability	1	2	3
Time to commit to coaching	1	2	3

I understand that my responsibilities as a youth coach are of great importance and that my actions have the potential to significantly influence the young athletes I coach. Therefore, I promise to uphold the following rights of young athletes to the best of my ability.

I. Right to participate in sports.

II. Right to participate at a level commensurate with each child's maturity and ability.

III. Right to have qualified adult leadership.

IV. Right to play as a child and not as an adult.

V. Right to share in the leadership and decision making of sport participation.

VI. Right to participate in safe and healthy environments.

VII. Right to proper preparation for participation in sports.

VIII. Right to an equal opportunity to strive for success.

IX. Right to be treated with dignity.

X. Right to have fun in sports.

I also promise to conduct myself in accordance with the Code of Ethics for Coaches as outlined here.

1. I will treat each athlete, opposing coach, official, parent, and administrator with respect and dignity.

2. I will do my best to learn the fundamental skills, teaching and evaluation techniques, and strategies of my sport.

3. I will become thoroughly familiar with the rules of my sport.

4. I will become familiar with the objectives of the youth sport program with which I am affiliated. I will strive to achieve these objectives and communicate them to my athletes and their parents.

5. I will uphold the authority of officials who are assigned to the contests in which I coach, and I will assist them in every way to conduct a fair and impartial competitive contest.

6. I will learn the strengths and weaknesses of my athletes so that I might place them in situations where they have a maximum opportunity to achieve success.

7. I will conduct my practices and contests so that all athletes have an opportunity to improve their skills through active participation.

8. I will communicate to my athletes and their parents the rights and responsibilities of individuals on our team.

9. I will cooperate with the administrator of our organization in the enforcement of rules and regulations, and I will report any irregularities that violate sound competitive practices.

10. I will protect the health and safety of my athletes by insisting that all of the activities under my control are conducted for their psychological and physiological welfare, rather than for the vicarious interests of adults.

With my signature, which I voluntarily affix to this contract, I acknowledge that I have read, understood, and will do my best to fulfill the promises made herein.

Sport _____   Signature of coach _____

Date _____   Director _____

Form 2.11   ASEP Coaching Appraisal Form

Coach name _____   Sport _____

Team _____   League _____

Appraiser _____   Date _____

Observation during: Practice   Competition

Minutes observed _____

Circle only one response using the following rating system.

	Unsatisfactory	Needs improvement	Adequate	Good	Excellent
Knowledge					
Knowledge of the sport (rules, skills, strategies)	1	2	3	4	5
Teaching of skills	1	2	3	4	5
Correcting errors	1	2	3	4	5
Management					
Organization of activities	1	2	3	4	5
Use of time	1	2	3	4	5
Involvement of athletes	1	2	3	4	5
Communication					
Provides clear instructions	1	2	3	4	5
Listens to others	1	2	3	4	5
Uses appropriate language	1	2	3	4	5
Health					
Provides safe environment	1	2	3	4	5
Conditions athletes properly	1	2	3	4	5
Is sensitive to child's self-esteem and emotions	1	2	3	4	5
Self-control					
Physical appearance	1	2	3	4	5
Control of emotions	1	2	3	4	5
Use of tobacco, alcohol, or other drugs	1	2	3	4	5
Relationships					
With athletes	1	2	3	4	5
With parents	1	2	3	4	5
With other coaches	1	2	3	4	5
With officials and directors	1	2	3	4	5

	Unsatisfactory	Needs improvement	Adequate	Good	Excellent
Motivation					
Motivates athletes appropriately	1	2	3	4	5
Shows enthusiasm for coaching	1	2	3	4	5
Coaching philosophy					
Appropriate perspective about winning and losing	1	2	3	4	5
Coaching style	1	2	3	4	5
Coaches to make sport fun to play	1	2	3	4	5
Overall rating of coach	**1**	**2**	**3**	**4**	**5**

Recommendations to coaching director:

_____

_____

_____

_____

_____

Form 2.12 | ASEP Parent Evaluation of Coach Form

Coach name _____ Sport _____

Team _____ League _____

We would appreciate your providing an honest evaluation of your child's coach as part of our efforts to provide the best youth sport program possible. Thank you.

A. Evaluate the degree to which you believe your child achieved the following (circle one):

	Not at all		Somewhat		Very much
Had fun	1	2	3	4	5
Learned how to play the sport better	1	2	3	4	5
Improved physical fitness	1	2	3	4	5
Learned to cooperate with teammates	1	2	3	4	5
Learned to compete appropriately	1	2	3	4	5
Increased motivation to continue playing this sport	1	2	3	4	5
Developed leadership skills	1	2	3	4	5
Learned sportsmanship	1	2	3	4	5

B. How did the coach do on the following items? (circle one)

	Not well		So-so		Very well
Treated your child fairly	1	2	3	4	5
Kept winning in perspective	1	2	3	4	5
Took appropriate safety precautions	1	2	3	4	5
Organized practices and contests	1	2	3	4	5
Communicated with you	1	2	3	4	5
Taught effectively	1	2	3	4	5
Showed self-control	1	2	3	4	5
Encouraged and recognized your child	1	2	3	4	5
Helped your child's self-esteem	1	2	3	4	5

C. Would you recommend that your child's coach be encouraged to continue coaching in the program?

Yes   No

D. If you could change anything about the coaching of your son or daughter, what would it be?

_____

_____

_____

E. How confident are you of your evaluation? (circle one)

Very confident   Moderately confident   Not too confident

Form 2.13 ASEP Athlete Evaluation of Coach Form

Coach name _____ Sport _____

Team _____ League _____

We would appreciate your providing an honest evaluation of your coach as part of our efforts to provide the best youth sport program possible. Thank you.

A. To what degree did you achieve the following? (circle one)

	Not at all		Somewhat		Very much
Had fun	1	2	3	4	5
Learned how to play the sport better	1	2	3	4	5
Improved physical fitness	1	2	3	4	5
Learned to cooperate with teammates	1	2	3	4	5
Learned to compete appropriately	1	2	3	4	5
Increased motivation to continue playing this sport	1	2	3	4	5
Developed leadership skills	1	2	3	4	5
Learned sportsmanship	1	2	3	4	5

B. How did the coach do on the following items? (circle one)

	Not well		So-so		Very well
Treated you fairly	1	2	3	4	5
Kept winning in perspective	1	2	3	4	5
Took appropriate safety precautions	1	2	3	4	5
Organized practices and contests	1	2	3	4	5
Talked and listened to you	1	2	3	4	5
Taught the skills of the sport	1	2	3	4	5
Showed self-control	1	2	3	4	5
Encouraged and recognized you	1	2	3	4	5
Helped you feel good about yourself	1	2	3	4	5

C. Would you like this coach to be your coach next season?

Yes   No

D. If you could change anything about your coach, what would it be?

_____

_____

_____

Managing Parents

If you've been a youth sport administrator for long, you know firsthand the influence that parents can have on the sport experiences of their children. You've observed the positive impact made by parents who reinforce with their youngsters the same goals your coaches have for their teams—such as developing players' self-esteem, fostering a sense of healthy competition, and creating an atmosphere of fun.

But chances are you've also witnessed parental behavior that has made you cringe: shouting at their own children or at players on the opposing team, getting into arguments with officials, badgering coaches to play their children, even getting into fights with other parents. Some journalists would have us believe that these are common parental actions, but in reality such misconduct occurs relatively infrequently. Nevertheless, it is your responsibility to minimize such behavior and take effective action when it happens.

As a youth sport administrator, you must be prepared to work with all kinds of parents, from those who genuinely want to help their children have a positive experience to those who need some help keeping their children's sport participation in proper perspective. This chapter will give you the tools you need to work effectively with all parents.

The objectives of this chapter are as follows:

1. To help you develop plans for involving parents in constructive roles in your sport program. To do this, we'll examine the responsibilities parents have to the program, the coach, the team, and, most important, their children.
2. To identify your responsibilities to the parents of the children participating in your sport program.
3. To tell you about ASEP's SportParent program, a constructive way to educate parents about their involvement in your program.
4. To discuss problem parents and propose guidelines for dealing with them.

We'll begin with an exercise to get you thinking about the responsibilities parents have to their children and to their children's youth sport program (see exercise 3.1).

Parent Responsibilities

Parents' foremost responsibility is to ensure that children's involvement is safe, beneficial, and enjoyable. With youth sport programs that are conducted primarily by volunteers, parents also have responsibilities to the team or pro-

---

Exercise 3.1　**Identifying Parent Responsibilities**

Name three responsibilities parents have to their children as participants in youth sport. Then determine three additional responsibilities that parents have to their children's youth sport program.

Parent responsibilities to their child

_____

_____

_____

Parent responsibilities to the youth sport program

_____

_____

_____

_____

gram. Parents should not treat these programs as babysitting services where they drop off their children so that other adults can look after them. In this section we examine parent responsibilities to children and to the team or program.

Responsibilities to the Child

1. The first responsibility of parents is to find out what their children want from sport and from them with respect to their sport participation. Most children want the opportunity to choose whether to participate. And then they want to choose which sport they participate in and at what level of competition. In other words, they want to set their own participation goals.

They may benefit from parental counsel, especially if they seek it, but they will resent parental dictums. Parents need to let their children choose to play, and to quit if they want to.

Parents may push their children into sports without recognizing they are pushing. They may want so much for their children to play, to become stars, to be extensions of their past athletic selves, that they unwittingly convey their expectations in subtle ways. Children easily sense these expectations, and if they feel compelled to play, it may diminish their prospects of obtaining the full benefits of sport participation. The full rewards of sport are available only when children play for intrinsic rewards, not extrinsic rewards such as parental praise or love.

2. Although parents should permit children to determine their own sports involvement, this does not mean that parents should play no part in their children's participation. Parents should provide a supportive atmosphere conducive to their children's participation. Parents ought to be the first to expose their children to the sports of our society. Research has shown that in homes where parents have favorable attitudes toward sports, where parents participate in sports, where they give their children some basic instruction in sports skills, and where they provide the equipment needed to play, children are much more likely to develop an intrinsic interest in sports. What parents must be alert to, however, is the subtle

difference between creating a positive atmosphere for sport participation and pressuring or nudging their children into sports.

3. Parents are also responsible for determining when their children are ready to begin playing sports, for setting limits on their participation, and for ensuring that the conditions for playing are safe. Additionally, they have an obligation to learn whether their children have any of the disqualifying conditions for participation in sports (see the American Academy of Pediatrics chart shown in appendix A).

4. Parents need to protect their children from abusive coaches. They should know what kind of person they are turning their children over to. They should evaluate whether coaches conduct themselves in ways that are beneficial to their children. Parents should know that an inquiry as to why their children never get to play in contests is not meddling. Neither is it meddling to question coaching practices that appear to imperil the health of their children or diminish their enjoyment of playing the sport. Parents always have the right to approach you, as the program administrator, about conditions that could be physically or psychologically harmful.

5. Parents have an enormous responsibility to help their children develop realistic expectations of their capabilities in sports. This of course requires that the parents have realistic expectations about their children—something that parents do not always have. When parents have excessively high expectations of their children, they may lead them to believe they are capable of doing more than they actually are. Children with unrealistically high expectations are often frustrated in sports, for even when they perform near their capabilities, their aspirations remain unfulfilled. Coaches, as well as parents, must help children form sensible goals if they are to experience full enjoyment from sports.

Sometimes children's expectations are quite realistic, while those of their parents are unrealistically high. This situation is also destructive to children's enjoyment of sports. Regardless of how well children perform, it never seems to be adequate for Dad or Mom. This, too, can frustrate children and thwart their motivation to participate. It can also result in children devaluing the worth of their parents' judgment.

Parents with excessively high expectations also frustrate themselves. They often find themselves in conflict with the coach, who may play their youngster only as a substitute. They demand to know why their child is assigned to play one position when they feel she is destined to be a star in another position. They blame the coach when their child fails to bring them vicarious fame. Coaches invariably report that the most frequent cause of coach–parent conflict is the discrepancy in their opinions about the child's capabilities to play the sport.

6. Parents have a responsibility to help their children interpret the experiences associated with competitive sports. Parents particularly can help children understand the significance of winning and losing. Psychologists have learned that the causes we assign to our experiences are important in shaping our personality and future behaviors. Parents are especially important in helping children assign appropriate reasons to why they won or lost, succeeded

or failed. Parents who can keep winning in perspective will help children do the same.

While some parents care too much about their children's sport participation, others do not care enough. They let their children participate without any knowledge of or interest in what they are doing. Uninterested parents neither meet their obligations to their children nor help other adults who provide the opportunity for children to participate.

Responsibilities to the Team or Program

Parents also have the following important responsibilities to the team or program in which their child participates, especially if the program is conducted largely by volunteers.

1. Parents should cooperate with the team's coaches by turning their child over to the coaches and supporting their actions as long as they are providing a physically and psychologically safe environment. Parents can also help their children meet their responsibilities to the team and the coach.

2. Parents are responsible for informing the coaches of their child's physical and mental

Parent's Role in Helping to Conduct Children's Sports Programs

Coach	PA announcer
Assistant Coach	Fundraiser
Scorekeeper	Business manager
Timer	First-aid attendant
Official/umpire	Team purchasing agent
Statistician	Team representative to league
Facility maintenance worker	Chauffeur/driver
Player and equipment transporter	Refreshments coordinator
Locker room supervisor	Ticket taker
Timekeeper	Usher
Registration coordinator	Janitor
Publicity director	

condition whenever this condition may place the child at risk. For example, parents should report to coaches any injuries to their child that the coaches may not know about and that further participation in the sport may aggravate. Parents should inform the coach of any allergies or special health conditions their child has. Parents should also make sure their child brings any necessary medications to competitions and practices.

3. Parents need to make sure that their children behave when participating in the sport and discipline them when they do not. Throughout the literature on children's sports—this guide included—the responsibility for the failure of children's sport programs is placed on the shoulders of adults. This is often justifiable, but sometimes children misbehave—they break the rules or are uncooperative and uncontrollable. Children do have obligations to their parents and coaches when they participate in sports. When a child misbehaves, parents should grant coaches the right to discipline the child within reasonable limits. Ultimately, of

course, the responsibility for disciplining a child belongs to the child's parents, and they must learn to use discipline wisely.

4. Parents should provide the equipment their child needs to play the sport safely. They also need to be sure the equipment stays in good repair and is used properly by their child.

5. Parents should behave appropriately as spectators. Consider the guidelines listed in "Dos and Don'ts." (You may have to modify them to meet your circumstances.)

6. Finally, parents should feel obliged to help conduct the sport program in which their child participates. Listed next are many ways that parents can help with a program.

Some parents are willing to help but don't know how. Others are shy and need encouragement. As an administrator, do you effectively call on parents to help? Do you provide them with the orientation they need to be useful helpers?

Director Responsibilities to Parents

As a youth sport program director, you have three major responsibilities to parents.

1. The first is to provide excellent leadership. You've been entrusted with the important responsibility of directing a youth sport program. Whether you are the director of a huge multisport program with hundreds of teams or a single league with six teams, whether you are a full-time paid professional or a part-time volunteer, you have the duty as program administrator to provide a safe, beneficial, and enjoyable sport program—foremost for the children who participate, but also for the adults involved.

Parents who see well-organized, well-run programs are less likely to find a reason to complain or interfere. Instead, they will find themselves playing an active part in their children's participation. When most parents are behaving appropriately, the isolated misbehaving parent is more likely to keep quiet.

Dos and Don'ts for Youth Sport Spectators

Do . . .
cheer for your team.
show interest, enthusiasm, and support for your child.
control your emotions.
help when asked by coaches or officials.
thank the coaches, officials, and other volunteers who conducted the event.

Don't . . .
leave the spectator area during competitions.
advise the coach on how to coach.
try to coach your child during the contest.
make derogatory comments to players, parents, coaches, or officials of either team.
drink alcohol at contests or come to watch contests intoxicated.

2. You should know that you cannot conduct a first-rate youth sport program without involving the parents, and you cannot expect parents to fulfill their responsibilities if they don't know them. As program administrator, you have a responsibility to the parents to educate them about their responsibilities to their children and to your program. In the next section of this chapter, we'll describe the SportParent program, ASEP's innovative parent education course.

3. Your third responsibility is to communicate with parents about the specifics of your youth sport program. Among the most frequent complaints parents have is that they receive inadequate information about their child's sport program. After you see the content of the SportParent Course, we'll show you how to prepare a handout or booklet containing the information that parents should receive about the sport in which their children participate.

SportParent Course

The SportParent Course helps you fulfill your responsibility to educate parents. The program shows parents how to team with coaches to

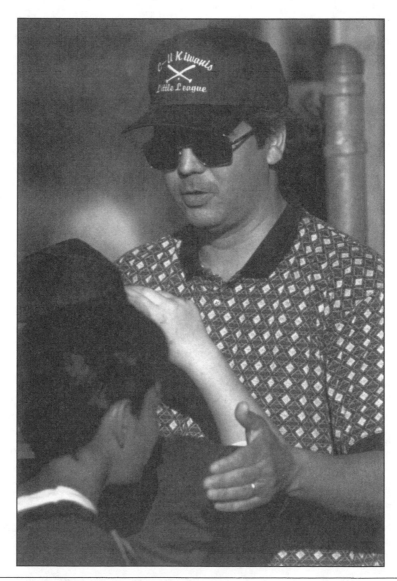

Involving parents in the sport program helps both children and adults share the sport experience.

give children fun, safe, and valuable sport experiences. In the process, parents will learn how to more fully enjoy the experience themselves. And youth sport administrators will benefit by having parents work in concert with them to make sports rewarding for children.

Through the SportParent Course, parents learn

- why kids play sports,
- what a parent's responsibilities are and how to fulfill them,
- how to develop a healthy sport perspective,
- how to help their children set performance goals,
- how to communicate and support their children in their sport experience,
- how to build their children's self-esteem,
- how to be a good role model,
- how to communicate with their children's coach, and
- how to help their children have fun and valuable experiences in sport.

It's recommended that you conduct the course yourself; but if time does not permit, appoint someone to conduct the course who is thoroughly familiar with your program and who shares your program philosophy. The course can be completed in one to two hours, depending on the options you choose. You need no training to present the course; the SportParent Facilitator Manual shows you how to prepare for and conduct the course step by step.

Besides the facilitator manual, the SportParent Course has three other resources:

- The *SportParent* video
- The *SportParent Survival Guide*
- The *SportParent* book

You'll use the *SportParent* video to raise parents' awareness and prime them to talk about key issues that affect their children's sport experiences. Following the video, you'll lead a discussion that allows parents to express their feelings about each issue and explore what those issues mean for them.

Next, you will want to give every parent a copy of the *SportParent Survival Guide*, which provides all the nuts-and-bolts information parents need to know. We also have available *SportParent*, a 96-page book that gives parents a thorough and complete understanding of their SportParent responsibilities. We recommend that you purchase several copies of *SportParent* and have them available for sale to parents at the SportParent Course.

The SportParent Course is really a two-step process for parents. First, they attend the meeting that you facilitate. Second, they read at home the *SportParent Survival Guide* and, we hope, the more complete *SportParent* book.

The SportParent course package is for you, the sport director. It contains the *SportParent* video, the *SportParent* book, and 10 *SportParent Survival Guides* (plus the facilitator manual). Appendix C offers price information on the package, as well as the price of the course components sold separately.

Once parents have completed the SportParent Course, we recommend that you provide them with the Parent Guide to your program. Next we'll discuss the specifics of this guide.

Communicating Program Specifics to Parents

In this section we'll help you develop a handout or booklet of the information parents need to know about the sport program their children participate in. We suggest that you develop this small publication for each sport in your program, although some sections will be the same for all sports.

Begin by selecting a specific sport and season to provide responses for, using the general format below, which includes a series of questions to address. Some of the questions may not be appropriate to your situation. Some of the specific information that a parent is looking for will probably come from the coach. However, some coaches forget to tell parents this information. In this case, your handout will serve as a useful reminder for the coaches and should be formatted in a way that allows them to easily insert the information that they should provide. Answering the questions below should prepare you to compile a handout for parents. We have also provided a sample handout on pages 89 to 90 that you can tailor to the various sports your organization offers.

Handout Format

Begin assembling your handout by compiling basic information: What should parents know about your organization?

- What is the organization's history?
- How is the organization supported financially?
- Is the organization affiliated with other groups?

What should parents know about the specific sport program?

- Who directs the program?
- Whom do they contact if they have a concern?
- How do they reach this person?
- When and how do they register for the program?
- What does it cost to participate in the program?

What should parents know about the upcoming season?

- What are the dates of the season?
- How many contests will be played?
- Where are the contests held?
- Are there postseason tournaments or other special events?
- When do practices begin?
- Where do practices take place?
- How long and how frequent are practices?
- May parents attend practices?
- What are the rule modifications to the sport?

What should parents know about equipment?

- Are parents responsible for purchasing equipment?
- Where do they purchase it?
- Generally, how much does the equipment cost?
- Is any equipment provided by the organization?
- Who cleans the uniforms?
- Who repairs the equipment and/or uniforms?

What should parents know about the coach?

- Who is this person?
- When will parents have a chance to meet the coach?
- What are the appropriate ways to communicate with the coach?
- What qualifications does the coach need?

What do parents need to know about eligibility requirements?

- Are there any age, height, or weight categories or restrictions?
- Are medical screenings or preparticipation examinations required?
- Is the league divided according to skill or experience?

What should parents know about transportation guidelines?

- How do athletes get to practices and competitions?
- Are coaches allowed to transport athletes?
- Are there additional costs for transportation?

What specific requests do you or your organization have of the participants' parents?

- Do they need to attend a parent orientation program?
- Do they have a specific role in assisting the coach with the team?
- Are there special rules or policies that parents need to adhere to?

Sample Program-Specific Handout

Stoughton Youth Basketball Program Guide

The Stoughton Youth Basketball Program is a community-supported nonprofit league designed for boys and girls ages 9-12. The Stoughton Youth Center has provided this program and 15 other youth sport programs since its inception in 1974.

The mission of the Stoughton Youth Center is to provide sport opportunities to area youth. The Center has adopted the philosophy of the AMERICAN SPORT EDUCATION PROGRAM by striving to place the athlete first and winning second in all its youth sport programs.

Listed below is important information about our youth basketball program. We hope that this information answers most of your questions about our program. If you have any additional questions, please contact the program director, Wayne Holden, or his assistant, Faye Cokinos. You may phone them at 555-____ or contact them at the Stoughton Youth Center at 245 South Franklin Street.

Registration dates/times	Tuesday and Wednesday, November 10 and 11 from 6-9 p.m.
Program Costs	$25 includes team T-shirt, handed out at first practice
Season Highlights	
Practices begin	November 12 (one practice per week lasting 45 minutes)
Practice sites	Stoughton Youth Center, 245 South Franklin Street and Hitchings School, 21 North Main
Practice times	Contact your child's coach or the Stoughton Youth Center for official practice times.
First game	November 26 (Ten weeks of games are scheduled)
Game sites	Stoughton Youth Center
Game dates I times	Saturday mornings excluding Christmas and New Year's Day weekends beginning at 9:00 a.m. at the Stoughton Youth Center. Check official schedule (to be handed out by coaches) for your child's team game times.
Final game	February 12

General Program Information

Equipment	Tennis shoes and shorts and/or sweats should be worn in addition to the team shirt (provided as part of the program). Mouth guards and eye goggles may also be worn but are not mandatory (these items may be purchased at the Stoughton Youth Center for less than $5 each).
Transportation	All athletes are responsible for their own transportation to and from games and practices. Coaches will not be allowed to transport athletes.

(continued)

Eligibility	Boys and girls ages 9-12 may participate in the program. School medical examination cards must be on file, or a complete physical screening must be completed prior to participating in the program. There are no height or weight restrictions.
Coaches	All Stoughton Youth Center coaches are required to attend and pass the ASEP Level One coaching course. We conduct criminal history checks on all volunteers. Coaches are introduced at the Parent Orientation Program (see below for more details) where they meet team parents and discuss their coaching philosophy along with any team rules and regulations.
Program Policies	You will receive a list of program policies at the Parent Orientation Program.
Parent Orientation	Program

Parents are invited to learn more about youth sports, their roles, and the Stoughton Youth Basketball Program at the Stoughton Youth Center Parent Orientation Program. The Parent Orientation Program utilizes ASEP's SportParent Course. At the orientation parents will learn why kids play sports, what a SportParent's responsibilities are and how to fulfill them, how to develop a healthy sport perspective, how to help your child set performance goals, how to communicate and support your child in his or her sport experience, how to build your child's self-esteem, the importance of being a good role model, how to communicate with your child's coach, and how to help your child have a fun and valuable experience in sport.

Date/Time	Thursday, November 10, 6:00 p.m. at the Stoughton Youth Center

There will also be a general question/answer period that will allow parents and athletes to address any of their concerns.

Parent Problems

It's not uncommon for coaches and administrators to blame parents for many of the problems in youth sport programs. In turn, parents often blame coaches and inept administrators for programs that fail to meet their expectations. Meanwhile, the kids snicker at the absurdity of the adults who make more out of the contest than they do.

In some programs parents have become such detriments that administrators have banned them from competitions. Other programs have resorted to having contests during the morning or early afternoon hours so that most parents cannot attend.

Banning parents from observing their children's games is a desperate last-resort solution and a sign that adults have lost perspective about the purpose of children's sports. Parents should not only be encouraged to attend contests, but should take an active part in their child's sport experience. Youth sports should be a family affair, not another experience that pulls the family apart.

Children want to share their experiences in sports with their parents; kids want their parents' support. But just as parents dislike being embarrassed by their children, young athletes dislike being embarrassed by their parents. Angry mothers and fathers who hurl epithets at opposing players, swear at officials, and bark orders to their children do more than embarrass their offspring (and themselves)—they have adverse effects on the entire program. Rather than sports serving as an opportunity for children to learn sportsmanship, they become an arena for parents to display contemptuous and derisive behavior.

Just as coaches, umpires, and players must conform to standards of behavior, so should parents. A few simply lose control of themselves when their children are competing. Such behavior is usually repugnant, and parents must be persuaded to behave appropriately. (Of course, occasionally the behavior of an overzealous parent can be quite funny and harmless. For example, in a peewee baseball game a mother standing on the sidelines was so engrossed in her daughter's batting that when the girl hit a ground ball to the shortstop, the mother ran alongside her daughter to first base. The umpire called the daughter out but ruled that the mother had beaten the throw!)

Overzealous parents create numerous other problems besides misbehaving as spectators. They are often guilty of pressuring their children into sports and of continuing to push once their children begin participating. Parents impose their own standards of performance on children, expecting them to meet their criteria of excellence rather than helping children to develop their own standards. Parents may prematurely place their children in evaluative situations, not giving them enough time to learn the skills before beginning to compete. Parents who push incessantly, set very high expectations, and constantly evaluate their child's behavior place great stress on the child. Confronted with these conditions, it is understandable that some children seek to avoid competitive sports. For them, the benefits of sport do not outweigh the risks.

Another problem is how some parents behave after the contest. What parents say to their child after competing is important in helping the child understand the significance of winning and losing as well as of other events that may have occurred during the contest. In a classic tale, Donald McNeil gives an example of the problem:

"One night last season my team lost a close game. I sat the whole team on the bench and congratulated them for trying, for acting like gentlemen. I said I couldn't have been prouder of them if they had won. Most of all, I said, it is as important to be a good loser as a gracious winner. As I talked I could see their spirits lifting. I felt they had learned more than just how to play baseball that night.

But as I mingled with the parents in the stands afterward, I was shocked to hear what they were saying to the boys. The invariable theme was, 'Well, what happened to you tonight?' One father pulled out a notepad and went over his son's mistakes play by play. Another father dressed down his son for striking out twice. In five minutes the parents had undermined every principle I had set forth."

Material from McNeil, D. R. "Little Leagues Aren't Big Leagues." *Reader's Digest*, June 1961, p. 142.

It is no tragedy, of course, for children to lose a contest, to make an error, or to perform poorly; the tragedy is when parents belittle their children, destroying their self-respect (and often their respect for their parents as well). Some parents seem to think that dealing with their children as athletes is somehow isolated from the rest of child rearing. They become so emotionally engrossed in their children's sports that they forget their child-rearing responsibilities. It is as though parents reverse roles. When their children do not perform like adults, the parents behave like children!

But, as with problem coaches, problem parents are a small minority. Although they may err occasionally, most parents have the best interests of their children in mind. They try to help, they offer encouragement, they control their emotions, and, most important, they show their children that they care. When parents err, it is often because they do not know what their responsibilities are with respect to their children's involvement in sports.

With education and skillful management on your part, most parents will eagerly contribute to the program in many ways. They will serve as coaches, officials, scorekeepers, maintenance workers, business managers, fundraisers, concessionaires, chauffeurs, and, of course, cheering fans.

Dealing With Problem Parents

Just as some coaches are problem coaches, some parents are likely to be problem parents. Coaches are the ones who most likely will have to deal with the problems presented by misguided parents. At contests, officials and supervisors, as well as coaches, may need to respond to misbehaving parents. Thus, it is important for you to have a set of policies on how to deal with problem parents.

As we recommend for coaches, the problems with parents should be classified as minor and major when considering how to address them. Minor problems include the following:

• Parents getting in verbal arguments with coaches, officials, and other parents

• Parents coaching their children or other children from the sidelines during the contest

• Parents yelling criticism to players or coaches of either team from the spectator area

Major problems include the following:

• Parents being repeatedly verbally abusive and disrupting the contest

• Any type of physical abuse

• Being out of control because of drinking alcohol or using other drugs

• Cheating on eligibility rules or by using illegal equipment

We recommend that coaches and supervisors be advised to deal with minor parental problems in the following way:

1. After the first incident or two the coach should meet the parent to explain that his behavior is not acceptable and describe clearly what behavior is expected.

2. After the next incident, the coach should request that the supervisor, if one exists, speak with the parent about the problem, conveying the same information as the coach did. If there is no supervisor, the coach should again speak with the parent.

3. If there is another incident, the coach or supervisor should advise the parent that this is the last warning. The parent needs to understand that continuing such behavior will result in her being banned from practices and games. The coach or supervisor should submit a brief written report of the complaint and warning to your office. Follow up by sending a written notice to the parent confirming the warning and possible repercussions.

4. If the parent further misbehaves, the coach or supervisor should report the parent to your office, recommending that the parent be banned from practices and games for the remainder of the season.

If a parent creates a major problem, the nature of that problem needs to be considered to determine what action you should take. All major problems should be reported to your office in writing by the coach or supervisor. If the parent's behavior directly violates your rules, the penalties as specified by your policies should be immediately enforced. If the problem is physical abuse, the severity of the behavior (from pushing an official to hitting a child) will determine your course of action, varying from calling the police to barring the parent from attending practices and games to meeting with the parent to discuss the problem.

Don't forget that you need to communicate your policies regarding problem parents to your coaches, officials, and supervisors so that they know what to do when an incident occurs. It's equally important that parents know your policies; this information should be contained in the parent guide you distribute.

Summary

Parents are vital to the success of your program. Most are eager to become involved in

their child's youth sport experience. But as a youth sport administrator you can't just sit back and expect the parents to come to you. If you are going to harness the abundantly positive energy that parents bring to your program, you must have a plan for involving them constructively in your organization. This chapter has given you the tools you need to develop your strategy for working with parents:

- You have examined parents' responsibilities to your program, the coach, the team, and most important, to their child.
- You have evaluated your responsibilities to the parents of the children participating in your sport program.
- You have learned about ASEP's SportParent program, a constructive way to educate parents about their involvement in your program.
- You have read about problem parents and have been given some guidelines for dealing with them.

Managing Risk

As a responsible administrator you want to provide a safe and equitable youth sport program. Thus, you'll need to think about ways to manage the risks of participating in your program. The best way is to have a comprehensive risk-management program, which we'll help you develop in this chapter. Our focus will be on nonprofit organizations that have volunteers serving as coaches and helpers in other capacities.

Risk refers to the probability of loss, either to people's well-being or to their property. As a youth sport administrator, you may or may not be responsible for developing a risk-management plan and developing policies that help reduce risk, but you certainly will be responsible for implementing policies to manage risk. You will want to manage risk for three groups:

1. The children participating in your program
2. Your coaches, officials, parents, spectators, and yourself and your staff
3. Your organization

We all recognize the litigious nature of our society. No doubt you've heard about some of the frivolous lawsuits filed against youth sport organizations and the ridiculous judgments that award astronomical sums of money to people for what seemed to be their own carelessness. These relatively few but highly publicized cases capture our attention and cause us concern about our own exposure to the risk of a lawsuit.

While we need to manage the risk of litigation, we want to focus on a more positive reason for managing risk: to provide the safest and fairest environment possible for your program's participants. The secondary reason for risk management is to reduce the risk of liability. In fact, the best way to reduce the risk of liability is to provide the safest, fairest environment possible.

Risk management is more than buying insurance. It's a systematic plan for identifying and reducing risk, while recognizing that in most cases you cannot entirely eliminate it. In this chapter we'll show you how to develop a risk-management plan that consists of four steps:

1. Identifying the risks in your program
2. Evaluating the risks to determine the probability and severity of their occurrence
3. Determining ways to deal with the risk by one or more of four means:
   a. Avoiding the risk, primarily by getting rid of the hazard or eliminating the activity. Since you're in the business of offering youth sport programs, eliminating the activity is contrary to your larger objectives. However, often we can get rid of a particular hazard within an activity.
   b. Reducing the risk by devising appropriate safety strategies, developing policies and procedures that make the play environment as safe as possible.
   c. Transferring the risk by purchasing insurance, warning participants of the inherent risks associated with participation, and having waivers and releases signed.
   d. Accepting the risk involved and being prepared with plans to deal with a loss.
4. Implementing and continually monitoring the risk-management plan

The next five parts of this chapter will provide you with essential information for preparing your risk-management plan, including:

- Your legal duties as a youth sport administrator and those of the adults you supervise
- What may happen when those duties are not performed properly
- What you can do to increase the safety of your participants
- How to transfer some of the risk to others
- How to manage specific risks, such as medical injuries and transportation of participants

Your Duties

Our society expects all of us to behave in specific ways in various circumstances. That is, we're expected to meet certain standards. When our actions are questioned, such as in a lawsuit, the court examines whether our behavior conformed to the standard—what prudent people with appropriate training for the particular position would do in the same situation. Sometimes these standards may also be prescribed by professional associations such as the National Operating Committee on Standards for Athletic Equipment (NOCSAE) or a sport-specific governing body such as the United States Tennis Association (USTA). As a risk manager, you will have the important duty of working with your staff to set and implement policies to reach these standards. You will also need to take the necessary steps to see that all those under your supervision conform to them.

As the administrator of your youth sport program, you have assigned responsibilities. Some of these responsibilities you delegate to others—paid staff, officials, or volunteer coaches. Failing to perform your duties properly can risk the safety of your staff, coaches, and participants. Failure of your staff, officials, and coaches to perform their duties properly can also risk the safety of the participants and lead to lawsuits against you and your organization. Thus, let's first look at the duties of your coaches and then at yours as an administrator.

Work with your faculty to keep equipment safe and up to date.

Coaches' Duties

The duties of your coaches include the following:

1. Providing a safe environment for practice and contests
2. Teaching skills in developmentally appropriate progressions
3. Providing appropriate supervision for the activity
4. Warning players of inherent risks in the activity
5. Enforcing the rules and regulations of the sport and your organization
6. Matching and equating players fairly for practice and contests
7. Providing proper first aid when injuries occur
8. Ensuring the civil rights of participants
9. Keeping records of injuries and other losses

Your Duties As an Administrator

You share the duties of your coaches, although you are not directly responsible for all of the duties—for example, instruction. However, for other duties, such as matching children for safe and equitable competition, you are likely to have more responsibility than your coaches. You have three additional duties:

1. To select qualified staff, officials, and coaches to conduct the program
2. To ensure that your staff, officials, and coaches are appropriately educated to perform their duties
3. To supervise all aspects of the program appropriately, especially the competitive events and the facilities in which they occur

When Duties Are Not Met

If you, your staff, or your volunteer coaches do not meet your duties, the most important consequence is the increased risk to the children in your program. These duties have evolved over the years because they have been shown to increase the safety of the children participating. A second consequence is that you, your staff, your coaches, and your organization may be sued for negligence. Thus you need to understand (a) what negligence is and (b) where you and your staff, coaches, and organization stand as a nonprofit volunteer organization with regard to protection from lawsuits.

Negligence

Negligence occurs when a person fails to act as a reasonable and prudent adult would in a similar situation, resulting in some loss or injury to another person. The courts judge the occurrence of negligence on four factors:

1. Did the person have a *duty* of care or responsibility to act prudently to the person harmed? As we just discussed, you and your volunteer coaches have duties to the participants in your program.

2. Was there a *breach* of this duty? The courts will consider (a) whether the person could have foreseen the injury and taken steps to prevent it and (b) whether there was a breach of duty in the standard of care given. Again, the standard of care is what a reasonable adult would do in a similar situation or, among professionals, what is considered accepted care by that profession.

3. Did the breach of duty cause the injury or loss? The court seeks to determine whether the negligence either directly caused the injury or indirectly helped cause the injury.

4. Was there *actual injury or loss?* Of course, there must be some actual injury or loss caused by the negligence for which the injured person seeks compensation.

The court must answer yes to each of these questions before negligence can be ruled to have occurred. The court considers two different types of negligence: ordinary and gross. *Ordinary* negligence is when a person makes an inadvertent mistake or fails to pay attention to something. For example, a coach divides her team into groups to rotate through three different skill stations. While she is busy instructing one group of players, an injury occurs at another station where players are practicing a higher-risk skill that requires the coach's supervision. Such negligence may not violate the duty of care. *Gross* negligence, however, occurs when a person is reckless or indifferent to the duty of care. An example of gross negligence on the part of a coach is to continue an outdoor swim practice during a violent storm, resulting in a swimmer being struck by lightning.

Your Vulnerability to Lawsuit

Some youth sport administrators are under the impression that nonprofit, charitable organizations are immune from lawsuits. It's not so. While most states have some type of immunity laws for volunteers, these laws do not provide blanket immunity to coaches, officials, or organizations (nor should they).

Your coaches and officials, paid or volunteer, can be held liable for failure to properly perform their duties. You and your organization may also be held liable under the legal doctrine of *respondeat superior,* which states that organizations can be held legally responsible for the acts of their employees, including volunteers, *when they are acting within the scope of their duties.* If coaches fail to act within the scope of their duties or perform their duties recklessly, they can be held liable, but usually not you or your organization.

Because your organization may be held accountable for your coaches' actions, it is important that you follow good personnel practices with these volunteers. As we discussed in chapter 2, you should follow an intelligent process in selecting capable coaches. Legally, you do not have to perform criminal background checks on volunteers, but checking references is certainly prudent for the safety of your participants. This is also why you should have job descriptions that define the coaches' duties; provide coaches with a basic training program; and supervise, evaluate, and provide feedback to your coaches about how to perform these duties. If an injury occurs because of a coach's action, evidence of training can establish that your organization acted prudently to ensure protection.

Lawsuits From Your Coaches and Others

Because volunteer coaches assume some risk of injury when they volunteer, to recover damages after injury they must show that negligence was not ordinary but gross. You need also to consider your vulnerability to lawsuit if it becomes necessary to relieve a coach of his position. Although volunteers are not employees, they have rights to due process and protection against discrimination. It's best that you honor the ethic of equal employment opportunity guidelines when working with coaches, paid or volunteer. These guidelines prohibit employers with 15 or more employees from discrimination in hiring and firing; compensation and terms; and conditions or privilege of employment on the basis of race, color, religion, disability, sex, pregnancy, or national origin. The penalties for violating these guidelines include back pay, compensatory and punitive damages, and reinstatement.

Additional considerations regarding your vulnerability to lawsuits from coaches and others arise from the Americans With Disabilities Act (ADA) of 1990, which mandates that policies, procedures, and practices that discriminate against persons with disabilities be eliminated.

Larry Anderson, who uses a wheelchair, is a case in point. Shortly after the ADA went into effect, Little League Baseball was challenged in court by Larry on its policy of barring people in wheelchairs from coaching on the field, on the grounds that it discriminates against persons with disabilities. Larry coached a Little League team in Arizona for three years without incident; he challenged a Little League ruling when he contended that Little League threatened to remove his local affiliate's charter if it continued to permit him to coach on the field. The U.S. District Court struck down the Little League policy on the basis that it violated the ADA.

The ADA is an important but potentially confusing piece of legislation. For additional information about the ADA, see pages 115 to 116 on personal rights.

You should also be aware that some states have laws requiring special protection for children and vulnerable adults (those with mental, emotional, and physical impairments). These states require that professionals, such as you and the coaches to whom you delegate duties, report any suspicion of the abuse or neglect of a child or vulnerable adult to the appropriate authorities.

Assumption of Risk Defense

When you, your coaches, or your organization is sued, your legal counsel will have several defenses to consider for the case. Of course, the obvious defenses are to prove that there was no duty of care, no breach of duty, the breach of duty did not cause the injury, or there was no actual injury. However, the law provides another line of defense—*an assumption of risk by the injured person.*

The injured person assumes responsibility for the injury because the person knew the risk and took it anyway. For example, coach Ralph Strickland instructed his baseball players to always slide feetfirst, but Billy Smith did a headfirst slide at home plate and lost four teeth. Billy's parents sued the coach and the park and recreation department, but the court determined that Coach Strickland had warned all the players it was dangerous to slide headfirst, never taught this method of sliding, and taught only the feetfirst sliding method. In this case, Billy assumed the risk and responsibility for the injury. This incident shows that it is critical for coaches to warn participants of the risks of any activity and teach them ways to reduce or eliminate the dangers associated with those risks.

What you must remember about the assumption of risk defense is that it is only a defense when the participants have been clearly informed about the risk. The athletes in your program, for example, cannot assume the risk if they do not know what the risk is. Thus, it is vital that you and your coaches properly warn participants of the risks involved in each sport and how to reduce or avoid these risks.

The courts also vary their expectation of the degree of risk assumed by people based on their age, skill level, and knowledge. In general, the younger, less skilled, and less knowledgeable the person, the less responsible the person is for her actions. A coach's responsibil-

ity, for example, decreases as athletes become older and more skilled and as they learn more about the risks involved in sport participation.

Comparative and Contributory Negligence

The injured person can also assume partial responsibility for an injury by contributing to the injury through negligent behavior. Others may also have contributed to the injury through negligence as well. In some states, awards for shared negligence between the injured person and others may be made on a percentage basis. This is called *comparative negligence*. For example, if according to a jury the person injured and his coach were equally at fault for the injury, under comparative negligence law the coach would be responsible for half of the damages awarded.

In other states, an injured person found to have contributed in any way to his injuries cannot collect anything from others who may have also contributed to the cause of the injury. This is called *contributory negligence*. For example, a football coach has a rule that forbids any of his players from practicing tackling without wearing their helmets. The coach consistently enforces the rule and reprimands any player he sees violating the rule. One day in practice, a player makes a tackle without wearing his helmet and suffers a serious injury. In a court of law the principle of contributory negligence would most likely prevent the athlete from bringing a successful negligence suit against the coach. Because the athlete did not heed the established rules set by the coach, he may be found legally responsible for his own injury.

Immunity Laws

It was stated earlier that volunteer coaches do not have immunity from lawsuits for negligence, but there is more to the story. In the 1980s, lawsuits against volunteer coaches increased substantially, with some of these cases being frivolous. The case of Joey Fort, a Little League baseball player in New Jersey, is an excellent example. Joey was hit in the eye while trying to catch a fly ball during warm-ups for a Little League all-star game, resulting in permanent loss of vision in the eye. Joey's parents filed a lawsuit against the four volunteer coaches, contending that he should not have been placed in the outfield because his normal position was second base. The suit was settled out of court, but it gained considerable national attention and led to New Jersey passing an immunity law for coaches. Several other states followed suit.

What protection do these immunity laws provide? They vary by state, but typically coaches and other volunteers are immune if they perform action in good faith and within the scope of their duties as a coach. The immunity is against ordinary negligence, not gross negligence. Who determines whether a breach of duty is ordinary or gross negligence? The courts, of course. Thus, when coaches act reasonably and prudently they are protected by general immunity law, reducing the number of frivolous lawsuits; but coaches may end up in court and held liable if the breach of duty is grossly negligent.

Immunity laws are a positive step toward protecting volunteer coaches from damages arising from frivolous lawsuits. But coaches should understand that this immunity does not exempt them from performing their duties properly. New Jersey, recognizing that coaches may not meet their duties as diligently with immunity available, requires that coaches complete a three-hour coaching education course that includes safety training.

States with immunity laws are closely scrutinizing them, and states without them are considering passing new laws. If you would like to know what your current state laws are about immunity, contact

Nonprofit Risk Management Center
1001 Connecticut Avenue, NW
Washington, DC 20036
Phone: 202-785-3891
Email: info@nonprofitrisk.org
URL: http://www.nonprofitrisk.org

This agency, part of the National Council of Nonprofit Associations, keeps tabs on legislative and judicial developments that affect the liability of charitable organizations and their volunteers. Among the resources it publishes is the manual *State Liability Laws for Charitable Organizations and Volunteers*.

What You Can Do to Make Your Program Safer

Remember, your main goal is to make your program as safe as possible—safe from injuries to your staff, coaches, spectators, and, of course, your participants. Another goal is to make your program as safe from lawsuits as possible. In this section we look at five things you can do to make your program safer. After that, we'll look at how you can transfer the risk of being liable for things you have little or no control over.

1. Develop a Risk-Management Plan

The first thing you can do is to develop a risk-management program, which begins with the development of a risk-management plan. Put that plan into effect as a proactive step to minimize the potential for loss.

One of the most important parts of your risk-management program is development of policies and procedures to help reduce injuries in your specific situation. For example, you may need to modify game rules because of limitations of a playing facility or restrict access to the number of people using a facility at one time. Careful study of what may create risks will help you develop policies that seek to minimize those risks.

2. Keep Knowledgeable About Current Standards

Standards determine the duties you and your coaches are to meet and how they should be met. Standards are continually evolving, so you need to stay abreast of any changes and pass on the appropriate information to your staff and coaches. But staying abreast of all these standards is not easy because there is no one central source. Standards, in the eyes of the judicial system, may come from any of the following sources:

a. Federal and state law, often based on previously litigated cases. These laws deal with negligence and immunity, employment standards, due process, contracts, and criminal acts.

b. National organizations. The National Operating Committee on Standards for Athletic Equipment (NOCSAE), in particular, is an organization you need to be familiar with if you are responsible for sports facilities and equipment purchasing and maintenance. You may contact the committee using the following information:

NOCSAE

P.O. Box 12290

Overland, KS 66282-2290

Phone: 913-888-1340

Fax: 913-888-1065

c. National governing bodies (NGBs) for each sport. A complete listing of these NGBs is found in appendix C. An NGB is the recognized national organization for establishing eligibility rules to participate in that NGB's competitive events, rules for participation, and in some cases facility and equipment requirements.

d. Other national and state governing bodies for certain levels of participation, such as the National Federation of State High School Associations and the 50 state high school activity associations that belong to the federation. These associations primarily set participation and playing rules for high school sports. The National Collegiate Athletic Association and the National Association of Intercollegiate Athletics set participation and playing rules for colleges and universities.

e. Health, physical education, and medical organizations offer recommendations on safe practices in sport, recommended ages for participation, conditions that disqualify participants from participation, preparticipation physical examinations, strength and conditioning guide-

lines, and drug use. Organizations offering such policies and their addresses are found in appendix D.

f. Periodicals that provide coverage of risk-management issues. Such publications include the following three:

From the Gym to the Jury
6917 Wildglen Drive
Dallas, TX 75230
Phone: 214-691-9476
URL: http://www.gym2jury.com/contact_info.htm

Sports and the Law
601 S. Kingsley Dr.
Los Angeles, CA 90005
Phone: 213-487-5590

Sport and the Law Journal
Manchester Metropolitan University
School of Law
Hathersage Rage
Manchester, Lancs, M13 0JA

g. Books that are important sources include the following:

Appenzeller, Herb. 1999. *Risk Management in Sport: Issues and Strategies.* Durham, NC: Carolina Academic Press.

Dougherty, Neil. 1998. *Outdoor Recreation Safety.* Champaign, IL: Human Kinetics.

Goldberg, Barry. 1995. *Sport and Exercise for Children With Chronic Health Conditions.* Champaign, IL: Human Kinetics.

3. Educate Your Staff and Coaches

Pass along to your staff and coaches the information they need to implement your risk-management program and to fulfill their duties. Help your staff understand that part of their responsibility is to be ongoing risk managers. You can't just talk about this once a year with them; you need to have regular sessions, written policies and guidelines, and periodic training for emergency procedures.

In chapter 2 you learned why you should educate your coaches. The education process must include preparing your coaches to provide a safe environment through proper instruction, good supervision, and appropriate response to emergencies. In your education program you should provide your coaches with specific written guidelines for safe use of your facilities and equipment (see page 104).

Educating your coaches also fulfills one of your duties as an administrator and minimizes your risk of being sued for assigning unqualified personnel. Doug Thornton, a YMCA youth sport program director writing in *Perspective* (September 1989), said: "Looking back on those 15 minutes on the witness stand in a packed courtroom, I was glad I was trained in the YMCA coaches training program and had implemented that program at our Y."

4. Supervise Your Program

You may develop a great risk-management program, become a legal encyclopedia, and educate your staff and coaches about all they need to know to provide a safe environment—but without supervision, all this could be for naught. Supervision is essential to see that your staff and coaches carry out your program in a safe way. Supervision involves fulfilling all the duties we discussed in chapter 2.

As an administrator you usually will have general supervisory duties over all areas, activities, and personnel participating in your program. You will often need to assign others to provide general and specific supervision. Specific supervision is usually provided by the coach and involves closely watching any activity in which there is a significant risk of injury.

You should have a policy shared by your staff, coaching committee, and coaches that a qualified adult is always assigned to supervise every practice and game. Coaches should never leave a practice or game unsupervised. Never!

Additionally, because of ever-increasing concerns about the safety and welfare of children, especially related to physical and sexual abuse, more than one adult should be present.

When you assign others to supervise a playing facility or special event, they must be competent to

- plan for the activity,
- present clear warnings of risks,
- provide age- and gender-appropriate supervision,
- know how to provide for a safe environment,
- be able to evaluate injuries and incapacities, and
- implement an emergency plan.

Following are some useful supervision guidelines for a youth sport program. Keep them in mind as you develop your risk-management plan.

Supervision Guidelines

- Provide general supervision for all your programs by either your staff or the coaches.
- Coaches should know how to provide close supervision for activities that pose greater risk to the participants.
- A competent adult should supervise all practices and contests.
- Coaches and officials should be able to carry out their supervisory duties.
- Have enough supervisors for the activities being monitored.
- Supervisors should not be too close to the activity or too far away. Some activities can be supervised by watching and others require hands-on supervision.
- Know the rules of the activity designed to protect the players from injury. Learn to anticipate potentially risky situations by athletes and coaches and quickly take precautionary action.
- Remember that when providing close supervision of one or more athletes, it does not reduce the need to continue providing good general supervision.
- When practicing, organize participants in such a way that they can be properly supervised.
- Never leave young participants unsupervised.

You are responsible not only for supervising your staff and the volunteers in your program, but also for general supervision of the facilities and equipment you use. This responsibility is not limited to the playing fields or gymnasiums but extends to locker rooms, showers, rest rooms, training and equipment rooms, and any other facility used in your program.

Here is a set of guidelines for supervising sports facilities, followed by further guidelines for supervising the use of sports equipment.

Guidelines for Supervising Sports Facilities

- Facilities must be adequate and appropriate for their use. *Adequate* means the facilities conform to the applicable rules, standards, and practices for the activity taking place. If your facility is not adequate, take steps to make it adequate. Modify the activity to reduce risk of injury, find an alternative facility, or, if necessary, terminate the activity.
- Facilities should be constantly monitored to ensure they remain adequate. Special supervision is required when conditions (such as bad weather) may render the facility unsafe.
- Control access to facilities that present potential risks, such as swimming pools, gymnastics centers, and weight rooms.
- Do not assume that coaches will conduct proper facility checks. This is your responsibility.
- Set procedures for correcting problems when you identify an inadequate aspect of your facility. Determine whether the problem warrants discontinuing facility use until the problem is corrected, or whether other action can protect participants from unnecessary risk (a warning, special padding, and so on).
- Require participants to perform basic safety inspections of the facilities they use.

Guidelines for Supervising the Use of Sports Equipment

- Equipment should meet existing standards. You or your staff is directly responsible for all equipment your program provides. If equipment is to be purchased by your coaches or the participants, make sure they have the information they need to know what to buy. Even if the participant buys the equipment, coaches and administrators are still responsible for it.
- Coaches should know how to properly fit equipment that players use, such as helmets, face masks, and eye guards.
- Coaches should know how to properly use all equipment in their sport.
- You, your staff, or the coaches should regularly inspect equipment that you provide. Set up a regular schedule and document the inspection.
- Equipment should be properly maintained and repaired.
- Require participants to perform basic safety inspections of their equipment before each practice and contest.

We have also provided you with a useful checklist for inspecting facilities (see form 4.1, pages 120-123) and another for checking equipment (see form 4.2, pages 124-127). Form 4.1 is an incomplete checklist provided as an example to help you develop a checklist specific to your facilities.

5. Keep Records

It's impossible to overemphasize the importance of keeping records. In the event of an alleged wrongdoing, without records it becomes your word against the accuser's. If you will keep the records using the forms provided in this guide, you should have sufficient documentation to show what has occurred.

Transfer of Risk

We've reviewed what you can do to directly and indirectly help make participation safer in your youth sport program and thereby reduce the risk of a lawsuit. But, by the inherent nature of sport, there is still the risk of injury or loss. You, your staff, and coaches may make a mistake, overlook something, or have an accident occur that is beyond your control. To reduce your risk, you'll want to transfer the financial responsibility for these risks to others. You can do this in two ways:

1. Have the parents of the participants in your program assume the risk by signing waivers/releases and consent forms.
2. Purchase insurance.

Let's look at each of these options.

Waivers/Releases and Consent Forms

A waiver/release is a contract between your organization and the participants (or parents of children who are not of legal age) that acknowledges that participation involves a risk of injury—even catastrophic injury—and that the participant or guardian accepts that risk. When participants sign the contract they waive their right to sue should an injury occur and thereby release your organization, its employees, and volunteers of liability for any such injury.

A consent form obtains an acknowledgment and acceptance by the participant (or parents) of the terms and conditions your organization puts forth, such as the right to seek emergency medical treatment for the participant if he is injured, consent to be transported to games, and participation in drug testing.

The use of waivers/releases and consent forms has been controversial. Some sport law advisors assert that these documents are not worth the paper they are written on. However, several sources have recently reported that these documents, when properly prepared and obtained, are useful in providing protection against ordinary negligence, but not gross negligence. Courts have held these documents to be valid under particular conditions, leading to summary judgments for the defense. The United States Olympic Committee's legal and insurance departments recommend and use them, as do many other major sports organizations and sports insurance companies.

A well-publicized case in California demonstrates the value of a waiver. As reported in the December 1991 issue of *Fitness Management*, an elite female cyclist was severely brain injured during a race sponsored by the defendant federation. She had signed two separate prospective releases and assumption of risk documents

before the event. The woman was injured in a race in which a novice racer was allowed to compete, despite the objections of the experienced cyclists. The association ignored the complaints and let the novice racer enter the event, which ultimately led to the plaintiff's brain injury. Testimony "clearly indicated that the plaintiff was aware of the risks associated with racing and that head injuries were a known hazard of cycling." Despite the plaintiff's claim that she did not assume the risk of the federation letting an inexperienced cyclist participate in the event, "the trial court felt that her execution of the release barred the claim and prevented her from recovering."

Failure to warn and lack of informed consent are the most common reasons for sport litigation. The waiver/release is foremost a method of obtaining acknowledgment that the participants have been warned. Second, they may hold you harmless should an injury occur from ordinary negligence, but not gross negligence. These documents also have the psychological effect of making participants assume more responsibility for their well-being, which discourages them from filing lawsuits.

While we recommend the use of waivers and releases, they are not guaranteed protection against being successfully sued. Waivers are least effective with minors, the participants you are most likely to have in your program, because minors cannot waive their own rights, and no one, not even parents, can waive their rights. Waivers and releases are one tool among many to help minimize your exposure to lawsuit.

Remember that consent forms work only when you collaborate with coaches to ensure that no one participates, even in practices, before submitting the required forms. Often, coaches' desires to help their athletes lead them to overlook the risks they take by permitting athletes to participate a few days before submitting consent and/or medical forms. Decide how to deal with this situation in advance (that is, check up on the status of participants, be ready to intervene to get a form signed and/or to deny participation) and make sure coaches know the importance of following your procedures.

Below are general guidelines for developing useful waivers/releases. Form 4.3 (pages 128-129) presents an example of a waiver/release form.

Guidelines for Developing Waivers/Releases

1. The waiver/release must be in writing and be complete and explicit about the harm that can occur, how it can occur, and the consequences thereof. Stating that "the participant accepts all responsibility for injury" is not complete and explicit.

2. It should be sport-specific, identifying what the injuries are in that sport and how they occur.

3. It should state how to prevent or reduce the risk of injury by using equipment correctly, obeying rules, and practicing skills as instructed.

4. It must be written clearly in language that the participant (or parent) can understand.

5. It should make clear the potential short- and long-term consequences of being injured in the sport.

6. It should specify the responsibility of the participants and their parents in preventing injuries, such as following medical advice and caring for equipment.

7. It must provide contractual release.

8. It must include the signature of a parent or guardian for minors.

You should work with an attorney or insurance company to develop your specific waiver/release form. Unlike other documents in this guide, you can't be sure that our sample waiver/release form (form 4.3, pages 128-129) will be valid in your state. Once you have a well-written waiver/release form, follow these steps:

1. Participants must be allowed to read the waiver/release before signing it.

2. Have participants (or parents) sign the waiver/release before they begin participating.

The most common uses for consent forms in youth sport programs are these:

1. To obtain consent to authorize emergency medical treatment for participants who become ill or injured when their legal guardians are not present or cannot be reached.

2. To be transported as part of participation in the sport. (These first two consents are often combined into one document, as shown in form 4.4 on page 130.)

3. To obtain participation consent for a child who has a known medical condition that puts her at special risk. A sample of this consent form is shown in form 4.5 on page 131.

Insurance

Insurance is a common and effective way of transferring the financial risk arising from an injury, loss, or lawsuit. Although the cost of insurance has increased tremendously, the potential expense to your organization, employees, and volunteers without insurance in the case of injury, loss, and lawsuit is far greater.

Wading through the insurance quagmire can be intimidating, but learning the types of insurance your organization does and does not need and educating your coaches about your program's coverage will help you meet the challenge head-on. There are several types of insurance that your agency needs to consider:

- *General liability insurance* typically covers your organization against bodily injury and property damage claims as well as personal liability arising from libel, slander, and invasion of privacy. It usually excludes intentional acts such as crimes and acts of war. The insurance should cover claims arising out of athletic participation and not exclude participant-versus-participant claims. It should also include coverage for all teams, sponsors, officers, directors, managers, coaches, umpires and referees, volunteers, and other managing personnel who engage in any activity associated with participation in the sport.

- *Comprehensive medical insurance* pays all or a major portion of expenses associated with illness and accidents, especially hospital, doctor, and medication expenses. Typically this insurance is provided only to full-time employees in your program.

• *Excess accident insurance* provides supplementary medical and dental expense benefits for those injured while participating in your program's activities. These covered expenses are those in excess of all other insurance coverage.

• *Directors and officers liability insurance* protects individual directors, officers, trustees, and sometimes volunteers from personal liability arising from such acts as discrimination, wrongful dismissal of employees or coaches, negligence in carrying out duties, waste of organizational assets, acts beyond recognized authority, and false or misleading reports.

• *Automobile liability insurance* agrees to pay on behalf of the insured all sums that the insured becomes legally obligated to pay as damages because of bodily injury, including death at any time resulting therefrom, sustained by any person, caused by accident and arising out of ownership, maintenance, or use of the automobile.

As the administrator of your youth sport program, you probably are not responsible for purchasing your program's insurance, but you certainly need to know exactly what insurance coverage your organization has. Exercise 4.1 guides you through the steps to getting the answers you need about your organization's insurance program.

Insurance is complicated but important business. Here are some tips to help you obtain more information about liability insurance:

1. Determine what coverage is available through the local organization and league.

2. If you are associated with a national organization, investigate whether it offers an insurance program. For example, the National Recreation and Park Association (NRPA) offers several insurance plans to member organizations:

- Liability and accident medical insurance plan for team sports, including football
- Blanket recreational accident medical insurance plan

- Business pursuits liability insurance plan
- Day care center/nursery school accident medical insurance protection plan
- Nonprofit directors and officers liability insurance
- Group term life insurance plan

For further information, contact NRPA's insurance administrators at

Aon Risk Services
10 Lanidex Center West
Parsippany, NJ 07054
Phone: 800-795-3248
URL: http://www.aon.com

Ask for the NRPA plan administrator.
The YMCA of the USA also offers an insurance program through its YMCA Services Corporation. If you are a YMCA, contact the following group about coverage:

YMCA Services Corporation
101 North Wacker Drive
Chicago, IL 60606
Phone: 800-872-9622 or 312-977-0031
Fax: 312-977-9063
URL: http://www.ymca.net

3. Contact the national organization of a specific sport. Many of these organizations—Little Dribblers Basketball, Inc., Pop Warner Football, Soccer Association for Youth, Little League Baseball, Inc., and U.S.A. Gymnastics, just to name a few—offer liability insurance programs to participating members. See the list of national sport organizations in appendix C.

4. The following is another major source of sports liability insurance:

K&K Insurance Group, Inc.
P.O. Box 2338
Fort Wayne, IN 46801-2338
Phone: 219-459-5000
Fax: 219-459-5500
E-mail: KK_General@kandkinsurance.com
URL: www.kandkinsurance.com

Exercise 4.1   Knowing Your Organization's Insurance Coverage

Let's see what you know or think you know about the insurance coverage your organization provides as it pertains to your youth sport program. Begin by circling "Yes" or "No" to indicate the coverages you think your organization has. Then enter the dollar limit of liability for each type. If you have no idea whether your organization has the type of insurance named, circle the "?" and then find out. You should know.

I. Insurance Coverage

	Coverage			Limit
Property Damage?	Yes	No	?	$ _____
Bodily damage?	Yes	No	?	$ _____
Injury to you and other employees?	Yes	No	?	$ _____
Injury to your coaches and other volunteers?	Yes	No	?	$ _____
General liability?	Yes	No	?	$ _____
Liability for your and your employees' actions?	Yes	No	?	$ _____
Liability for your coaches' and volunteers' actions?	Yes	No	?	$ _____
Medical insurance for employees?	Yes	No	?	$ _____
Excess accident insurance for coaches and players	Yes	No	?	$ _____
Transportation?	Yes	No	?	$ _____
Directors' and officers' liability?	Yes	No	?	$ _____
Legal fees?	Yes	No	?	$ _____
Other?_____	Yes	No	?	$ _____

II. Do you know . . .

• How the coverage applies?	Yes	No
• If the policy covers traveling to practice?	Yes	No
• If the policy covers before, during, and after practices and contests?	Yes	No
• Whom to call when you have a question about your insurance or a claim to file?	Yes	No

---

5. Develop good rapport with a local insurance provider. This insurance agent can help you sort through the types of insurance described on pages 106-107, decide what types of policies suit your particular program, and determine whether the company can provide or obtain the type of insurance your program needs.

It's especially important that you know whether your current liability insurance policy covers your coaches and other volunteers. If it doesn't, it should. If coaches are willing to donate their time and complete your coach education program, then you should protect them against financial loss from a lawsuit when they are acting within their coaching duties. If your organization cannot provide this insurance, then you have an obligation to notify coaches at the time they are selected that you will not provide insurance coverage and that you recommend they obtain coverage themselves.

The best way to educate your volunteer coaches about insurance is to discuss the subject during your coach orientation program. Tell all your coaches exactly what is and is not covered by your program's liability insurance. Make copies of the liability policy available to those who request it.

Your organization's liability insurance will usually provide adequate coverage for your coaches, but in some cases coaches may want to obtain additional insurance. Each coach needs to evaluate whether the liability coverage through the youth sport program insurance policy is adequate for his particular situation. Only after learning the specifics about the liability coverage of the youth sport program can a coach decide whether she needs additional coverage in the form of a secondary policy, umbrella, or an excess policy.

Volunteer coaches should have their own personal general liability insurance. If they'll be transporting athletes at any time, they should also have automobile insurance that covers transporting these players. Coaches can obtain general liability insurance in several ways, including:

1. *Homeowner/renter policy.* If the coach has such a policy, it should be reviewed to determine what exactly is covered and excluded, and how much the coverage is for. It is unlikely that a primary liability insurance policy will cover a person while he is coaching. Most insurance providers suggest that the coverage be for $500,000 liability. If the policy doesn't provide sufficient coverage, the coach may be able to have the insurance agent add an endorsement for a minimal fee.

2. *Personal umbrella, secondary, or excess liability policy.* This type of policy typically provides coverage for bodily injury, personal injury, and property damage as secondary coverage to the primary coverage of automobile, homeowner/renter, or other policies. The policy often provides broader coverage and higher limits, such as for libel and slander, than does a homeowner/renter policy.

For those who feel they have greater exposure to lawsuit because of their personal worth, a personal umbrella, secondary, or excess liability policy may be appropriate. Let's say Coach Elliott volunteers for a park district whose liability insurance covers him for up to $500,000. But Coach Elliott has personal assets of about $1 million. To raise his total liability to $1 million, Coach Elliott takes out a secondary or umbrella policy for the additional $500,000. His insurance agent will coordinate the secondary policy with the park district policy to provide that extra coverage. In the event of a lawsuit, should the primary or base policy reach its limit or not be effective, the secondary policy will take effect.

As a matter of course, don't advise your coaches to purchase additional liability insurance. Only your coaches can decide whether the coverage provided by your insurance is sufficient or whether they need additional coverage.

Just as your coaches need to determine whether they need additional coverage, the person or group purchasing your agency's insurance needs to evaluate whether your organization needs or wants to provide excess accident insurance for your coaches and players. The National Youth Sports Coaches Association is one youth sport organization that offers an excess liability program to members. The National Recreation and Park Association insurance program also offers an excess accident insurance plan.

When you investigate the value of excess insurance programs, be sure to get these questions answered:

- Does this excess policy become a primary policy in the event that no other policy exists (either from the coach or organization)?
- What is the length of the policy period?
- When does the policy go into effect?
- Is the policy in effect for the duration of the policy period, no matter which sport the coach chooses to coach?

It's not recommended that you advise volunteer coaches seeking additional insurance to obtain a professional liability policy. This type of secondary insurance policy is designed for professional coaches, not volunteers.

Managing Specific Risks

Unfortunately, no matter how much you try to prevent them, accidents are going to happen and injuries result. Your duties are to do all that you can to (a) minimize accidents and injuries and (b) keep your organization from being held liable for accidents and injuries. To achieve these objectives, you need a medical response plan, an emergency plan, and a policy regarding transportation of your participants. We'll discuss each of these in the sections that follow.

Medical Response Plan

Children playing sports may be injured regardless of how well your coaches are trained, how safe your facilities and equipment are, and how good your supervision is. You will also have medical emergencies involving officials, coaches, parents, and other spectators. When children are injured playing sports, your coaches will probably be the first responders who will need to provide first aid and, if the injury is serious enough, implement an emergency plan to obtain qualified medical assistance fast.

Your first priority is to have a medical response plan that provides the best care possible to everyone involved in your youth sport program. Second, you want to minimize your risk of being held liable because you failed to provide the standard of care that society judged you should. In this section we describe elements to consider in developing a medical plan. We recommend that you develop your specific plan in consultation with a local physician, preferably a sports medicine specialist.

Being prepared for on-the-field accidents can eliminate time and money in the long run.

For youth sport programs, we recommend that you seek a pediatrician who has taken additional training in sports medicine. Check the yellow pages or contact the following to obtain names of pediatricians in your area:

American Academy of Pediatrics

141 Northwest Point Boulevard

Elk Grove Village, IL 60007-1098

Phone: 847-434-4000

Fax: 847-434-8000

E-mail: kidsdocs@aap.org

URL: www.aap.org

The American Running and Fitness Association (ARFA) also offers a referral system. To inquire about sport-oriented medical professionals in your area, contact them:

American Running & Fitness Association

4405 East West Highway, Suite 405

Bethesda, MD 20814

Phone: 800-776-ARFA

E-mail: run@americanrunning.org

URL: www.americanrunning.org

Consider these elements in preparing your medical response plan:

1. All participants should provide you with medical histories (see form 4.6, pages 132-133, for a sample medical history form you can use).

2. For screening purposes, all participants should have a preparticipation physical examination, which, combined with their medical histories, identifies potential medical problems (see form 4.7, page 134). The specific objectives of the examination are

   a. to detect conditions that may limit participation,

   b. to detect conditions that may predispose participants to injury, and

   c. to meet legal and insurance requirements.

If you are responsible for arranging preparticipation physical examinations or working with the medical personnel in your community to conduct these examinations, you should purchase a copy of *Preparticipation Physical Evaluation* (1992), a joint publication of the American Academy of Family Physicians, American Academy of Pediatrics, American Medical Society for Sports Medicine, American Orthopaedic Society for Sports Medicine, and the American Osteopathic Academy of Sports Medicine. Order copies of this book from the publisher.

McGraw-Hill Companies Inc.

1221 Avenue of the Americas

New York, NY 10020

(212) 512-2000

www.mcgraw-hill.com

This book contains the latest guidelines. Share it with the physicians in your community who will conduct the examinations for your participants. You yourself do not need to know the technical aspects of a good preparticipation physical examination, but you should know that the five medical groups that prepared *Preparticipation Physical Evaluation* recommend the following:

• Schedule a complete physical examination with medical history prior to the child's first participation in sports, followed by an annual reevaluation.

• Ideally, the evaluation should be performed at least six weeks before the season begins.

• The physical examination should include height and weight measurements, an assessment of physical maturity, and an examination of the eyes, cardiovascular system, pulmonary system, abdomen, skin, musculoskeletal system, and genitalia (male).

3. Obtain a consent form for participation. Certain conditions may disqualify a child from playing, as recommended by the American Academy of Pediatrics. These conditions are described in appendix A. To obtain consent, use form 4.4 for children without medical conditions and form 4.5 for children with medical conditions. Children should not be allowed to participate until they have submitted a consent form.

4. Have all participants fill out an emergency information card, including the names and numbers of parents or guardians to contact in the event of an emergency (see form 4.8). This card should also contain information to alert you to any preexisting medical conditions an athlete may have that could influence treatment. Emphasize to your coaches that a youngster cannot be allowed to participate until you have received an emergency information card.

5. Train your coaches and supervisors about what to do and what not to do when players are injured. Ideally, every coach should be qualified to administer cardiopulmonary resuscitation and first aid, but this is often not required. Your supervisors and coaches have four basic duties:

a. To protect the athlete from further harm (and to do so judiciously)

b. To attempt to maintain or restore life to the injured youngster

c. To comfort and reassure the injured youngster

d. To immediately activate the emergency medical response plan (see page 113)

6. Coaches should have a first-aid kit at every practice and contest and know how and when to use it. The contents of a basic first-aid kit are listed in figure 4.1.

7. Develop an emergency plan to obtain medical assistance fast. If there are no phones at the playing site, arrange to have cellular phones available at practices and games. See pages 113 to 114 for the steps to consider in an emergency plan.

8. Keep good records of the accident. You may use the accident report form (form 4.9) on pages 136 to 137.

Steps in an Emergency Plan

The coach is responsible for the care of each of her athletes. Immediate care for an injured athlete is of the utmost importance for ensuring the best treatment for the athlete and for maintaining a safe environment. Listed here (in order of preference) are the people who should first respond to the needs of an injured athlete:

Stocking the First-Aid Kit

A well-stocked first-aid kit should include the following items:

List of emergency phone numbers

Change for phone calls

Plastic bags for crushed ice

4-inch and 6-inch elastic wraps

Triangular bandage

Sterile gauze pads—3-inch and 4-inch squares

Saline solution (for eyes)

Contact lens case

Mirror

Penlight

Tongue depressors

Cotton swabs

Butterfly strips

Bandage strips (assorted sizes)

Alcohol

Peroxide

Antibacterial soap

First-aid cream

Petroleum jelly

Tape adherent

Tape remover

1 1/2-inch white athletic tape

Prewrap

Sterile gauze rolls

Insect sting kit

Safety pins

1/8-inch, 1/4-inch, and 1/2-inch foam rubber

Examination gloves

Mouth shield for CPR

Figure 4.1   Contents of a well-stocked first-aid kit.

- Team physician
- Team trainer
- Emergency medical personnel
- Coach

Having medically trained personnel, when they are available, to assist the injured athlete allows the coach to tend to the safety and needs of the rest of the team. However, if no medical personnel are present, the coach is responsible for the immediate care of the athlete. The first step is for the coach to decide whether the injury is an emergency. This decision requires good judgment and is greatly helped by taking a sport first-aid or regular first-aid course. If the coach decides the injury is an emergency, he activates the emergency medical response plan.

Activating the Emergency Medical Response Plan

1. Delegate the responsibility of seeking medical help to the following (in order of preference):

> Assistant coach
> Parent
> Responsible adult near the athletic site
> Athlete

Whoever is responsible for seeking medical assistance must be calm, responsible, and familiar with the emergency medical plan. This person should be present at each practice and competition to ensure consistency with the plan. When the person cannot attend, be sure the coach appoints another person to this position in advance.

2. Prepare in advance a list of emergency phone numbers that coaches should take to every competition and practice.

> Rescue unit
> Hospital
> Physician
> Police
> Fire department

For away contests, talk with the host coach(es) prior to the event to learn about their emergency procedures.

3. Take each athlete's emergency information card (see form 4.8, page 135) to each competition and practice. This card will assist medical personnel in administering proper care and assist the coach in contacting the athlete's parents or guardians.

4. Give an emergency response card (see form 4.9, pages 136-137) to the person responsible for calling for medical assistance. This card provides critical information to assist the caller and help him keep calm, knowing that everything he needs to say is on the card.

5. Complete accident report form (see form 4.10, page 138) to keep on file.

Emergency Medical Steps

If an injury occurs, follow these steps:

1. Assess the injury.
2. Send your contact person to activate the emergency medical response plan and call the injured athlete's parents.
3. Administer basic first aid.
4. Help emergency medical personnel prepare to transport the athlete to the medical facility.
5. Designate someone to go with the person if the parents are not available. This person should be responsible and calm and should know the athlete. Assistant coaches or parents are good candidates for this job.
6. Complete an injury report form while the details of the event are fresh in your mind.

Most injuries won't require emergency medical attention. Coaches will face an array of minor injuries, from bruises to sprains. Such injuries, though minor, require attention from the coach to prevent further complications. Take these steps in the event of a minor injury:

1. Evaluate the injury.
2. Administer basic first aid.
3. Remove the youngster from the contest if he is in pain or can no longer walk, run, jump, or throw.

4. Contact the athlete's parents.
5. Discuss the injury with the parents and the athlete.
6. Suggest that the athlete see a physician to rule out a serious injury.
7. Fill out an injury report form while the incident is fresh in your mind.

Transportation

Numerous lawsuits have resulted from the sponsoring agency—or volunteers as part of their duties with the sponsoring agency—transporting athletes. It is not uncommon for coaches and parents to transport groups of youngsters to practices and games across town, the state, or the country. Most youth sport administrators, volunteer coaches, and parents do not fully understand their risk of lawsuit under various transportation options. In this section we'll examine what the laws generally say, remembering that laws vary from state to state.

Ideally, it is best to transport athletes by licensed commercial carriers because they have the liability insurance necessary to cover the participants in the case of an accident. But this ideal choice is also usually the most expensive choice. The next best option is to use your agency's vehicles, finding qualified drivers. Of course, the vehicles should be in good repair and properly insured. The worst choice is for you or your volunteers to transport youngsters using your personal vehicle. You, your organization, and your volunteers are exposed to the greatest liability risk under this option. For example, in most cases, if you are compensated for transporting players, your automobile insurance policy is likely voided because you become a public rather than private operator. You should know that if you or your staff or volunteers regularly transport athletes, you may be judged to be providing public transportation and therefore need a chauffeur's license.

As the administrator of your youth sport program, you need a policy on transportation. You should have answers to these questions:

- Do you ask your coaches to transport youngsters using their personal vehicles

routinely; on occasion, such as to a tournament; or in emergencies?
- Do you provide auto insurance for volunteer drivers?
- Are your volunteers licensed to drive in your state? Are the vehicles properly insured with the maximum liability insurance coverage permitted under your state's laws?
- Should you purchase an umbrella policy on top of the base liability policy for agency-owned vehicles?
- Should your organization be listed as an additional insured party on your volunteers' automobile insurance policies?
- Do you provide rules, procedures, and expected behaviors for volunteers who drive on your behalf? (For example, prohibit drivers from drinking alcohol for at least six hours before driving and at all times while driving the vehicles.)
- Do you use agency vehicles? If yes, who is qualified to drive them? Who checks the drivers' qualifications and regularly inspects the vehicles to ensure they are safe?

Be sure to address the transportation of athletes in your organization's risk-management plan. Reexamine your transportation policy every year.

Participant Rights

You need to develop policies and procedures that permit you to control your program while maximizing the benefits and minimizing the risks to your participants. However, you cannot develop policies and procedures that deny people their basic rights. Doing so opens you and your organization to the risk of being sued for denying people these basic rights. In this section, we'll look at

- basic personal rights such as freedom of speech, religion, and personal appearance,
- the implications of the Americans With Disabilities Act on your youth sports program,

- due process and conducting searches (and drug testing as a form of conducting searches), and
- child abuse.

Personal Rights

People have the right to free speech as long as it does not disrupt the activity or risk harm to others. You have the right as program administrator to determine whether a person's form of expression is vulgar or otherwise offensive and to take steps to control these expressions.

People have the right to free exercise of religious beliefs without official sponsorship or interference. Thus, your agency can neither impose religious practices on all participants nor deny any participant the right to engage in a religious practice (for example, prayer). In other words, your best legal position is to be neutral.

Youth sport programs sometimes set rules regarding the personal appearance of participants. Considering past court rulings, it is recommended that you follow these guidelines when developing any such rules:

1. The rule should be specific, not vague. The rule should be succinct and explicit, minimizing the chances for interpretation and personal discretion. For example, a rule that prohibits the wearing of jeans, T-shirts, and sneakers to out-of-town athletic contests is less vulnerable to individual interpretation than one that simply prohibits the wearing of casual clothes. Ten different people would define "casual clothes" 10 different ways.

2. The rules must relate directly to the safety of participants or to the quality of the activity. Prohibiting jewelry is appropriate in most sports because it pertains to the safety of the players. Requiring everyone to wear white shorts is probably not appropriate.

3. The benefits of the rule must outweigh the restrictions imposed on your participants' constitutional rights. For example, requiring all swimmers to wear bathing caps and to shower before swimming and prohibiting swimmers from wearing cutoffs or gym shorts would most likely be justified because the sanitary gains significantly outweigh the breach of individual freedom.

4. When restricting a person's rights for the safety of others, choose the least restrictive of the alternatives available. For example, long hair can be a sanitation problem in swimming pools and should be prohibited. Although you could require that all hair be cut short, a bathing cap also solves the sanitation problem and is less restrictive (because it is a temporary solution) than requiring a person to cut her hair.

Americans With Disabilities Act

You've probably heard discussions about the Americans With Disabilities Act, but do you know what it says and means? The easiest way to understand the act is to view it as an extension of the 1964 Civil Rights Act, which states that people cannot be discriminated against because of their race, color, sex, national origin, or religion. The ADA simply adds *disability* to that list.

The ADA general rule states the following:

"No individuals shall be discriminated against on the basis of disabilities in the full and equal enjoyment of goods, services, facilities, privileges, advantages or accommodations at any place of public accommodation by any person who owns, leases or operates a place of public accommodation.

Benefits provided for the disabled cannot be separate or different from those provided for others, unless they are as effective as those provided for others."

A *disability* is a physical or mental impairment that substantially limits one or more of the major life activities of an individual. The law states that an agency, including almost all sports organizations (private clubs and religious groups are excluded), should provide reasonable accommodation to those with disabilities. What is *reasonable accommodation*? Those interpreting the act answer by saying: actions that provide meaningful access to programs, services, and benefits without requiring substantial, fundamental, or undue burden on the agency.

What does this act mean for operating youth sport programs? We wish we could answer this important question definitively, but the full interpretation of this far-reaching act continues to be determined by the courts. For example, the definition of "substantial, fundamental, or undue burden" is open to wide interpretation and thus requires resolution through litigation.

Although much remains to be resolved, based on our reading of the ADA and recently published literature, we can offer the following guidelines:

1. The intent of the act is to integrate people with disabilities into all dimensions of society wherever possible. Thus, wherever you can accommodate those with disabilities in your sport programs without a substantial burden to you or risk to other participants, you should do so. The right to participate in sport programs is not absolute. You must determine on a case-by-case basis whether people can participate within the parameters of the activity in spite of their conditions. You need not change your programs to make accommodations that disrupt the activity or fundamentally alter it.

2. You need not accommodate disabled persons when they pose a significant risk or direct threat to themselves or other participants. However, you should have some basis for this decision such as medical, professional, or legal opinion or documented evidence of the risk.

3. You cannot exclude from participating in your sport programs, including contact sports, young people who have lost an organ, limb, or appendage on the basis of that condition alone. However, you should warn them of the risks involved and obtain a medical clearance just as you would with all other participants.

4. You should make your sport facilities accessible to those with disabilities whenever reasonable accommodation can be made, but the ADA does not mandate such accommodation if the cost is excessive. For now, "excessive" remains open to interpretation.

5. Without undue hardship, your communications about your youth sport programs should be made available to those with dis-

abilities—for example, to people with visual impairments and hearing loss.

6. When people with disabilities cannot be accommodated in your sport programs, strive to offer equal programs for those with disabilities if sufficient demand for such a program exists. The ADA recognizes that separate programs may be appropriate ways to provide equal opportunities for persons with disabilities.

7. If insurance is provided to coaches or players, it must be extended to cover those with disabilities as well.

8. Inform your staff and coaches of the ADA regulations and encourage them to accommodate youths with disabilities whenever it is prudent.

For further assistance with understanding the ADA and its impact on your program, contact your national sport organization (see appendix C), the United States Olympic Committee, or the United States Department of Justice.

U.S. Olympic Committee
Department of Disabled Sports Services
One Olympic Plaza
Colorado Springs, CO 80909-5760
Phone: 719-632-5551
URL: www.usoc.org

U.S. Department of Justice
Civil Rights Division
Coordination and Review Section
P.O. Box 66118
Washington, DC 20035-6118
Phone: 202-514-0301

Due Process

Due process refers to the procedures used to protect and preserve people's rights. Government and its institutions are required to ensure that no person is deprived of life, liberty, or property without due process of law. Private agencies are not required to provide due process, but should consider the merits of doing so. Here are some guidelines established from legal rulings regarding due process:

1. State all rules and regulations in simple language.
2. Presume all persons innocent until you have a reasonable body of proof to the contrary.
3. The admission of guilt removes the possibility of bias or error and thus fulfills the legal requirement for due process.
4. Grant the accused a reasonable and fair hearing before imposing disciplinary sanctions. For minor offenses this hearing could take the form of an opportunity for the accused to discuss the matter with the person imposing the sanctions. For situations in which the effects of the sanctions can be long term or costly, a formal hearing is appropriate.
5. For major offenses, give the person accused written notice of a hearing and a written statement of the charges and the grounds that, if proven, justify the imposition of sanctions. The accused should be given the opportunity to present evidence to support his position and to examine the evidence used against him. A written or taped record of the proceedings is a good idea as well.
6. Grant people the right to appeal a decision.
7. Impose punishment appropriate for the severity of the offense and administer it consistently and fairly among offenders.

Searches and Drug Testing

While we wish that searches were not needed for youth sport programs, the alarming increase in the use of weapons and drugs and the rise in theft among younger people are making searches increasingly necessary. We know of no legal precedent for searches in youth sport programs, but we recommend that you follow the guidelines established for searches within school programs, which include the following:

1. Search only when you have a *reasonable suspicion*. The test for reasonable suspi-cion is if you believe the search will reveal evidence that the person in question is violating or has violated the law or the rules of your program.
2. Search in a way that avoids unnecessary intrusion on the privacy of the person being searched. Never conduct a strip search. Call the appropriate law enforcement authorities.
3. Search in a way to maintain control over any evidence found.
4. Involve the police when appropriate.

Drug testing has been a controversial means to try to police the use of drugs in sports. In May 1994, random drug testing of public school athletes was ruled unconstitutional by the 9th U.S. Circuit Court of Appeals. "Children, students, do not have to surrender their right to privacy in order to secure their right to participate in athletics," the court ruled. In light of this recent ruling, it is recommended that you not engage in any drug testing of athletes in your program.

Child Abuse

Child abuse includes nonaccidental physical injury, neglect, sexual molestation, and emotional abuse. Sadly, incidences of child abuse continue to increase today. The 1974 Child Abuse Prevention and Treatment Act requires certain professionals—and coaches fall into this category—who know or have reasonable cause to suspect that a child is abused or neglected to report the matter to the state department of social and rehabilitation services. As the director of a program that comes into contact with hundreds, even thousands, of youngsters every year, insist that your agency develop guidelines and policies to help your staff and volunteer coaches comply with the law and deal with this critical problem. Provide your staff and coaches with training and information about the signs and symptoms of possible child abuse. Designate a specific person in your program to serve as the first contact for coaches to go to if they suspect child abuse. Make sure your coaches understand the reporting procedures your organization develops.

Some Signs and Symptoms of Possible Child Abuse

Physical abuse

Unexplained bruises

Unexplained cuts or scrapes

Unexplained stomach injuries

Fear of adults

Withdrawn behavior

Fear of parents

Fear of going home

Physical neglect

Underfed or constant hunger

Unattended medical needs

Constantly tired

Constantly unclean

Sexual abuse

Difficulty walking or sitting

Poor peer relationships

Stomachaches

Sudden onset of behavior problems

Emotional/psychological abuse

Speech problems

Antisocial behavior

Habit of sucking, biting, or rocking

Loss of appetite

Learning difficulties

Self-destructive behavior

Mistreating children has no place anywhere, including youth sports. Unfortunately, you'll need to be on guard against child abuse that originates in the youth sport setting. This abuse is defined as actions taken by an adult (most likely a coach) that cause direct or indirect physical and/or emotional harm to a child.

The two most common types of abuse in the sport setting are verbal abuse (such as negative comments about a child's performance, which demean a youngster's integrity) and emotional abuse (such as coaches having unrealistic goals and expectations for youngsters).

Less common are physical abuse (touching in a way that causes physical pain to a child, such as slapping, grabbing, or hitting) and sexual abuse (touching or fondling, implicit or explicit sexual comments, and sexual harassment).

Depending on their own sport experiences, some coaches may not think their behavior is racist, sexist, harassing, or abusive. At your coach training session, provide examples of behaviors that would constitute abuse to ensure that coaches understand what is inappropriate.

Devise and enforce a code of conduct to guide coaches in their relationships with children. Some elements of the code might include these:

1. Treat all children with equal respect.
2. Keep the reason for the competition in perspective.
3. Use appropriate discipline.
4. Take injuries seriously.
5. Replace putdowns with instruction.
6. Motivate with praise, not name-calling.
7. Do not accept abusive behavior.

Clearly defined management practices related to the recruitment, training, and supervision of coaches (as detailed in chapter 2) will help your program make sports a safer haven for children.

For more information on this subject, contact any of the following organizations:

National Committee to Prevent Child Abuse

332 S. Michigan Avenue, Suite 1600

Chicago, IL 60604-4357

Phone: 312-663-3520

Fax: 312-939-8962

National Council on Child Abuse and Family Violence

1155 Connecticut Avenue NW, Suite 400

Washington, DC 20036

Phone: 202-429-6695 or 800-222-2000

American Humane Association, Children's Division

63 Inverness Drive East

Englewood, CO 80112

Phone: 303-792-9900

Summary

We've provided you with considerable background with regard to managing risk. Now you can put all of this information to use by developing your risk management plan, as described in exercise 4.2.

Exercise 4.2   ## Designing Your Risk-Management Plan

Follow the steps of this exercise to create a risk-management plan for your program. Take your time and be thorough. It could pay off in preventing an injury or lawsuit.

1. Identify each risk in your program by describing it under the "Source of Risk" heading in form 4.11. Remember you are considering two major types of risk: risk to the well-being of your participants and risk to you, your staff, and volunteers regarding legal liability and subsequent financial loss. Use the checklist of general risks in sport given in form 4.12 as a starting point to identify the specific risks of your program.

2. Determine the probability of the risk occurring by circling high, moderate, or low on the form. If you have minimal experience, you may want to ask others about the probability of this risk occurring.

3. Indicate your estimate of the potential severity of this risk by circling high, moderate, or low on the form.

4. Now for the critical step: What can you do to deal with this risk in some way by (a) avoiding the risk, (b) reducing the risk, and (c) transferring the risk? Write in the space provided the actions you believe are the best for your situation.

5. Implement your recommendations, constantly monitor the plan to add items you missed in your initial evaluation, and communicate the plan to all those who need to know.

Facilities Inspection Checklist

Name of inspector _____

Date of inspection _____

Name and location of facility _____

Note: Form 4.1 is an incomplete checklist provided as an example. Use it to develop a checklist specific for your facilities.

Facility Condition

Circle Y (yes) if the facility is in good condition and N (no) if it needs something done to make it acceptable. In the space provided note what needs to be done.

Gymnasium

Y N Floor (water spots, buckling, loose sections) _____

Y N Walls (vandalism free) _____

Y N Lights (all functioning) _____

Y N Windows (secure) _____

Y N Roof (adverse impact of weather) _____

Y N Stairs (well lighted) _____

Y N Bleachers (support structure sound) _____

Y N Exits (lights working) _____

Y N Basketball rims (level, securely attached) _____

Y N Basketball backboards (no cracks, clean) _____

Y N Mats (clean, properly stored, no defects) _____

Y N Uprights/projections _____

Y N Wall plugs (covered) _____

Y N Light switches (all functioning) _____

Y N Heating/cooling system (temperature control) _____

Y N Ducts, radiators, pipes _____

Y N Thermostats _____

Y N Fire alarms (regularly checked) _____

Y N Directions posted for evacuating the gym in case of fire _____

Y N Fire extinguishers (regularly checked) _____

Other (list) _____

_____

Locker room(s)

Y   N   Floor _____

Y   N   Walls _____

Y   N   Lights _____

Y   N   Windows _____

Y   N   Roof _____

Y   N   Showers _____

Y   N   Drains _____

Y   N   Benches _____

Y   N   Lockers _____

Y   N   Exits _____

Y   N   Water fountains _____

Y   N   Toilets _____

Y   N   Trainer's room _____

Other (list) _____

_____

Field(s)/outside playing area

Surface

Y   N   Too wet or too dry _____

Y   N   Grass length _____

Y   N   Free of debris _____

Y   N   Free of holes and bumps _____

Y   N   Free of protruding pipes, wires, lines _____

Y   N   Line markers _____

Stands

Y   N   Pitching mound _____

Y   N   Dugouts _____

Y   N   Warning track and fences _____

Y   N   Sidelines _____

Y   N   Sprinklers _____

Y   N   Garbage _____

Y   N   Security fences _____

(continued)

121

Y   N   Water fountain _____

Y   N   Storage sheds _____

Concession area

Y   N   Electrical _____

Y   N   Heating/cooling systems _____

Other (list) _____

_____

Pool

Y   N   Equipment in good repair _____

Y   N   Sanitary _____

Y   N   Slipperiness on decks and diving board controlled _____

Y   N   Chemicals safely stored _____

Y   N   Regulations and safety rules posted _____

Lighting—adequate visibility

Y   N   No glare _____

Y   N   Penetrates to bottom of pool _____

Y   N   Exit light in good repair _____

Y   N   Halls and locker rooms meet code requirements _____

Y   N   Light switches properly grounded _____

Y   N   Has emergency generator to back up regular power source _____

Exits—accessible, secure

Y   N   Adequate size, number _____

Y   N   Self-closing doors _____

Y   N   Self-locking doors _____

Y   N   Striker plates secure _____

Y   N   No obstacles or debris _____

Y   N   Office and storage rooms locked _____

Ring buoys

Y   N   20-inch diameter _____

Y   N   50-foot rope length _____

Reaching poles

Y   N   One each side _____

Y   N   12-foot length _____

Y   N   Metal stress _____

Y   N   Good repair _____

Guard chairs

Y   N   Unobstructed view _____

Y   N   Tall enough to see bottom of pool _____

Safety line at break point in the pool grade (deep end)

Y   N   Bright color floats _____

Y   N   3/4-inch rope _____

First-aid kit

Y   N   Inventoried and replenished regularly _____

Stretcher, two blankets, and spine board

Y   N   Inventoried and in good repair _____

Emergency telephone, lights, and public address system

Y   N   Accessible _____

Y   N   Directions for use posted visibly _____

Y   N   Powered by emergency generators as well as regular power system _____

Y   N   Emergency numbers on telephone cradle or receiver _____

Emergency procedures

Y   N   Sign posted in highly visible area _____

Track

Surface

Y   N   Free of debris _____

Y   N   Free of holes and bumps _____

Y   N   Throwing circles _____

Y   N   Fences _____

Y   N   Water fountain _____

Other (list) _____

_____

Recommendations/observations: _____

_____

_____

_____

Form 4.2   Equipment Inspection Checklist

Name of inspector _____

Date of inspection _____

Football

Y   N   Helmet _____

Y   N   Mouth guard _____

Y   N   Jersey _____

Y   N   Pants _____

Y   N   Shoulder pads _____

Y   N   Hip pads/girdle _____

Y   N   Thigh pads _____

Y   N   Elbow pads _____

Y   N   Hand pads _____

Y   N   Shoes/spikes _____

Y   N   Ball condition _____

Y   N   Inflation level _____

Other (list) _____

_____

Basketball

Y   N   Jersey _____

Y   N   Shorts _____

Y   N   Shoes _____

Y   N   Mouth guard (optional) _____

Y   N   Eye guard/goggles (optional) _____

Y   N   Knee pads _____

Y   N   Elbow pads _____

Y   N   Ball condition _____

Y   N   Inflation level _____

Other (list) _____

_____

Wrestling

Y   N   Singlet _____

Y   N   Shoes _____

Y   N   Headgear _____

Other (list) _____

_____

Baseball

Y   N   Jersey _____

Y   N   Pants _____

Y   N   Sliding pants/pads _____

Y   N   Leggings _____

Y   N   Protective cup _____

Y   N   Mouth guard (optional) _____

Y   N   Eye guard/goggles (optional) _____

Y   N   Cap _____

Y   N   Cleats/shoes _____

Y   N   Ball condition _____

Y   N   Bats _____

Y   N   Batting glove _____

Y   N   Bases _____

Y   N   Glove _____

Other (list) _____

_____

Softball

Y   N   Jersey _____

Y   N   Pants/shorts _____

Y   N   Leggings _____

Y   N   Sliding pants/pads _____

Y   N   Protective cup _____

Y   N   Mouth guard (optional) _____

Y   N   Eye guard/goggles (optional) _____

(continued)

Y N Cap _____

Y N Cleats/shoes _____

Y N Ball condition _____

Y N Bats _____

Y N Batting glove _____

Y N Bases _____

Y N Glove _____

Other (list) _____

_____

Tennis

Y N Shirt/jersey _____

Y N Shorts _____

Y N Shoes _____

Y N Mouth guard (optional) _____

Y N Eye guard/goggles (optional) _____

Y N Racquet _____

Y N Ball condition _____

Optional (list) _____

_____

Volleyball

Y N Shirts/jersey _____

Y N Shorts _____

Y N Shoes _____

Y N Mouth guard (optional) _____

Y N Eye guard/goggles (optional) _____

Y N Knee pads _____

Y N Elbow pads _____

Y N Ball condition _____

Y N Inflation level _____

Other (list) _____

_____

Soccer

Y	N	Jersey _____
Y	N	Shorts _____
Y	N	Shoes _____
Y	N	Mouth guard (optional) _____
Y	N	Eye guard/goggles (optional) _____
Y	N	Shin guards _____
Y	N	Ball condition _____
Y	N	Inflation level _____

Other (list) _____

Hockey

Y	N	Helmet/chin strap _____
Y	N	Mouth guard _____
Y	N	Jersey _____
Y	N	Pants _____
Y	N	Protective cup/supporter _____
Y	N	Ankle guard _____
Y	N	Shoulder pads _____
Y	N	Suspenders/belt/garter _____
Y	N	Stick _____
Y	N	Shin pads _____
Y	N	Thigh pads _____
Y	N	Elbow pads _____
Y	N	Gloves _____
Y	N	Socks _____
Y	N	Shorts/long underwear _____
Y	N	Skates _____
Y	N	Puck: number _____
		Condition _____

Other (list) _____

Form 4.3   Sample Waiver/Release Form for _____ (fill in sport name)

I realize that ____(name of sport)____ is a vigorous physical activity that involves (characterize the elements of the activity: for example, height, flight, and rotation; violent body contact; rapid directional change) _____

_____

I understand that participation in ____(name of sport)____ involves certain inherent risks and that regardless of the precautions taken by ___(name of organization providing program)___ or the participants, some injuries may occur.

Give examples, being sure to include the most common and most severe injuries, such as blindness, quadriplegia, death.

List circumstances that might bring about the types of injuries cited above. Again, be sure to include the most common hazards, such as being struck by a racquet or ball, making initial contact with head while blocking or tackling.

The likelihood of such injuries may be lessened by adhering to the following safety rules:

1.

2.

3.

4.

5.

In order to properly protect my own safety and that of my fellow participants, I agree to follow these rules as well as any others that may be given by my (coach/instructor). Further, in recognition of the importance of shared responsibility for safety, I agree to immediately report any noted deviations from the safety rules as well as any observed hazardous conditions or equipment to my (coach/instructor).

I further certify that my present level of physical condition is consistent with the demands of active participation in _____(name of sport)_____. Following is a complete list of all of my known health conditions that might affect my ability to participate:

_____

_____

_____

_____

_____

_____

I have carefully read the foregoing document. I have had the opportunity to ask questions and have them answered. I am confident that I fully know, understand, and appreciate the risks involved in active participation in _____(name of sport)_____.

Having been informed of the above program to provide games for girls and boys, I, the parent of the above-named registrant, do hereby give my approval of his/her participation in any and all of the activities during the current season. I assume all the risks and hazards incidental to the conduct of the activities, and I do further release, absolve, indemnify, and hold harmless the _____(name of group)_____, the organizers, sponsors, supervisors, volunteers, and officials, any or all of them. In case of injury to my son/daughter, I hereby waive all claims against the organizers, the sponsors, or any of the supervisors appointed by them. I am voluntarily requesting permission for my son/daughter to participate.

_____   _____
Signature of parent or guardian   Date

_____   _____
Signature of child   Date

Form 4.4   Sample Medical Release and Transportation Consent Form

As a parent and/or guardian, I do herewith authorize the treatment by a qualified and licensed medical doctor of the following minor in the event of a medical emergency which, in the opinion of the attending physician, may endanger his or her life, or cause disfigurement, physical impairment, or undue discomfort if delayed. The authority is granted only after a reasonable effort has been made to reach me.

We, the undersigned, also give the child permission to be transported by _____

_____ as part of his/her participation in the program, by whatever means of

transportation the _____ deems appropriate.

Name of minor _____ Relationship _____

Dates when release is intended: _____

This release form is completed and signed of my own free will with the sole purpose of authorizing medical treatment under emergency circumstances in my absence.

Signed _____ Date _____
                 (Father/mother/legal guardian)

Address _____ Phone _____

Family physician _____ Phone _____

Other contact in case of emergency:

Name _____ Relationship _____ Phone _____

Form 4.5   Sample Form for Consent to Participate With Known Medical Condition

Participant's name _____

Sponsoring organization _____

In consideration of my knowledge that I have been diagnosed as having the medical condition _____ and having been informed that I am medically at risk for participation in the sport of _____ by representatives of _____, the sponsoring organization, because of this diagnosed condition, and that I and my physician have been fully informed by these representatives that further participation in this sport would indeed bring an unusually high risk of fatal or permanent severe disability, I acknowledge, agree, and assert that:

1. I hereby demand the right to continue participation in this sport in accordance with my athletic skills and in compliance with all rules that apply to such participation;

2. I know that I risk experiencing a fatal or severe and permanently disabling outcome from such participation due to my medical condition;

3. I knowingly and with full appreciation for this unusual risk freely assume all responsibilities arising from participation for any illness, injury, paralysis, dismemberment, or death.

This is to certify that as a parent/guardian of this participant and on my own behalf I do agree to all that has been stipulated as acknowledged, understood, agreed, and asserted by the minor and do consent to his/her release of the sponsoring organization from any and all liabilities incident to his/her participation and medical condition, and I join in the release. If, despite this release, I, the minor, or anyone on the minor's behalf makes a claim against any person released, I agree to indemnify and save and hold harmless those released and free each of them from any litigation expenses, attorney fees, loss, liability, damage, or cost they may incur due to the claim, whether the claim is based on the negligence of those released or otherwise.

Name _____ Date signed _____
(print name)

Relationship _____

Form 4.6 Medical History

History   Date _____

Name _____ Sex _____ Age _____ Date of Birth _____

Grade _____ Sport _____ _____ _____

Personal physician _____ _____ _____
                                                              Address   Physician's phone

Explain "yes" answers below: Yes   No

  1. Have you ever been hospitalized?   ☐   ☐

    Have you ever had surgery?   ☐   ☐

  2. Are you presently taking any medication or pills?   ☐   ☐

  3. Do you have any allergies (medicine, bees, or other stinging insects)? ☐   ☐

  4. Have you ever passed out during or after exercise?   ☐   ☐

    Have you ever been dizzy during or after exercise?   ☐   ☐

    Have you ever had chest pain during or after exercise?   ☐   ☐

    Do you tire more quickly than your friends during exercise? ☐   ☐

    Have you ever had high blood pressure?   ☐   ☐

    Have you ever been told that you have a heart murmur?   ☐   ☐

    Have you ever had racing of your heart or skipped heartbeats? ☐   ☐

    Has anyone in your family died of heart problems or a sudden death before age 50? ☐   ☐

  5. Do you have any skin problems (itching, rashes, acne)?   ☐   ☐

  6. Have you ever had a head injury?   ☐   ☐

    Have you ever been knocked out or unconscious?   ☐   ☐

    Have you ever had a seizure?   ☐   ☐

    Have you ever had a stinger, burner, or pinched nerve?   ☐   ☐

  7. Have you ever had heat or muscle cramps?   ☐   ☐

    Have you ever been dizzy or passed out in the heat?   ☐   ☐

  8. Do you have trouble breathing or do you cough during or after activity? ☐   ☐

  9. Do you use any special equipment (pads, braces, neck rolls, mouth guard, eye guards, etc.)? ☐   ☐

 10. Have you had any problems with your eyes or vision?   ☐   ☐

    Do you wear glasses or contacts or protective eyewear?   ☐   ☐

11. Have you ever sprained/strained, dislocated, fractured, or broken or had
    repeated swelling or other injuries of any bones or joints?   ❐   ❐

    ❐ Head   ❐ Shoulder ❐ Thigh ❐ Neck ❐ Elbow ❐ Knee ❐ Chest

    ❐ Forearm ❐ Shin/calf ❐ Back ❐ Wrist ❐ Ankle ❐ Hip ❐ Hand ❐ Foot

12. Have you had any other medical problems (infectious mononucleosis,
    diabetes, etc.)?   ❐   ❐

13. Have you had a medical problem or injury since your last evaluation?   ❐   ❐

14. When was your last tetanus shot? _____

    When was your last measles immunization? _____

15. When was your first menstrual period? _____

    When was your last menstrual period? _____

    What was the longest time between your periods last year? _____

Explain "yes" answers:

_____

_____

_____

_____

_____

_____

I hereby state that, to the best of my knowledge, my answers to the above questions are correct.

Date _____

Signature of athlete _____

Signature of parent/guardian _____

Form 4.7   Preparticipation Physical Evaluation

Physical Examination   Date _____

Name _____ Age _____ Date of Birth _____

Height _____ Weight _____ Blood pressure _____ / _____ Pulse _____

Vision R 20/ _____ L 20/ _____ Corrected: Y N Pupils _____

		Normal	Abnormal findings					Initials
Cardiopulmonary								
Pulses								
Heart								
Lungs								
Tanner stage		1	2	3	3	4	5	
Skin								
Abdominal								
Genitalia								
Musculoskeletal								
Neck								
Shoulder								
Elbow								
Wrist								
Hand								
Back								
Knee								
Ankle								
Foot								
Other								

(Left margin labels: **Complete** spanning all, **Limited** spanning Cardiopulmonary through Skin)

Clearance:

A. Cleared

B. Cleared after completing evaluation/rehabilitation for _____

C. Not cleared for: ❑ Collision

                 ❑ Contact

                 ❑ Noncontact ___ Strenuous ___ Moderately strenuous ___ Nonstrenuous

       Due to _____

Recommendation: _____

_____

Name of physician _____ Date _____

Address _____ Phone _____

Signature of physician _____

EMERGENCY INFORMATION CARD

Athlete's name _____

Address _____

Phone _____ S.S. # _____

Sport _____

List two persons to contact in case of emergency:

Parent or guardian's name _____ Home phone _____

Address _____ Work phone _____

Second person's name _____ Home phone _____

Address _____ Work phone _____

Relationship to athlete _____

front

Insurance co. _____ Policy number _____

Physician's name _____ Phone _____

Important

Are you allergic to any drugs? _____ If so, what? _____

Do you have any other allergies? (e.g., bee sting, dust) _____

Do you have ___ asthma, ___ diabetes, or ___ epilepsy? (Check any that apply.)

Are you on any medication? _____ If so, what? _____

Do you wear contacts? _____

Other: _____

Signature _____ Date _____

back

Accident Report Form

1. Name _____ Home Address _____

2. Organization _____ Sex M ❑ F ❑ Age _____ Sport _____

3. Time accident occurred: Hour _____ AM _____ PM _____ Date: _____

4. Place of accident: _____

5. Nature of injury: (check)

Abrasion	❑	Concussion ❑	Puncture	❑
Amputation	❑	Cut	Scalds	❑
Asphyxiation	❑	Dislocation ❑	Scratches	❑
Bite	❑	Fracture	Shock (elec.)	❑
Bruise	❑	Laceration ❑	Sprain	❑
Burn	❑	Poisoning ❑	Other (specify)	❑

Part of body injured: (check)

Abdomen	❑	Eye	❑	Other	❑
Ankle	❑	Face	❑	Leg	❑
Arm	❑	Finger	❑	Mouth	❑
Back	❑	Foot	❑	Nose	❑
Chest	❑	Hand	❑	Nose	❑
Ear	❑	Head	❑	Tooth	❑
Elbow	❑	Knee	❑	Wrist	❑

Description of accident

6. Protective equipment worn? Yes ❑ No ❑

7. Degree of injury: Death ❑ Permanent impairment ❑ Temporary disability ❑ Nondisabling ❑

8. Coach in charge when accident occurred (name) _____

   Present at scene of accident? No ❑ Yes ❑

9. Immediate action taken: _____

   First-aid steps taken? ❑ By (name) _____

   Sent to physician? ❑ By (name) _____

   How transported _____

   Physician's name _____

10. Sent to hospital ❑ By (name) _____

   How transported _____

   Hospital name _____

11. Was parent or other individual notified? No ☐ Yes ☐ When? _____

How? _____ Name of individual notified _____

By whom? (enter name) _____

12. Witnesses: 1. Name _____ Address _____

2. Name _____ Address _____

Remarks:

Signed: (Youth Sport Director) _____ (Coach) _____

CALL 911   Police:
                                  Fire:
                                  Ambulance:

INFORMATION FOR EMERGENCY CARD

(Be prepared to give this information to the EMS dispatcher.)

1. Location

   Street address _____

   City or town _____

   Directions (cross streets, landmarks, etc.) _____

   _____

2. Telephone number from which the call is being made _____

3. Caller's name _____

front

4. What happened _____

5. How many persons injured _____

6. Condition of victim(s) _____

7. Help (first aid) being given _____

Note: Do not hang up first. Let the EMS dispatcher hang up first.

back

Source of risk

_____

_____

Probability of occurrence: Low   Moderate   High
Severity if it occurs: Low   Moderate   High
Method to reduce risk

_____

_____

_____

Source of risk

_____

_____

Probability of occurrence: Low   Moderate   High
Severity if it occurs: Low   Moderate   High
Method to reduce risk

_____

_____

_____

Source of risk

_____

_____

Probability of occurrence: Low   Moderate   High
Severity if it occurs: Low   Moderate   High
Method to reduce risk

_____

_____

_____

_____

Form 4.12　Checklist of General Risks in Sport

Identify the general risks in your youth sport program by answering Yes or No to the following questions.

Do Coaches . . .

	Yes	No
Provide a safe environment for practice and contests?	☐	☐
Teach skills in developmentally appropriate progressions?	☐	☐
Provide appropriate supervision for activities?	☐	☐
Warn players of inherent risks in the activity?	☐	☐
Enforce the rules and regulations of the sport and your organization?	☐	☐
Match and equate players fairly for practice and contests?	☐	☐
Provide proper first aid when injuries occur?	☐	☐
Keep records of injuries and other losses?	☐	☐
Ensure the civil rights of all participants?	☐	☐
Understand the difference between ordinary negligence and gross negligence?	☐	☐
Know the signs and symptoms of possible child abuse?	☐	☐
Know that by law they must report to the appropriate authorities any reason they have to believe a child or vulnerable adult is being abused or neglected?	☐	☐
Know whether the immunity laws in your state protect them against ordinary negligence?	☐	☐
Know if they are covered under your organization's insurance program?	☐	☐
Have a plan for obtaining medical assistance quickly?	☐	☐
Submit reports on all injuries and accidents?	☐	☐
Transport youngsters using their personal vehicles?	☐	☐

Do you . . .

	Yes	No
Follow a formal procedure for selecting qualified staff, officials, and coaches to conduct the program?	☐	☐
Ensure that your staff, officials, and coaches are appropriately educated to perform their duties?	☐	☐
Monitor all aspects of the program appropriately, especially the competitive events and the facilities in which they occur?	☐	☐
Keep up-to-date job descriptions that define the coaches' duties?	☐	☐
Supervise, evaluate, and provide feedback to your coaches about how to perform their duties?	☐	☐

	Yes	No
Honor equal employment opportunity guidelines when hiring or terminating a coach?	❏	❏
Follow ADA mandates that policies, procedures, and practices that discriminate against the disabled population be eliminated?	❏	❏
Keep your risk-management plan up-to-date?	❏	❏
Ensure that you and your staff are knowledgeable about certain standards regarding sport facilities and equipment purchasing and maintenance?	❏	❏
Keep up-to-date with health, physical education, and medical organizations that offer recommendations on safe practices in sport, recommend ages for participation, conditions that disqualify participants from participation, preparticipation physical examinations, strength and conditioning guidelines, and drug use?	❏	❏
Receive periodicals that provide coverage of risk-management issues?	❏	❏
Educate your staff and coaches?	❏	❏
Supervise all aspects of your program or assign others to provide general specific supervision?	❏	❏
Assign others to supervise a playing facility or special event only after making sure they are competent to plan for the activity?	❏	❏
Ensure that your staff members follow guidelines and a checklist for supervising sports facilities?	❏	❏
Keep up-to-date supervision guidelines for all your programs?	❏	❏
Ensure that all staff members follow guidelines and a checklist for supervising the use of sports equipment?	❏	❏
Maintain a careful system of recordkeeping that could serve as legal documentation in case of a lawsuit?	❏	❏
Ensure that the parents of the participants in your program assume risk by signing waivers/releases and consent forms?	❏	❏
Ensure that your organization purchases all the types of insurance it needs for staff and volunteer coaches?	❏	❏
Keep an up-to-date emergency medical response plan that you developed in consultation with a local physician, preferably a sports medicine specialist?	❏	❏
Require all participants to provide you with a medical history?	❏	❏
Require all participants to have a preparticipation physical examination to identify potential medical problems?	❏	❏
Ensure your awareness of the conditions that may disqualify a child from playing as recommended by the American Academy of Pediatrics?	❏	❏
Ensure that all participants fill out an emergency information card?	❏	❏

(continued)

	Yes	No

Train your coaches and supervisors about what to do and what not to do when players are injured? ☐ ☐

Ensure that all athletes in your programs are transported by licensed commercial carriers? ☐ ☐

Ensure that athletes who are not transported this way are transported instead by vehicles of your agency? ☐ ☐

Ensure that all drivers of your agency's vehicles are qualified? ☐ ☐

Ensure that the vehicles are in good repair and properly insured? ☐ ☐

Keep up-to-date policies to ensure that all personnel and athletes in your program are afforded due process? ☐ ☐

Managing
Finances

This is the nuts and bolts of running a program. You need money to run the program. You need to budget for your expenses, live within your means, and keep records to account for it all. For those who love sports and making them possible for children, managing finances is at best a distraction and at worst an insurmountable obstacle.

The purpose of this chapter is to make it as easy as possible for you to manage your program's finances. When youth sport administrators were asked what they especially wanted help with, they mentioned two things:

1. They want to know how to increase the funding of their program, especially through special-event fundraising and commercial sponsorships.

2. Those responsible for budgeting and recordkeeping want a simple system they can learn without having to be a CPA.

This chapter provides help for these two purposes.

Sources of Funds

Let's begin by looking at where your funds are coming from now. Exercise 5.1 will help you assess your program budget and identify your current sources of funding. Then we'll consider what you can do to obtain more money from the sources listed, especially through fundraising events and sponsorships.

The two funding sources often underutilized are special-event fundraising and commercial sponsorships. Special-event fundraising is distinguished from other sources of funds in that you provide people with a product or service for which they are willing to pay rather than patronage—relying on people to give you money. With commercial sponsorship, for the purpose of commercial advantage, a business pays an organization for certain rights to be associated with an event and/or the organization. We'll now look more closely at these two funding sources.

Special-Event Fundraising

Numerous ways can be used to raise funds through special events that are both fun and profitable. For example, you can conduct any or all of the following:

- Food sales (bake sales, fruit, candy)
- Service sales (car washes, cleanup work, collecting recyclable items)
- Auctions (goods and services offered by members, silent bids, donated items of value)
- Raffles and lotteries
- Social events (parties and dances)
- Camps and clinics
- Activity-a-thons (walking, swimming, running, biking, dancing)
- Eating events (banquets, pie eating contests, celebrity dinners, pancake breakfasts)
- Celebrity sports contests (softball, basketball, golf, tennis)
- Entertainment (shows, exhibits, benefit productions)
- Publishing (production of cookbooks, newsletters, directories)

If you're interested in fresh, creative ways to raise funds to help you pay for your program or event, we recommend *More Fantastic Fundraisers for Sport and Recreation* by William F. Stier (Human Kinetics). Released in 1997, this book includes 70 fundraising activities organized into four parts by the amount of funds the event can potentially generate. Stier explains how to conduct the event, lists the resources you need, indicates the complexity of the event, and alerts you to the risks involved.

Conducting a fundraising event is similar to conducting a sport event. As the administrator, you need to do many of the same tasks, but for a different purpose. If you decide to conduct a fundraising event, adapt the Sport Event Planner in chapter 6 to help you plan the event. Fundraising can be a good source of income for your program when you

1. have a good image in the community,
2. plan an event that appeals to sufficiently large numbers of people,
3. organize the event effectively (see chapter 6),
4. promote the event well,

Exercise 5.1   Your Sources of Funds

Assess your current budget and consider which sources might be able to provide additional funding.

1. What is the total sum of money you have for operating your program? $ _____
   (For our purposes here use only the money that you have control over or the operating budget of the program.)

2. Provide the best estimate you can of the percentage of income from each of the sources of funds listed below.

   Local and state taxes   _____

   United Way contributions   _____

   Federal and state grants   _____

   Registration and entry fees   _____

   Membership fees   _____

   Admission fees   _____

   User fees for facilities and equipment   _____

   Concession sales   _____

   Other sales   _____

   Private gifts and donations   _____

   Special event fundraising   _____

   Commercial sponsorships   _____

   Other _____

   Other _____

                                                         Total 100%

3. Now review each source of funds to determine the potential for you to obtain more funds from this source. Circle Yes or No for each item. If your answer is yes, identify how you may be able to obtain more funds from this source.

   Taxes allocated to your agency   Yes   No

   _____

   _____

   _____

   _____

   United Way contributions   Yes   No

   _____

   _____

   _____

   _____

(continued)

Federal and state grants   Yes   No

_____

_____

_____

_____

Registration and entry fees   Yes   No

_____

_____

_____

_____

Membership fees   Yes   No

_____

_____

_____

_____

Admission fees   Yes   No

_____

_____

_____

_____

User fees for facilities and equipment   Yes   No

_____

_____

_____

_____

Concession sales   Yes   No

_____

_____

_____

_____

Other sales   Yes   No

_____

_____

_____

_____

Private gifts and donations   Yes   No

_____

_____

_____

_____

Fundraising events   Yes   No

_____

_____

_____

_____

Sponsorships   Yes   No

_____

_____

_____

_____

Other   Yes   No

_____

_____

_____

_____

Other   Yes   No

_____

_____

_____

_____

4. Now review your list, talk with other youth sport administrators about how they are funding their programs, and list the highest potential step you can take to raise more funds for your program.

_____

_____

_____

_____

5. select a time that does not compete with other events and when many people can attend,
6. avoid events where you have considerable expenses upfront that risk a potential loss,
7. have the financial resources to fund the upfront costs, and
8. have the support and help of the members of your organization to conduct the event.

Commercial Sponsorships

Sponsorships exploded in college and professional sports in the 1980s. They are becoming an increasingly necessary source of funds for high school sport programs, and they may provide you with an additional income if pursued correctly. Many sports have had team sponsors for a long time. Generally these sponsorships do not require too much effort because the dollar amount requested is small and the sponsors in many cases are not looking for commercial gain. Instead they are donating money to your program as a patron. In this section we're not discussing patronage, but sponsorships, where companies are looking for commercial gain.

Sponsorships are business agreements. A business is willing to pay you for the opportunity to communicate a message by being associated with your organization. Therefore, sponsors will have various expectations and possibly demands of you to be certain that they are able to deliver their message to those promised in this business agreement. Some youth sport organizations want the money from sponsors but are not prepared to take the steps to deliver the message effectively. Then the organization

Sponsorship is a great way for companies to contribute to the community.

really wants patrons, not sponsors. You will find that sponsorships must be earned if they are to be retained. So before you jump into sponsorships, be sure you are ready to earn this source of funds.

Once you've decided to try the business of sponsorships—or to get into it in a bigger way than you have before—how do you do it? Let's take a look.

Know What You Have to Sell

Fundamentally, you are selling a way for the company to communicate a message with an audience that you reach. Listed below are various components of this communication process that you can sell to a company.

- Enhanced corporate awareness through association with your organization or event
- Building or reinforcing a corporate image
- Opportunity to develop new markets by exposure of a product
- Opportunity to promote sales of a product
- A means to build and enhance community relations
- Opportunity to compete favorably with competitors in the community

Sponsorship is an attractive means to communicate with potential customers because it is a "soft sell" in contrast with the "hard sell" of advertising. Youth sport programs invariably are seen as contributing to society, and by helping to sponsor these programs a company may also be seen as contributing to society.

Know What Sponsors Are Looking For

If you know what sponsors are seeking, you can better prepare a proposal to meet their needs. Following is a list of questions that companies ask themselves when they consider sponsoring an event.

- Does sponsoring the event provide a good fit with our company or product?
- Does the event have legitimacy and an identity of its own?
- Will our sponsorship get lost among other sponsors?

- Does the event have a clean image?
- Can the sponsor's name be associated with the event?
- How visible will the sponsorship be?
- What level of media coverage is expected?
- Will the media include the sponsor's name?
- Will signage be available? How much and where will it be located?
- What other forms of recognition are available?
- Who is the audience for the event and is this a fit for the sponsor?
- How many participants and spectators will be reached?
- Does the sponsorship have the potential to affect sales directly or only indirectly?
- Are there any distribution benefits from the sponsorship?
- How easy is it to become a sponsor?
- Is it a one-time or multiple-exposure event?
- Is the organization capable of conducting the event successfully?
- Is the amount of money requested fair value for what is gained by the sponsorship?

Reviewing these questions when preparing your proposal for a potential sponsor will help you make it more appealing to the business. Now let's look at the four steps for obtaining a sponsor.

1. Identify the specific events or components of your program that have potential to be sponsored. Here is a list to stimulate your thinking.

- Sponsor a league
- Sponsor a team
- Sponsor a player
- Sponsor a tournament
- Sponsor a fundraising event
- Sponsor a facility
- Sponsor uniforms and other equipment
- Sponsor the awards for an event
- Sponsor food and drinks during the event

- Sponsor registration for the event
- Sponsor the promotion for the event

Obviously, it is easier to service one sponsor willing to pay for an entire event than to service many sponsors who each pay less. However, you will find that it is easier to sell sponsorships when you ask for less money than when you ask for more. Most youth sport organizations take the approach of seeking sponsors for larger components of their programs first, and if that fails, seeking sponsors for smaller components. Consider tying in your sponsorship proposal to a cause-related initiative. For example, create a "safety sponsorship" package to provide and promote safety in youth sport. Resources would be used to purchase the safest equipment and facility materials.

2. Identify potential sponsors.

Begin by creating a list of potential sponsors. You can create a card file or a database on your computer for this purpose. Sources for names of potential sponsors can be obtained from community business directories. The yellow pages of the telephone directory is the obvious first place to look, but often the local chamber of commerce will have useful directories as well.

Theoretically every company is a potential sponsor, but in reality some businesses certainly offer better sponsor potential. Consider companies whose products and/or services are compatible with your program's philosophy and goals. Two questions to ask as you are evaluating potential companies in your community are:

1. Can you think of a way that the sponsorship will benefit the company?
2. Do you have a contact with this organization that will help you get inside the organization?

Here are other suggestions to consider as you seek to identify potential sponsors:

- See whether any parents in your program are executives in companies that may have an interest in sponsoring an event.
- Watch the local newspaper ads to see what companies are advertising, searching for

ways to connect your sponsorship to their products or services.
- Identify those companies that have sponsored other sports events in the community.
- Look for businesses that are expanding, have recently moved to the community, or are introducing a new line of products. They may welcome the exposure.
- Identify those companies that will directly benefit from your event. Stores that sell sporting goods are obvious targets. If people will be coming to your community for the event, hotels, motels, and restaurants will directly benefit.
- Remember, you are selling more than sports. You are selling exposure, publicity, enhanced image, and goodwill. Identify those companies in your community that benefit most from these. How do you do this? Request annual reports and corporate brochures from larger businesses to reveal their goals and what they've spent for promotion in the past.
- Identify companies that have the potential budget to support the dollar amount of your sponsorship. It doesn't make sense to go to a two-chair barbershop to ask for a $5,000 sponsorship.

3. Prepare the sponsorship proposal.

Prepare a generic proposal at this point, one that you can easily modify for a specific business. Keep the proposal succinct—about two to three pages. If the business wants more information, you can provide it later. Outlined below are the key components of the proposal.

- **Event to Be Sponsored:** Give a brief description of the sport or event to be sponsored. Provide the date(s) of the event and explain who is involved and where it will take place. How many participants will be involved? How many spectators? Is the event a fundraiser?
- **Your Organization:** Remember that you are selling not only the identification with the event to be sponsored but also the association with your organization. Describe your organization in terms that make association with it appealing.

• **Sponsorship Request:** What specific component of the event are you offering the company to sponsor? Is it an entire league or tournament? A clinic? A facility? Is this an exclusive or nonexclusive sponsorship? How much money or other forms of payment do you want for the sponsorship? Explain what the money will be used for.

• **Sponsorship Benefits:** Review the list of what you are selling and what companies seek in sponsorships. Promote the items that you believe meet the company's goals, giving specific information wherever possible. State how the company will be recognized, how many people will be exposed to the message, and who those people are.

On pages 152 and 153 are two examples of proposals prepared for youth sport organizations. One is to sponsor a local baseball league, and the second is to sponsor a local playing facility. Each proposal takes a slightly different approach.

4. Contact potential sponsors.

You've narrowed the list to those companies that you think are a good match for the sponsorship you want to sell. Now you should do the following:

1. Identify who in the company is responsible for deciding about sponsorships and how that person would like to be approached—by telephone, mail, or personal meeting. Often you can get this information from the president's administrative assistant or the marketing director.

2. If you have identified someone who can introduce you to the company representative, or an associate of this representative (networking), ask her to do so. Have your contact suggest to the company representative that this may be a worthwhile opportunity and encourage the representative to receive your proposal. Then you should follow up by calling to schedule an appointment.

3. If you do not know someone who can open the door for you, call the company representative directly. Briefly explain the purpose of your call and request an appointment, indicating that your meeting will be brief.

4. When you obtain an appointment, follow up immediately by modifying the proposal to the specific goals of this company as you can best determine. Send the proposal early enough to allow the sponsor time to review it before your meeting.

5. Meet with the sponsor to review the proposal. Begin the meeting by seeking to understand more about the company's goals in the community. This information will help you to reinforce the benefits of its sponsoring this event.

Now you may develop a sponsorship proposal for some aspect of your program. Follow the instructions in exercise 5.2.

Once you have a sponsor, it is a good idea to draw up a letter of agreement to specify the terms of your business relationship. We recommend that you have an attorney prepare this legal contract (expect to pay over $125 per hour), including the following elements:

• The date of the agreement
• The names and addresses of your organization and the sponsor
• The event or activity to be sponsored (be as specific as possible)
• The dates or time period for the event
• The specific rights the sponsor has (the benefits you promised) and who is responsible for their delivery (use exercise 5.2 to help you prepare this part of the agreement; clarify which rights are exclusive and nonexclusive)
• The specific rights the sponsor does not have, if there is any potential for confusion
• What the company agrees to do and when (When will the money be paid? What other products and services will it provide?)
• What happens if the event is canceled (What are your responsibilities and what are the company's responsibilities? What happens if the money is paid but the promised benefits are not derived?)
• Any other termination clauses

You need to be aware that the Internal Revenue Service has been scrutinizing the taxation

Sample Sponsorship Proposal #1

Event to Be Sponsored

The Whitman Park District is seeking sponsorship from the Whitman Cafe for our PONY Baseball League, now in its 25th season. Approximately 200 local boys between the ages of 13 and 15 will compete on 10 teams. They will play a 20-game schedule, starting May 10 and ending July 28. All-star games against other towns begin July 30 and extend into mid-August. Each team will have a head coach and two assistant coaches and play an average of two games per week. Coaches may also schedule up to two practices per week. On August 30, an awards banquet will conclude the season. All games will be held at Summer School Field, Dodds Park Field, and Duncan Park Field.

Our Organization

The Whitman Park District, one of the oldest in the state, has been providing quality programs for the 61,000 youths, adults, and seniors of Whitman since 1958. Last year we offered over 300 programs, 75 of which were sport programs for youngsters 16 and under. The district oversees 505 acres of park land and open space, and there are 27 major parks within the city limits, one within walking distance of every residence in the city. Seven out of every 10 Whitman families with children under 16 participate in a park district program at some point during the year.

Our operating budget is currently $4.5 million. We are governed by a full-time general manager and five elected officials who serve six-year terms. The district employs 48 full-time year-round employees and over 200 additional part-time employees at different times during the year (as lifeguards, umpires, day camp counselors, ground crews, and so on). We conduct our youth sport program entirely with volunteer coaches. Last year, an impressive 2,741 volunteer coaches donated more than 29,000 hours to teams and special events.

Twice since the inauguration of the award in 1972, the Whitman Park District has won the National Gold Medal Award for excellence in park and recreation services for communities smaller than 500,000. We have also been a finalist several times over the past 20 years.

Sponsorship Request

We are offering the Whitman Cafe the exclusive title sponsorship of the Whitman PONY Baseball League. Your $5,000 contribution would cover the cost of the players' uniforms and equipment.

Sponsorship Benefits

As the exclusive sponsor, the Whitman Cafe will associate its good name with a quality baseball program, now in its jubilee year. In addition, your company will receive these benefits:

- Your company's name and logo on the players' uniforms
- A banner displaying your company's name and logo at the three playing fields
- Equipment bags that bear the company's name and logo for each team
- Your company's name and logo on all promotional material about PONY League Baseball released by the Whitman Park District

- Your company's name in any media coverage of PONY League Baseball
- Distribution of coupons or flyers about the Whitman Cafe's fabulous food line and catering service to all parents during registration
- Mailing list of all the league's coaches and parents
- A special awards presentation to your company at the season-ending banquet

The Whitman Park District appreciates the past support of the Whitman Cafe. We are happy to offer you this unique sponsorship opportunity by which you will positively impact youth baseball in our community and benefit from an effective advertising avenue.

Sample Sponsorship Proposal #2

Our Organization

The Beasley YMCA has a proud heritage, serving the community of Athens for nearly eight decades. The Beasley YMCA is a fully equipped facility that reaches out to the 35,000 residents of Athens and the 40,000 others in surrounding communities.

The Beasley YMCA offers over 350 different programs annually for community members of all ages, ranging from preschoolers to seniors. The YMCA is a nonprofit organization supported financially through its membership, United Way dollars, and community support. Through the Max Beasley Scholarship Fund ($80,000), the YMCA reaches out to thousands of needy people in the Athens community. A part of the YMCA's mission is to serve all community residents. The YMCA has not refused and never will refuse access to its facilities or programs to anyone because of financial status.

Event to Be Sponsored

Through the generosity of an anonymous donor, an eight-acre tract of land adjacent to the Athens Power Plant was donated to the Beasley YMCA on March 1. To make full use of this wonderful gift, the YMCA board of directors has voted to convert the land into a much-needed multisport field complex.

Original plans are to convert the land into two softball/baseball complexes with an additional playing field for soccer and football. There would also be a two-and-a-half–acre parking lot built to accommodate athletes and fans attending sport events at the site.

Sponsorship Request

This wonderful gift can and should be a blessing to the entire community of Athens. However, the YMCA had not anticipated such a gift. The YMCA is now seeking support for the project from the Ball-4 Sports Supply Company.

The $5,000 contribution made by Ball-4 will cover the cost of converting the land into a viable multisport field complex (including fences, lighting, parking lot, and field development).

Because of the limited playing sites now available, the YMCA can offer only limited sport programs for area youth. Developing this land into a multisport complex will address our need for more room.

(continued)

Sponsor Benefits

The benefits of Ball-4 becoming the title sponsor are numerous:

- Have a positive, lasting influence within the community by being associated with the project.
- Increase Ball-4's visibility within the community by having the Ball-4 name commemorate the sport complex.
- Increase Ball-4's revenue—sport complexes create sport opportunities, which generate more sales of sport-related products for Ball-4, the leader in the sporting goods industry.
- Help improve the economy of Athens—additional sport opportunities will require additional staff. Officials, scorekeepers, field maintenance personnel, and new program staff will be needed to effectively operate new sport programs.
- Help the YMCA offer more sport opportunities to a wider age range of youngsters.

The Beasley YMCA has the unique opportunity to serve the Athens community and positively affect lives. We hope that Ball-4 will join us in this effort and sponsor the new Ball-4 Sports Complex.

Exercise 5.2   Developing a Sponsorship Plan

Success in pursuing sponsorships requires a well-constructed plan. This exercise takes you through the steps for developing such a plan for use in your community.

Step 1. Make a list of the five components of your program that have the greatest potential to be sponsored.

1. _____

2. _____

3. _____

4. _____

5. _____

Step 2. Identify five types of businesses, with an example of a specific business in your community that is of this type, as potential sponsors.

Type of business	Name of business
_____	_____
_____	_____
_____	_____
_____	_____
_____	_____

Step 3. Prepare a sponsorship proposal for any one of the components you identified in step 1. For our purposes in this exercise, indicate the key points to be made under each of the four parts of the proposal.

The Event to Be Sponsored

_____
_____
_____
_____
_____

Your Organization

_____
_____
_____
_____

Sponsorship Request

_____
_____
_____
_____
_____

Sponsorship Benefits

_____
_____
_____
_____

Step 4. Outline below how you will go about contacting the potential sponsors of this proposal to get the most favorable consideration possible. Who will you network with? What particularly will you emphasize to one business compared to another on your list?

_____
_____
_____
_____
_____

of corporate sponsorships. If the IRS deems that the sponsorship benefits are substantial and commercially valuable to the sponsor, the sponsor's support will be taxable to the non-profit agency receiving the support. Because the issue of taxation of sponsorships is currently unresolved, we can only advise that you seek advice from a tax consultant who is familiar with this aspect of the law.

More Suggestions in Working With Sponsors

After you have succeeded in obtaining a sponsor, you will want to operate in a way that strengthens the business bond between you. We recommend the following:

- Deliver on what you've promised. Know who your contact person will be within the company and agree with that person how your two organizations will work together to achieve a successful sponsorship.

- Keep a historical record or file on the sponsor so that you don't overuse any one corporate partner.

- Approach a company for sponsorship support only once a year during its budget cycle. Bundle a year's worth of sponsorships into one package, with funding level options for the corporate partner to choose from.

- Recognize the potential "in-kind" sponsorship resources offered by companies (coaches, practice space, printing and advertising, and so on). These should be given an equitable cash value if they serve to reduce your overhead costs.

- Finally, acknowledge and recognize the gifts of corporate partners and honor their commitment in a public way.

If you would like to learn more about sponsorships, consult *The Sponsorship Seeker's Toolkit* by Anne-Marie Grey (McGraw-Hill) or *The Athlete's Guide to Sponsorship: How to Find an Individual, Team, or Event Sponsor* by Jennifer Drury (Velo Press).

Budgeting and Recordkeeping

Budgeting is the work you must do before your sport program begins, and *recordkeeping* is what you must do throughout your management of the program. They are both vital aspects of good management.

Budgeting

Budgeting is estimating anticipated income and expenditures. It's easier to do if you have (a) records of previous program income and expenses, and (b) good plans for your program—the type of planning we describe in chapter 6. To assist you in preparing a budget, this chapter includes a budget model for youth sport programs that lists the income sources discussed earlier and describes the probable sources of expenditures (see form 5.1, pages 159-161).

Use this budget model as just that—a framework for guiding you in developing your specific budget. The keys to developing an accurate budget are to

- have thorough plans for your program,
- be realistic about estimating income,
- gather facts about expenses (don't guess at quantities and prices), and
- build in some flexibility, as plans are likely to change and the unexpected should be expected.

Recordkeeping

Recordkeeping is a pain, but as the sign hanging outside the outhouse says, "You're not done until you've finished the paperwork."

The recordkeeping system you need depends on how large a program you have and what may be required of you by your superiors. You may have few recordkeeping responsibilities, needing only to submit any income received and expenses incurred to your office bookkeeper. You're fortunate if that is your situation. But if you are responsible for recordkeeping, consider three possible approaches to this task.

1. Create a simple income and expense journal, as shown in form 5.1 on pages 159 to 161. For income, simply record the date, source of funds received, and the amount in the income column, just as if it were a checkbook register. For expenses, record the date, who you paid

Discuss the budget with your staff so they are aware of what's possible for their programs.

and for what purpose, and how much in the expense column. This is as basic as you can get, but if your program is small it may suffice.

2.   You can create a more complete "paper" system on your own that builds in some checks and balances and lets you categorize income and expenses more completely. This is beneficial if you want to compare actual income and expenses with what you budgeted—not a bad idea. The following two books can help you set up your own system:

> Pinson, Linda, and Jerry Jinnett. 1993. *Keeping the Books*. Dover, NH: Upstart Publishing Company.

> Wilson, Earl R., Leon E. Hay, and Susan C. Kattellus. 1998. *Accounting for Governmental and Nonprofit Entities*. 11th ed. Burr Ridge, IL: Irwin/McGraw-Hill.

If you prefer not to set up your own set of books, you can purchase printed bookkeeping systems for small businesses, which work very nicely. A local office supply store should carry these products for under $15. Dome produces

weekly and monthly ledgers that will help you keep track of income and expenses, deductions, payroll for up to 25 employees, important tax dates, net profit, and more. Providence Business Forms also produces a general ledger and trial balance book.

3.   You can keep your records on the computer. We recommend a software program by Intuit called QuickenBooks Pro 2000. It's the easiest, most user-friendly program available. Over a million people use it for their personal financial records, and it has a business option that works ideally for a youth sport organization. When you set up the accounts, use those that you selected for your budget, and you're in business. This latest version gives you all the tools you need to manage your program's finances. Here are just some of the tasks that can help:

- Set up and adjust a budget for your income and expenses

- Keep track of tax-related activities earnings, deductions, and so on

- Track all your financial activity and automatically update the register and balances

- Print payroll checks and pay bills electronically

- Generate customized reports for income and expenses, cash flow, balance sheets, and budget

Use Quicken to organize your program's finances, and you'll see how quick and easy it is to keep track of where the money goes. And there is a bonus to using Quicken for your youth sport program: You'll learn how to set it up for your personal finances, as well. Quicken is available for about $180 wherever software is sold.

Summary

Working with coaches and parents can be the most rewarding aspect of your job. Managing the program's finances, on the other hand, is much less fulfilling but is a task you must do well if your organization is to succeed. In this chapter, we have given you the following:

- Ideas for increasing your funding through special-event fundraising and commercial sponsorship

- Methods for determining, approaching, and developing sponsorship proposals to woo potential sponsors

- Suggestions for computer and paper budget and recordkeeping systems

Model for Youth Sport Budget

Sources of Income

	Actual	Budget	Over/under budget
Local and state taxes	_____	_____	_____
United Way contributions	_____	_____	_____
Federal and state grants	_____	_____	_____
Registration and entry fees	_____	_____	_____
Membership fees	_____	_____	_____
Admission fees	_____	_____	_____
User fees for facilities and equipment	_____	_____	_____
Concession sales	_____	_____	_____
Other sales	_____	_____	_____
Private gifts and donations	_____	_____	_____
Special-event fundraising	_____	_____	_____
Commercial sponsorships	_____	_____	_____
Other	_____	_____	_____
Other	_____	_____	_____
Total income	_____	_____	_____

Sources of Expenditures

	Actual	Budget	Over/under budget
Personnel Expense	_____	_____	_____

Subcategories may include full- and part-time employees, officials, coaches, and supervisors. You also will record your benefits expenses here.

	Actual	Budget	Over/under budget
Education and Training Expense	_____	_____	_____

This expense is not in many youth sport budgets, but it should be, just as it is in most companies now. Record expenses for the education of coaches, officials, parents, and your permanent staff here.

(continued)

	Actual	Budget	Over/under budget
Facility Expense	_____	_____	_____
Equipment and Uniform Expense	_____	_____	_____
Supplies Expense	_____	_____	_____
Food Service Expense	_____	_____	_____
Housing and Transportation Expense	_____	_____	_____
Promotion and Public Relations Expense	_____	_____	_____
Legal and Accounting Expense	_____	_____	_____

Facility Expense
Subcategories may include facility operating expenses, maintenance, rental, and utilities. This category of expense does not include capital expenses for building new facilities or remodeling.

Equipment and Uniform Expense
Each of these could be separate accounts, with purchasing and repair as subaccounts for equipment and purchase and cleaning as subaccounts for uniforms. If you operate a multisport program, you could further divide these accounts by each sport.

Supplies Expense
These may include office supplies, cleaning supplies, and toiletries.

Food Service Expense
If you provide food or drink without charge, this will be an expense to track. If you sell food and drink, then this is where you will record the purchases of the items sold.

Housing and Transportation Expense
This is not a likely expense for a residential program, but if you have an event where you travel to a tournament, it may be an expense.

Promotion and Public Relations Expense
Expenses associated with letting potential participants and volunteers know about the events in your program.

Legal and Accounting Expense
This expense category is for any legal work you have done such as facility leases, sponsorship agreements, review of waiver forms, and any formal litigation action. It also is where you record any expense associated with keeping these records.

	Actual	Budget	Over/under budget
Insurance Expense Expenses include a wide range of possible insurances you may wish to purchase depending on your situation, See chapter 4 for further information.	_____	_____	_____
Publications Expense Your costs to prepare schedules, rules, policy manuals, programs, and other materials to communicate with your constituents.	_____	_____	_____
Awards and Recognition Expense The purchase of trophies, medals, ribbons, certificates, banquets, and other forms of recognizing participants and volunteers in the program.	_____	_____	_____
Communication Expense Telephone and postage are the two major expenses here.	_____	_____	_____
Other Expense Whatever doesn't fit into the aforementioned accounts.	_____	_____	_____
Total expenditures	_____	_____	_____
Net income/loss	_____	_____	_____

Managing Events

In this chapter you'll find practical information on managing the events that make up your program. *Events* are the practices, league play, tournaments, and other special contests and meets that make up your program. Whether you are a professional administrator of a multisport program that offers many events, or the voluntary administrator for a league of six teams, you'll find this chapter loaded with the information you need for running successful events.

As you may know, sport administration is a specialty in which you can get a bachelor's, master's, or even PhD degree. We won't cover the theory of sport management here, nor will we address the complex aspects of personnel management (although we have given you help in managing coaches and parents in chapters 2 and 3). What we will do is address the essentials of event management by examining the following:

1. The most critical element in managing the event is you. We'll ask you to evaluate yourself as a manager.

2. ASEP's Sport Event Planner, the most comprehensive checklist for planning events available today. We'll explain each task in planning a sports event and provide you with forms and references to help you in your planning process.

3. The computer. You will be pleasantly surprised to see what a computer can do to improve the management of your program.

Now let's see what kind of manager you are.

Your Management Skills

In the first chapter we discussed your leadership skills as a youth sport director. Leadership, of course, is essential for good management. But good management is more than having a vision for the future—it's also having the skills to guide people to use the resources available to achieve those visions. All of us want to think we are good managers. Yet the most common complaint about youth sport administrators, whether they are paid professionals or unpaid volunteers, is that they orga-nize poorly, manage time ineffectively, and manage people inadequately. In this chapter you will find guidelines, checklists, and useful computer software to help you organize your program—but if you lack the organizational skills to use these tools, the program will fail because of you.

Let's begin by checking in with a disorganized youth sport administrator. Does he remind you of anyone?

Frank Stewart is a youth sport administrator for a park district in upper New Jersey. A great guy who's very popular and lives life on the run, Frank arrives at his office every morning with a full head of steam. He leaves his office door open all day because he thinks he must always be available, regardless of how busy he may be. Frank's open-door policy invites colleagues to drop in for visits, to ask him questions, or to update him on projects. Frank prides himself on never turning anyone away.

On this particular day, Frank is trying to complete his budget for the next fiscal year. After numerous interruptions from passersby, around midmorning his assistant stops by for help on a sponsorship proposal. The assistant should be able to complete the proposal independently, but after listening to the assistant's difficulties, Frank agrees to finish the proposal himself rather than reassign it to another staff member. Frank puts the unfinished proposal on top of a large, sloppy stack of papers—his high-priority pile, supposedly. Frank spends precious time every day looking for various reports, invoices, brochures, proposals, and so on that disappear into the piles of paper stacked on his desk and work table.

He finally gets back to his budget work, but 10 minutes later interrupts himself when he remembers that he has to finish preparing for an interview with a local reporter about the new aquatics program. As Frank hastily looks for his notes for the interview, he receives two phone calls, one from an applicant who's upset about not being hired for a position at the park district, and another from a parent who's concerned about her daughter's coach. Frazzled after the two calls, Frank tries to get back into the groove of number-crunching for his budget proposal, but after 15 minutes gives up and heads out the door for lunch.

With renewed purpose, Frank returns from lunch ready to tackle that budget. Midway through the second page, however, he suddenly remembers another priority—writing a letter to the top candidate for a position opening to arrange an interview. If he doesn't get the letter out soon, Frank fears the applicant will think the district isn't interested in her. Frank gets within one paragraph of finishing the letter when he suddenly rears back in his chair as he realizes it's 2:30 and he needs to get over to three soccer fields. Today's the last day he can conduct safety and equipment inspections on the fields before Saturday's season-opening games. Frank drops everything, grabs his coat and clipboard, and flies out the door.

Unfortunately, today was not an unusual day for Frank. His poor management skills do more than leave him feeling scattered and disorganized. His entire program—staff, coaches, officials, and children—suffer the negative consequences of his mismanagement. It may be only a matter of time before his management weaknesses lead to a disaster.

Effective management of events requires that you have

- organizational skills,
- time-management skills,
- communication skills, and
- sport-specific management knowledge.

Now complete each of the four self-evaluation tests we've constructed to help you identify your strengths and weaknesses as a youth sport director. Answer each item honestly, thinking about how you typically are in that aspect of management. Then, after you total your score, consider our recommendations for how you can improve this aspect of your management.

Organizational Skills

First, let's see how you rate in organizational skills. Exercise 6.1 helps you step back and evaluate these skills and gives you some ideas on how to improve them.

Good adminstrators are organized, efficient, and posses strong communication skills.

Exercise 6.1　Evaluating Your Organizational Skills

Read each item below carefully and then rate your organizational skills from the scale shown here. Be honest.

1	2	3	4	5
Weak				Excellent

_____ 1. You periodically step back from the day-to-day program management to determine direction for the program *versus* you are so caught up with all the work in running the program that you have little or no time to determine the program's direction. *How good are you at determining direction for the program?*

_____ 2. You delegate duties to others with significant time to complete the task *versus* you tend to try to do it all yourself and ask for help only at the last moment when you are desperate. *How good are you at delegating?*

_____ 3. You motivate others to action by your good organizational skills *versus* you stifle and frustrate others who could help you because of your disorganization. *How good are you at motivating others to help you achieve the program goals?*

_____ 4. You seek help when you need assistance with solving problems *versus* you seek to solve the problems on your own, even when doing so wastes your time and increases the risk of solving the problem incorrectly or less than optimally. *How good are you at knowing when to seek help?*

_____ 5. You anticipate impending events and plan for them appropriately *versus* waiting until the last moment to organize the event, often resulting in improper planning and the need to manage crises. *How good are you at planning ahead?*

_____ 6. You give clear and complete directions to those you supervise *versus* giving vague and incomplete directions, often because you are unclear yourself what needs to be done or because you are in too much of a hurry. *How effectively do you give directions?*

_____ 7. You have a good personal organizational system that helps you keep track of things to do each day and over the year *versus* you rely too much on your memory and have difficulty finding records and other items in your office because you do not have or maintain a personal organizational system. *How good is your personal organizational system?*

_____ 8. You supervise the work of others well by making sure they have clear direction, monitoring their work, and taking action when necessary for the task to be done correctly *versus* you assign work but tend not to check to see if it is being done correctly. *How effective are you in supervising those who work for you and taking corrective action when needed?*

_____ 9. When faced with a crisis you can size up a problem and direct others to solve it appropriately *versus* you tend to avoid dealing with crises because you don't manage them well or become too flustered or emotional to help solve the problem. *How good are you at managing crises?*

_____ 10. You encourage co-workers to suggest ways to manage the program better and give thoughtful consideration to these suggestions *versus* you feel that it is your job to direct the program and prefer that others not tell you how to do your job. *How good are you at encouraging and utilizing the suggestions of others?*

Now add up your score and see how you rate on the following scale.

41-50 Excellent organizational skills

31-40 Average to good organizational skills

21-30 You need assistance to be a better manager

10-20 Consider a career change

If you would like to improve your skills in organizing details, staying on schedule, creating lists of goals and things to do, and managing the myriad of records associated with running a program, follow these three steps:

1. Take a course in self-management. These may be offered by a local college or continuing education program or by professionals holding seminars at hotels in your community. Here's information about two organizations that offer adult self-management seminars:

Institute for Professional Businesswomen

A Division of Pryor Resources, Inc.

P.O. Box 70106, Station A

Toronto, ON MSW 2X5

Phone: 800-255-6139

CareerTrack

Thayer Capital Partners

1455 Pennsylvania Avenue N.W., Suite 350

Washington, DC 20004

Phone: 202-371-0150

URL: http://www.thayercapital.com

2. Read more about self-management. Here are two good books to begin with:

DeWaele, M. 1993. *Self-Management in Organization: Defining & Achieving Survival & Triumph*. Kirkland, WA: Hogrefe & Huber Publishers.

Timm, Paul R. 1996. *Successful Self-Management: A Psychologically Sound Approach to Personal Effectiveness*. Iowa City, IA: Crisp Publications, Inc.

3. Use a personal organizer, either in print form or on a computer. In fact, given today's explosion of information and the pressing time-management needs we all share, now's a great time to put the computer to work in managing yourself, if you have not already done so. You need a computer and a personal organizer software program such as Lotus Organizer, ACT!, or Microsoft Outlook. These powerful and very user-friendly programs help you plan events, schedule appointments, keep notes on goals, maintain a database of business contacts, and much more. Once you learn to use these programs—which are easily adapted to your personal needs—you'll wonder how you ever got along without them.

Excellent printed personal planners are also available from such companies as DayRunner Personal Planners, DayTimer, Franklin Covey Organizer, and Collins Personal Planners. These planners and others may be purchased through your local office supply store.

Time-Management Skills

As a busy administrator, your challenge is to balance many responsibilities at once. You might think you don't have time to stop and take stock of your ability to manage time. But no skill will take you farther than being able to effectively manage your time. It is probably the most important skill you need to succeed at your job. Your ability to successfully manage your time will pay dividends for your program. It should even improve the quality of your life. Use exercise 6.2 to help you evaluate your time-management skills.

Exercise 6.2   Evaluating Your Time-Management Skills

Evaluate your time-management skills by reading each question carefully and then rating yourself from 1 to 5.

1	2	3	4	5
Weak				Excellent

_____ 1. You monitor your work by keeping a record of what you are doing throughout the day.

_____ 2. You prioritize your goals, distinguishing between urgent tasks and less important ones.

_____ 3. You set limits on how much time you spend on any given project.

_____ 4. When several problems need to be resolved at once, you try to identify the most critical problem and take care of it before trying to resolve the others.

_____ 5. To complete a large task, you plan the necessary steps to complete the task, working back from the due date to the starting date.

_____ 6. You plan out your daily schedule instead of skipping from task to task until more pressing tasks come to mind.

_____ 7. You establish routines you can follow regularly as a method of eliminating unimportant details.

_____ 8. You control interruptions to the extent possible.

_____ 9. You prepare in advance for meetings and keep the meeting focused on its objective.

_____ 10. You establish a timeline so the pressures of your immediate responsibilities don't prevent you from thinking about the future.

Now add up your score and see how you rate on the following scale.

41-50   Excellent time-management skills

31-40   Average to good time-management skills

21-30   You need assistance to be a better manager of your time

10-20   Consider a career change

If you want to improve your time-management skills, here are some things to try:

1.   Take a course or seminar on this popular topic. Check with the continuing education programs in your community. The following companies also conduct seminars on time management in cities across the country. Contact them to find out when they are near you.

SkillPath Seminars
6900 Squibb Road
P.O. Box 2768
Mission, KS 66201-2768
Phone: 913-677-3200
Email: custserv@skillpath.net
URL: http://www.skillpath.net

3.   Read more about time management. Here are a few suggestions:

Blanchard, Kenneth, Sheldon Bowles, Don Carew, and Eunice Parisi-Carew. 2000. *High*

Five! The Magic of Working Together. New York: William Morrow & Co.

Bly, Robert. 1999. *101 Ways to Make Every Second Count: Time Management Tips and Techniques for More Success With Less Stress.* Franklin Lakes, NJ: Career Press.

Johnson, Spencer. 2000. *Who Moved My Cheese? An Amazing Way to Deal With Change in Your Work and in Your Life.* New York: Putnam Publishing Group.

Morgenstern, Julie. 2000. *Time Management From the Inside Out: The Foolproof System for Taking Control of Your Schedule—and Your Life.* New York: Henry Holt.

Smith, Hyrum. 1995. *The 10 Natural Laws of Successful Time and Life Management: Proven Strategies for Increased Productivity and Inner Peace.* New York: Warner Books.

Communication Skills

More administrators fail because of poor communication skills than any other aspect of management. That's why we've made a separate section for you to evaluate how well you communicate with those you work with and for. Exercise 6.3 will help you evaluate your skills in sending effective messages.

Exercise 6.3   Evaluating Your Communication Skills

Read each item below carefully and then rate your communication skills from 1 to 5.

1	2	3	4	5
Weak				Excellent

_____ 1. You organize your thoughts before you speak.

_____ 2. You use language that is appropriate for the person or group you are speaking to.

_____ 3. Your verbal and nonverbal messages are consistent with each other.

_____ 4. You provide clear directions in a supportive, "nonbossy" tone.

_____ 5. When you give feedback about mistakes (criticism), you do so in a constructive rather than destructive way.

_____ 6. You listen well to others, showing respect for their viewpoints.

_____ 7. You express to your co-workers that you are open to their constructive criticism.

_____ 8. You let people know you understand their messages through verbal and nonverbal feedback (active listening).

_____ 9. You avoid resolving conflicts until your emotions are under control.

_____10. In conflict situations, you focus on the issue rather than on the person.

Now add up your score and see how you rate on the following scale.

41-50   Excellent communication skills

31-40   Average to good communication skills

21-30   You need assistance to be a better communicator

10-20   Consider a career change

If you want to improve your communication skills, follow these steps:

1. Take a course in communication skills. These may be offered by a local college or continuing education program or by professionals holding seminars at hotels in your community. Here's one organization to check with regarding adult communication seminars:

CareerTrack

3085 Center Green Drive

Boulder, CO 80301-5408

2. Read some books on improving communication skills. The following are good references to get you started:

Barnes, Gregory. 1993. *English Communication Skills for Professionals.* Lincolnwood, IL: NTC Publishing Group.

Ludden, Marsh. 1992. *Effective Communication Skills: Essential Tools for Success in Work, Social, & Personal Situations.* Indianapolis, IN: JIST Works, Inc.

Sport-Specific Management Knowledge

Sport-specific management knowledge refers to how well you know each of the sports you administer—the equipment and facilities needed; the methods for scheduling events; the knowledge for planning, promoting, funding, staffing, financing, and conducting the event. We're not talking about general management skills, but what you need to know that is specific to a particular sport. Complete exercise 6.4 to help you take stock of your sport-specific management knowledge.

Good communication skills will aid you in working with referees, coaches, parents, players, and sponsors.

Exercise 6.4 Evaluating Your Sport-Specific Management Knowledge

Read each item below carefully and then rate your sport-specific management knowledge from 1 to 5.

1	2	3	4	5
Weak				Excellent

_____ 1. You know how to thoroughly and correctly plan for conducting the events in your program.

_____ 2. You know how to schedule regular and special events for the sports you supervise.

_____ 3. You know how to modify facilities, equipment, and rules to adjust for the various age groups and skill levels in your program.

_____ 4. You know how to maintain, schedule, and supervise facilities.

_____ 5. You know how to purchase the proper equipment and supplies for the sport.

_____ 6. You know the personnel requirements to run an event effectively and how to prepare each person to do his or her job correctly.

_____ 7. You know how to effectively promote and manage public relations of events in your program.

_____ 8. You know how to recruit volunteers to help conduct your program.

_____ 9. You know how to solicit sponsorships.

_____10. You know how to budget and mange the finances for your program.

Add up your scores for the 10 items and evaluate yourself on these standards:

41-50 Excellent technical knowledge

31-40 Average to good technical knowledge

21-30 You need to improve your technical knowledge

10-20 You are potentially dangerous in this position

If you're not as well prepared to administer your program as you'd like to be, you've taken a big step toward becoming a much better administrator by studying this guide. When you do so, we recommend that you do the exercises, read the recommended references, and complete the activities we've suggested. If you would like to do additional study to become a better sport administrator, consider the following:

1. Contact the universities in your region to see whether they offer a sport administration or sport management course through a continuing education program.

2. Read the following books to learn more about the technical aspects of sport management:

Mull, Richard F., Kathryn G. Bayless, Craig M. Ross, and Lynn M. Jamieson, eds. 1997. *Recreational Sport Management*. Champaign, IL: Human Kinetics.

Parks, Janet B., Beverly R. K. Zanger, and Jerome Quarterman, eds. 1998. *Contemporary Sport Management*. Champaign, IL: Human Kinetics.

3. Spend a week or two working with a mentor who can teach you what is not written anywhere.

Steps to Improve

Good managers identify what needs to be improved, develop plans for improving, and then systematically work at making the improvement. In exercise 6.5, try to identify three goals for improving your management skills and develop a plan for meeting these goals.

Exercise 6.5   Goals for Developing Your Management Skills

Now that you've taken an honest appraisal of your management skills, list three specific things that would help you most to become a better administrator. Then describe your plan for making the improvement.

1. Goal _____

   Plan for improvement: _____

   _____

   _____

2. Goal _____

   Plan for improvement: _____

   _____

   _____

3. Goal _____

   Plan for improvement: _____

   _____

   _____

Event Planning

Managing an event is planning the tasks to be done and seeing that they are completed. Planning an event is deciding in advance what to do, how to do it, when to do it, and who will do it. Plans are your road map for reaching your goals. If your plans are vague, you'll take an indirect course or get lost trying to get there. If they are wrong, you will not reach your goal. Good plans will get you to your destination, although sometimes you'll run into obstacles along the way. Then you'll need to detour—adjust your plans based on the circumstances—to reach your goal. Approach revising your plans with the same enthusiasm as your original plans. Successful events occur because of planning. Remember the seven Ps of planning—prior proper planning prevents pretty poor performances.

Planning consists of four steps:

1. Establish your goals or objectives.
2. Collect relevant information about how to achieve the goal.
3. Identify and evaluate alternatives to achieve the goal.
4. Choose a course of action from the alternatives.

Fortunately you don't need to do all the planning alone. You will want to involve others, especially in establishing your goals. Although you are the appointed administrator, youth sport programs are for your constituents, so make certain your goals are consistent with

Establishing goals for a special event really helps make an event successful.

theirs. You will also want to involve others if you lack experience and knowledge of reaching the goals you've established.

The Sport Event Planner

When there is much to plan and organize, a checklist of tasks to complete is essential. ASEP's Sport Event Planner is a comprehensive checklist of tasks to be completed in planning and conducting a sport event. In preparing the planner, we considered individual and team sports; regular events, such as league play; special events, such as tournaments and all-star games; and small and large events. The tasks are organized into logical categories, and each task is briefly explained with suggestions to consider during the planning process. When it is helpful, we also refer to additional sources of information about the task and include sample forms that you can modify to suit your needs. We've even created a computer software version of the planner to make it easier to use.

Here's how to use the Sport Event Planner:

1. Read through the entire planner. If you have not managed an event before, don't be overwhelmed by what appears at first to be an endless amount of work. If you are planning a small event, many of the tasks will not be applicable. If you're planning a large event, the more reason to do the planning thoroughly so that you can delegate the work to others.

2. Make a copy of the planner to keep as a template for later copying, or better yet, use

the software version for greater speed and versatility. Planning often involves making changes, and computers make changes easy.

3. Now begin with "Planning the Event Objectives." Read the task and the explanation. Write out your response for that task as completely as you can. If you need more information to complete this task, note in the margin what you need to find out.

4. Likely you'll find tasks that are not appropriate for your event; perhaps even entire categories of tasks will not be relevant. Just mark out those tasks on the planner or zap them if you are using the software version. You may also have planning tasks that we omitted or are unique to your event that you should add to the planner.

5. Recognize that the way you plan each task may influence other tasks. For example, you may plan a large event with terrific awards, but when you complete your budget you'll find you can't afford them. Thus, you'll need to revise your plans for the scope of the event and the awards to be given.

6. Use form 5.1 on pages 159-161 to complete your financial planning. You are likely to revise this form often in the early stages of planning.

7. As you work through the event planner, use form 6.6 on pages 215-217 to detail your specific staffing needs.

8. Share your plan with those who will benefit from reading it or be able to help you in further planning or conducting the event.

1. PLANNING THE EVENT OBJECTIVES

Complete the tasks below if you are responsible for determining the objectives of an event. If it is a special or very large event, it might be a good idea to form a committee to help you. If the objectives of the event are already determined, record your interpretations of the objectives here and share them with those who created the objectives to be sure that you are in agreement. Share the objectives with those who help you conduct the event.

A. Determine for whom the event is planned.

For starters, be sure that all those responsible for planning the event agree about who should participate. Age range, gender, residence, special needs, and qualifications of the participants all need to be considered. Are there other criteria that include or exclude participants for this event?

Your response: _____

_____

_____

_____

B. Determine the type of event.

The event could be league play over a season, various types of tournaments, a match, a meet, an all-star game, or something else. Describe specifically the type of event you will hold. If it is a team event, be specific on how teams will be formed (for example, based on friends, skills, or tryouts).

Your response: _____

_____

_____

_____

C. Determine the size or scope of the event.

To help determine facility and equipment needs, personnel requirements, and the budget, you need to set some limits on how many participants or teams your event will involve. Also set criteria as to how the limit will be reached (such as first come first served, number of teams, or past participation in the event).

Your response: _____

_____

_____

_____

(continued)

D. Determine the categories of competition to be offered.

Decide how you will organize competition to be safe and equitable for all involved. Matching children on ability and size generally makes for safer, more enjoyable competition. Organize competitive events by age, gender, grade, residence, height, weight, skill level, qualifications through previous play, and disability.

Your response: _____

_____

_____

_____

E. Determine the dates and duration of the event.

Consider these factors when deciding on the duration of the event and specific dates:

- Number of days needed to complete all competition while allowing participants adequate rest between contests. Include travel time.
- Number, availability, cost, and size of facilities.
- Convenience of the dates for participants, coaches, officials, and other personnel.
- Transportation needs.
- Availability of officials and other personnel to conduct the event.
- Weather or weather provisions.
- Competing events and holidays.
- Probability of delays, cancellations, rain-outs, and conflicting events.
- A refund policy in the event of cancellation or postponement.

Your response: _____

_____

_____

_____

F. Determine the location(s) of the event.

The event may require a single location with a facility that you control, making this task easy to complete. On the other hand, the event may require multiple sites to complete all the contests, contracts with other agencies to obtain rights to facilities, and a transportation system for moving participants from one site to another—all making the planning far more complex. Also consider if your community is the best location for this event or if another community with better facilities, weather, accommodations, and housing availability would be more suitable.

Your response: _____

_____

_____

_____

2. FINANCIAL PLANNING

Although money should not be the most important planning concern, finances play a major part in feasibility. Thus, an initial financial plan is necessary at this stage because your budget will influence your subsequent planning. Then, as you plan the steps in the other categories, you can be more precise in your financial estimates, permitting you to refine your budget. See chapter 5 for more information on financial planning and on how to prepare your financial plan. If the event is large, consider assigning or hiring a financial manager to assist you.

A. Prepare a budget for the event.

Use the budget model in chapter 5, form 5.1, to develop the categories for income and expenses for the event. Then determine which categories of funds are or may be sources of income for your event. Separate your income estimates into two categories: committed funds and potential funds. *Committed* funds are those you know are available to you for this event—for example, budgeted funds by your agency, registration fees, and sponsorships. *Potential* funds are good prospects not yet locked up. These will require additional steps to obtain the funds—such as sponsorships, admission fees, donations, fundraising events, or food sales.

Next, enter the expenses for conducting the events and calculate the difference between the anticipated income and expenses. Compare the committed funds to expenses first. If these funds cover the expenses, then you have no financial worries. If the committed funds do not cover your expenses, then determine if the committed and potential funds combined cover your expenses. If they do not, you obviously need to develop plans for reducing your expenses or increasing income. If the combination does cover your expenses, calculate the amount that comes from potential funds and give careful thought to the probability of obtaining these funds. Continue revising your budget as you obtain more accurate information about the funds available and actual expenses.

Your response: _____

_____

_____

_____

B. Develop plans to obtain all income and implement these plans.

First, take any steps necessary to obtain the committed funds. (If these funds are from registration fees, be sure you have plans for collecting these fees in the registration category of this planner.) Second, develop specific plans for obtaining the potential funds from each source and then implement those plans. It is often difficult to get help with fund raising, so it is vital that you organize and supervise this task effectively. See chapter 5 for assistance with fundraising.

Your response: _____

_____

_____

_____

(continued)

C. Keep accurate records.

You will want to set up a recordkeeping system for income and expenses. Keep the income and expenses completely separate from your personal finances so that there is no impropriety or appearance thereof. If others collect income, you need a system of receipts and verifications of income received with income deposited. If others are permitted to make expenditures, you need a system for authorizing the type and amount of expenditures, verifying the expenditure, and recording it. See chapter 5 for information on simple recordkeeping systems.

Your response: _____

_____

_____

_____

3. RULES AND OFFICIAL PLANS

You will need to make decisions about the rules you will use to govern the event. These rules should cover participant eligibility, the playing of the contests, and managing disputes and unsportsmanlike behavior. You will also need to determine how to officiate the contests and what officials you will need (such as referees, scorekeepers, timers, or judges). Commonly the person coordinating the officials is responsible for directing the rules planning. Having a tournament or event director make final decisions on rules disputes is a good idea.

A. Select the eligibility rules to follow.

The eligibility rules can be those of a local program, those of a state, national, or international sport governing body, or any combination of these. These rules should be clearly written out and distributed to all involved.

Your response: _____

_____

_____

_____

B. Decide what contest rules to use.

Rules for most sports are set by professional sports leagues such as Major League Baseball, college sports associations such as the NCAA, the National Federation of State High School Associations, or a national or international sport governing body. For a list of the prominent rule-making authorities, see appendix C. A useful reference is *Sports Rules Book* by Thomas Hanlon, available from Human Kinetics, P.O. Box 5076, Champaign, IL 61825, 800-747-4457. This revised and greatly expanded second edition includes the rules to 52 sports. You'll find the official rules of play as approved by the governing body, playing area specifications, equipment requirements, and more.

Your response: _____

_____

_____

_____

C. Modify rules to suit your event.

If the event is part of sanctioned competition under a sport governing body, you may not be allowed to modify the rules. However, when you can, modify rules to improve safety or equitable competition to suit the limitations of a facility, equipment, time, and participant abilities. Be sure to communicate all rule modifications to those involved in the event.

Your response: _____

_____

_____

_____

D. Determine who will officiate the contests and obtain their services.

Decide if volunteers are sufficiently qualified or can be trained to officiate the contests or if it is best to hire trained, experienced officials. Then be sure you obtain the services of officials well in advance and that you have a liability waiver and contract or letter of agreement that states the dates they will be officiating, how many contests they will officiate, their payment, and what happens in the event of cancellation or postponement.

Your response: _____

_____

_____

_____

E. Determine procedures to follow when a protest is made by a player, coach, or team official.

Many sports have complex rules enforced by officials who must make judgments about events during the contest. Inevitably participants will disagree with some of these judgments and rule interpretations. Many sports rules specify the procedures for protesting various rules, but you may want to modify these procedures.

Your response: _____

_____

_____

_____

F. Determine the procedures to follow when participants, coaches, and spectators display unsportsmanlike behavior or criminal acts.

The rules of many sport governing bodies specify how to deal with unsportsmanlike behavior by coaches and players. If the rules do not cover this area, you'll need to develop a set of procedures and communicate them to all involved. You should also have clear guidelines specifying when an individual's behavior crosses over the line from being unsportsmanlike to being criminal or potentially criminal. Establish when the appropriate law enforcement agency will be called for such actions as damage to property, illegal use of alcohol and other drugs, stealing, threats of violence, and actual violence.

(continued)

Your response: _____

_____

_____

_____

G. **Determine what other officials you need (such as scorekeepers, timers, judges, and announcers) and plan to obtain their services.**

Depending on the sport, you may need little or considerable help to conduct the event properly. Plan your needs now and then see form 6.6 (pages 215 to 217) and the Staffing section on pages 203 to 205 for further tasks to complete. If your event has the potential to expand, have a contingency plan to secure more staff if necessary.

Your response: _____

_____

_____

_____

4. **COACH DEVELOPMENT PLANS**

The recruitment, selection, education, and evaluation of coaches is a vital part of planning for most youth sport events. See chapter 2 for extensive plans regarding this aspect of youth sport program management.

A. **Develop plans for recruiting coaches.**

See chapter 2 for specific steps to follow in recruiting coaches.

Your response: _____

_____

_____

_____

B. **Develop plans for educating your coaches.**

See chapter 2 for guidance in using the ASEP SportCoach Volunteer Level coaching education program.

Your response: _____

_____

_____

_____

C. **Develop plans for evaluating your coaches.**

See chapter 2 for specific steps to follow in evaluating your coaches.

Your response: _____

_____

_____

_____

D. If your coaches are to conduct the parent education program, prepare them to do so.

See chapter 3 for more specific information on this parental education process.

Your response: _____

_____

_____

_____

5. **RISK AND EMERGENCY PLANS**

It is a good idea to analyze risks and develop a plan for reducing the chance of injury to those participating in or attending the event. The steps you take to reduce the risk of harm will also reduce the likelihood of a lawsuit. As part of a risk plan, you need to plan for emergencies. Chapter 4 provides a good summary of risk management to use in forming your risk and emergency plan.

A. Prepare a risk-management plan for this event.

If the risk-management plan you prepared in chapter 4 using exercise 4.2 and form 4.11 did not include this event, then use form 4.11 now to prepare a separate plan for this event. Inspection of the facilities and equipment should be done both before and during the event (use forms 4.1 and 4.2 for this purpose). If the event includes providing housing and transportation, be sure to include these in your risk analysis.

Your response: _____

_____

_____

_____

B. Determine if you should use a waiver or release form.

If you can reduce your risk of lawsuit by using a waiver/release form, have copies made of the form to be completed by all participants during registration. Adapt the sample in form 4.3 to suit your purposes.

Your response: _____

_____

_____

_____

(continued)

C. Determine if you need a medical release and transportation consent form.

If you determine that this form is needed, have copies made of the form to be completed by all participants during registration. Use or adapt form 4.4 for this purpose.

Your response: _____

_____

_____

_____

D. Determine your need for insurance to reduce your risk in managing this event.

Purchase additional insurance if you determine you need more than your usual coverage for this event. Inform all appropriate personnel what insurance coverage is provided.

Your response: _____

_____

_____

_____

E. Determine if you will be in compliance with local fire and safety ordinances for this event.

Call the officials in your area to find out what regulations affect your event.

Your response: _____

_____

_____

_____

F. If food is to be sold, determine what steps are necessary for compliance with local or state food inspection laws.

Contact your local health department to find out what regulations pertain to your event.

Your response: _____

_____

_____

_____

G. Prepare an emergency plan for this event.

Your emergency plan should specify how players and others will be treated when injured. It should include what medical personnel and supplies will be present at the first-aid station at the event, how injured persons will be transported to emergency care facilities, and who is responsible for supervising an emergency. Use the emergency plan in chapter 4 as a guideline for developing your event emergency plan.

Your response: _____

_____

_____

_____

H. Develop a plan for managing spectators if large numbers are expected.

Most youth sport events do not attract so many spectators that you need to be concerned about planning for them. However, if the event could attract a large number of spectators, you will need a plan for adequate seating, communication with spectators, inclement weather, restrooms, food service, supervision of facilities, and safety and security (crowd control). Other sections of this event planner will indicate planning tasks if sufficient spectators are expected.

Your response: _____

_____

_____

_____

6. REGISTRATION PLANS

Depending on the event, you will likely need to have a registration period to obtain eligible candidates to participate. You need to plan this part of the event carefully so that you obtain all the information you need during registration and for the registration to be convenient for the participants or their parents and efficient for you.

A. Determine what information you need to get during registration.

Review this list of information you may need for individual and team registration.

- Name, address, gender, birth date, age, height, and weight of participant
- Information about parents
- Evidence of eligibility (such as a birth certificate) and/or proof of residency
- Indication of special services required by the individual
- Sizes for fitting of equipment
- Collection of any fees
- Waiver/release form
- Medical history (may be a separate form that coaches collect at the first practice)
- Medical release and transportation consent form (may be a separate form that coaches collect at the first practice)

Your response: _____

_____

_____

_____

(continued)

B. Determine when the registration period begins and ends.

Consider whether it is better to have a short or long registration period. This may depend on the estimated number of registrants and how many you will have to process registrations. It may also depend on how quickly you must have the information in order to schedule the competition. Set up a schedule for this process.

Your response: _____

_____

_____

_____

C. Determine the registration process to be followed.

Plan a way for potential participants to receive registration forms and how the forms may be returned to you or your office. Will you accept mailed or telephoned registrations, or will registration be at a certain location only? How much help will you need to process the registrations and what will each person's assignment be? How many registrations will you accept? How will you process the registration information to assign players to teams, teams to leagues, leagues to playing facilities, and so on?

Your response: _____

_____

_____

_____

D. Prepare the appropriate forms for the registration process.

Form 6.1 is a sample form for obtaining the usual information for registration. Adapt it to suit your purposes.

Your response: _____

_____

_____

_____

7. SCHEDULING PLANS

This category of tasks does not concern the dates of the event but involves scheduling the practices and contests for participants. If facilities are at a premium, which they often are, you may need a system for scheduling practice times. The scheduling of contests can involve such duties as making league round-robin schedules, double elimination tournament brackets, pairings for a wrestling meet, and so on. Scheduling the contests may be simple or quite complex, depending on the event. A good reference on this subject is John Byl's *Organizing Successful Tournaments*, available from Human Kinetics, P.O. Box 5076, Champaign, IL 61825, 800-747-4457. This book will help you work through the mind-twisting combinations of tournament players and games. Chapters are devoted to five major tournament types—single elimination, multilevel, double elimination, round robin, and extended—and their variations.

A. Determine what facilities are available and compute the maximum number of practices and contests that can be held.

If you anticipate needing more facilities than are available to you, determine if you can get access to other facilities in the area. If you are using multiple sites, remember you will have to plan for transportation and communication among the sites. Beepers, phones, cellular phones, and walkie-talkies are excellent ways to bridge distance.

Your response: _____

_____

_____

_____

B. Determine the time of day to schedule practices and contests.

When preparing the schedule, consider the preferences of your participants, availability of the facilities, maintenance time, and other factors unique to your situation. Don't forget to plan for inclement weather with cancellation procedures and a refund policy. Also consider other options, such as cutting the event short, rescheduling on another date, delaying the event, and so on.

Your response: _____

_____

_____

_____

C. Compute the actual number of practices that can be scheduled for the facilities and the number of contests to be played.

Set up a schedule book or purchase one of the many software packages on the market that make it easier to schedule practices and contests in many different formats. Packages range from $300 to $1,800. Here are three to check out: HK's Sport Director Volunteer edition, © 2001, Human Kinetics, 1607 North Market Street, Champaign, IL 61820, 800-747-4457; *All American SportsWare*, 90 High Street, Newtown, PA 18940, 215-860-8535; and *RecWare* by Active.com, Inc., 937 Enterprise Drive, Sacramento, CA 95825, 916-925-9096.

Your response: _____

_____

_____

_____

D. Determine the need to schedule practice times because of facility demand.

If you determine that to be fair and reduce disputes you need to schedule practice times, then you'll need to develop such a schedule. In doing so, consider the availability of the facilities, the times of day to schedule practices, the actual number of practices that can be held, and any other factors that may influence the schedule. For example, you may want to choose early times and smaller sites for younger teams (players) and later times and larger sites for older teams (players). If so, arrange your practice schedule accordingly.

(continued)

Your response: _____

_____

_____

_____

E. Prepare the schedule for the contests.

Consider these factors when preparing the schedule:

- The facilities available for contests
- How long each contest will take
- The maximum number of contests that can be held with these facilities
- The actual number of contests to be played for this event
- How much rest is required between contests
- Determine a method to make the competition as equitable as possible. For example, you may seed players or teams in tournaments, use a handicap system such as in golf or bowling, create classes based on ability, or have qualifying rounds to determine who advances to further competition. Plan for postponements, forfeits, and delays in the schedule by building some catch-up time into the schedule.

Your response: _____

_____

_____

_____

F. Print and distribute the schedule.

Once your schedule is complete, copy it and distribute it to all who need to see it. Participants, coaches, parents, officials, and those assisting in conducting the event will need a copy. Also don't forget the facility staff, maintenance staff, garbage staff, and so on. If many spectators are expected, you may want to develop a program that contains the schedule and some information about the contestants. If the event is a tournament, plan how to update the schedule and make the information available to participants and spectators. If your program or event has a headquarters, designate a central location to post updated brackets along with other important information.

Your response: _____

_____

_____

_____

8. FACILITIES PLANNING

This section regards facilities management *for the event you are planning* and is not intended as a comprehensive guide to designing or managing facilities. Good planning of facilities is essential to running a successful event. Following the steps listed here will decrease the likelihood of your forgetting an important aspect of facility management for your event.

A. Determine your facility needs.

Your facility needs consider not only playing facilities but also locker rooms, rest rooms, spectator seating, parking, traffic flow, and food service. Think about your needs for special lighting, temperature control, scoreboards, and timing systems. Is the facility handicap accessible, including doorways, rest rooms, and spectator areas? You should also plan for many alternative facilities in case of bad weather. If you expect spectators, you need to plan for (a) sufficient access and exits to the site, (b) rest room facilities, (c) parking facilities, (d) ticket taking if admission is to be charged, (e) procedures for cancellations and postponements, (f) how to deal with disorderly people, and (g) plans for evacuation in case of emergency.

Your response: _____

_____

_____

_____

B. Reserve the facility.

If you control the facility, reserve it to be certain there are no conflicts of schedules. If you do not control the facility, seek permission to use it by contracting with the controlling agency. Be sure you get an agreement in writing so that you are assured of having the rights to use the facility for the dates you desire. The facility rental agreement should also specify clearly what parts of the facility are included or excluded in the rental (such as the locker rooms, toilets, and food service areas) as well as who will be responsible for supervising and maintaining the facility and the compensation, if any, for its use. A sample facility rental agreement is shown in form 6.2.

Your response: _____

_____

_____

_____

C. Determine who will supervise the facility.

If you are responsible for the facility, it is your duty to assign and properly train a supervisor. If you rent the facility from another agency, the agency may stipulate that it will provide a certain level of supervision and maintenance, or it may pass that responsibility on to you. If it is your responsibility, you will want to assign supervisors to each facility for the duration of the event. See the Personnel section of this checklist for a list of recommended duties for facility supervisors.

Your response: _____

_____

_____

_____

(continued)

D. Arrange for access to the facility.

If you are renting the facility and supervision is provided by the rental agency, you need to coordinate with the supervisor access to the facility at the appropriate times. If you are responsible for supervising the facility, you need to be sure you have all the keys you need, including keys to buildings, gates, equipment storage areas, locker rooms, toilets, and lighting, sound, and temperature control panels.

Your response: _____

_____

_____

_____

E. Prepare the facility prior to the event.

Prior to the event determine if you need to do any of the following:

- Clean the facility and schedule cleaning during the event (sweeping and mopping floors, etc.)
- Modify the facility for the event
- Eliminate or reduce any hazards as a result of your risk analysis
- Prepare the playing area (cut the grass, mark the field, paint lines, erect nets, and so on)
- Prepare the spectator area
- Prepare the locker rooms or other dressing accommodations
- Prepare the scorer's and timer's areas
- Make arrangements for the officials' area
- Prepare signs to direct people
- Prepare the sound and lighting systems
- Prepare rest rooms for participants, other personnel, and spectators
- Make certain the facility has adequate water supplies for drinking and maintenance

Your response: _____

_____

_____

_____

F. Arrange for maintenance of the facility.

Depending on the sport, there may be a great deal of maintenance involved. If the maintenance is your responsibility, consider the following:

- Determine who will be responsible for maintenance.
- Develop and use a facility inspection schedule. All indoor facilities should be inspected daily. For outdoor facilities, do an inspection two to four months before the start of the season so there is time to correct any problems or complete any upgrades. Once the season starts, site supervisors should perform a daily inspection and report any problems to the agency. Facilities should be inspected before and after contests. Use form 4.1 to develop an inspection checklist specific for your facilities.
- Determine the maintenance schedule for the playing area during and after the event.

- Determine the maintenance schedule for other facilities such as the locker room, toilets, and spectator area.

Your response: _____

_____

_____

_____

G. Arrange for security for all facilities.

Security will most likely be the responsibility of the supervisor of the facility, but if it is not, make sure that someone is assigned to securing all parts of the facility.

Your response: _____

_____

_____

_____

H. Arrange for adequate parking if this is a need.

Determine how much parking is needed, if reserved areas are required, if directional signs or attendants to direct parking are needed, and if security for vehicles is required.

Your response: _____

_____

_____

_____

9. EQUIPMENT, UNIFORMS, AND SUPPLIES PLANNING

It may or may not be your responsibility to provide some or all of the playing equipment, uniforms, and other supplies needed for your event. If it is the responsibility of the players or their parents to purchase uniforms or equipment, recommend to them what items need to be purchased, the quality to consider, the price range, and where it can be purchased. If you are responsible for equipment, uniforms, and supplies for the event, the following steps should help you.

A. Inventory what is available.

Know what you have by taking inventory and determining its condition. See forms 6.3A and B for two kinds of simple inventory forms that you can use or adapt. For supplies, you will need to take inventory regularly since these are consumables.

Your response: _____

_____

_____

_____

(continued)

B. Determine what is needed for the event.

Calculate what your need will be based on the number of participants (and previous records, if available) and subtract what you have on hand to determine what you need to purchase.

Your response: _____

_____

_____

_____

C. Purchase what is needed.

If you permit others to make purchases for the event, you'll need to develop a system for controlling these purchases. Otherwise the amount spent may exceed your budget and the type of equipment and supplies bought may not meet your requirements. If you are making the purchases, consider these guidelines:

- Know what you are purchasing. Do the necessary research to become educated about the equipment.
- Purchase from reputable dealers who stand behind their products. Specify the turn-around time you need and be sure the vendor can meet your time frame.
- Compare prices among dealers or bid out the purchase.
- Make certain the equipment meets the recommended safety standards.
- Purchase the best quality and durability you can afford.
- Purchase in quantity to get better prices.
- See if you can return unused inventory.
- Find out if you can quickly purchase additional equipment and supplies if you run out during an event.

Your response: _____

_____

_____

_____

D. Inventory new purchases.

Make sure that the quantity and style of what you ordered is what you got. Mark each uniform and piece of equipment to identify it for inventory. Identify your organization, the unit number, date of purchase, serial number, size, and so on as appropriate for the item.

Your response: _____

_____

_____

_____

E. Distribute the equipment, uniforms, and supplies.

Create procedures for distributing and collecting these items. Keep a record of where all equipment is located, who has uniforms, and where supplies are distributed.

Your response: _____

_____

_____

_____

F. Plan for storage and security.

Develop plans for short-term storage of equipment, uniforms, and supplies so that they can be accessed readily by those with permission to do so. Also develop plans for the long-term storage of these items during the off-season. Give careful consideration to the security of these items during their short- and long-term storage.

Your response: _____

_____

_____

_____

G. Inspect and maintain the equipment.

As part of your risk-management plan, the equipment should be inspected regularly (you can combine this inspection with your inventory check). Use (or modify) form 4.2 to conduct your equipment inspection. When equipment is found damaged, write down the item, location, and if it should be repaired or replaced. Proper maintenance will reduce the risk of injury and extend the life of the equipment.

Your response: _____

_____

_____

_____

10. AWARDS AND RECOGNITION PLANS

We all like to be recognized for our accomplishments, yet awards and recognition are controversial in children's sport programs. As you plan your event, decide if you want to offer awards and recognition to the players, teams, coaches, and other helpers. Do some awards undermine the long-term objectives of children's sport programs? What forms of recognition are appropriate and inappropriate? As you plan for awards and recognition, think carefully about how they contribute to your program objectives (see chapter 1).

A. Determine for what achievements awards will be given and how they will be given.

For young players, do you give awards for merely participating, for sportsmanship, or for achievement in the sport? Will you give awards to those who place first, second, third, and so

(continued)

on? Do you give awards to recognize teams only or individuals too? What criteria should you use for selecting individuals or teams to receive awards? How can you make the selection as fair as possible?

Your response: _____

_____

_____

_____

B. Determine the types of awards to be given.

First decide how much money to spend on the awards. This decision should be based on your overall budget. Then select the type of award from such items as trophies, medals, plaques, ribbons, certificates, pins, T-shirts, hats, jackets, sports equipment, and photographs.

Your response: _____

_____

_____

_____

C. Purchase the awards.

Get bids from vendors who will provide you with the product and service you need for your awards. Consider not only the price and quality but also the reliability of the vendor delivering what you need on time.

Your response: _____

_____

_____

_____

D. Plan for the storage of the awards before the event.

Keep the awards properly stored and secure. Some awards require considerable space and because of their value need to be kept under lock and key.

Your response: _____

_____

_____

_____

E. Plan for the display of the awards during the event.

Often awards are displayed during the event for participants and spectators to view. You should decide if you wish to do this, and if so, how to prevent the awards from being stolen or vandalized.

Your response: _____

_____

_____

_____

F. Plan for the presentation of awards.

If awards are to be given, give them with class. Determine the best time to give the awards, who will present them, what ceremony if any will accompany the presentation, and what is to be said about the award and its recipient. Consider the need for a PA system. Determine if you want to send news releases to the media about the awards given.

Your response: _____

_____

_____

_____

G. Plan for recognizing those who have contributed to the event in various ways and implement those plans.

It is valuable to recognize those who have contributed to making your event successful. Sponsors, coaches, officials, scorekeepers, timers, facility maintenance staff, and others who have helped put on the event should be considered for recognition. During the presentation of awards, you can recognize these contributors with a verbal thank you. You can also list them in the tournament brochure and perhaps give them a commemorative souvenir, like a T-shirt or cap.

Your response: _____

_____

_____

_____

11. FOOD SERVICE PLANS

First decide what food and drink service you want and need to provide. Of course you will need water for the participants and others, but what beyond that? The sale of food and drinks is one way to raise additional revenue, but doing this requires well-organized service, perhaps a contract with a professional concessionaire. If you get into selling foods, be aware of and in compliance with local health department regulations. Find out about any facility policy regarding food and drink in gyms or other facilities (indoor and outdoor). If you plan to have extensive food and drink service, you will want to delegate someone to oversee this function.

A. Drinks for participants

Determine what your needs will be. They will vary depending on the temperature and the intensity of the activity. Consider these questions:

- Where will you get the water?

(continued)

- How will it be stored?
- How will it be served safely and cost-effectively?

Your response: _____

_____

_____

_____

B. Food for participants

First determine what food you wish and need to make available to participants. Then decide where the food will come from, how it will be stored, when it will be made available, and how it will be served.

Your response: _____

_____

_____

_____

C. Refreshments for other personnel

Decide the same issues for other personnel as you have for the participants. What food and drink will you provide, where will it come from, how is it to be stored, when will it be dispensed, and how will it be served? Consider having a hospitality room.

Your response: _____

_____

_____

_____

D. Refreshments for spectators

Determine what service you wish to provide parents and other spectators. Consider if a concessionaire should handle this service, freeing you of another item to manage.

Your response: _____

_____

_____

_____

12. TRANSPORTATION PLANS

Often in children's sport programs parents are responsible for transporting their children. But on occasion (such as when traveling out of town, or if children do not have access to transportation) you may need to develop a transportation plan. If you do become involved in transportation, give careful consideration to the legal liability involved. See chapter 4, page 114.

A. Determine what transportation is needed.

You must first evaluate if you need to offer transportation for the event or if it is the responsibility of the participants. If the event involves traveling to another city, you may wish to coordinate travel plans for the team or group. If the event brings a number of teams into your city, you may need to plan transportation from hotels to the playing sites. If the event involves multiple sites, also consider how players will travel from site to site. You also need to think about the transportation needs of officials and others helping to conduct the event.

Your response: _____

_____

_____

_____

B. Communicate what transportation will be offered.

If you decide you need to provide transportation, you will need to inform those to be transported how the service will work. When is the transportation provided? How often will vehicles run? From where will vehicles depart? Will there be room for equipment and baggage? How many people can travel in a vehicle at once? Is the vehicle wheelchair-accessible? If teams are traveling from out of town, they will want to know all the details about transportation. Make sure transportation details are included in the information sent to each team prior to their arrival. Have signs made and placed where transportation information may be needed.

Your response: _____

_____

_____

_____

C. Arrange the vehicles to provide the transportation.

If you'll be using public transportation, you'll need to contract for it. If you're using private vehicles, you'll need to find volunteers. Make sure that all vehicles are properly insured and that a responsible, licensed driver is assigned to each.

Your response: _____

_____

_____

_____

13. HOUSING PLANS

Planning for housing becomes necessary when teams travel out of town and participate in events lasting more than one day. You will need to consider whether to use a hotel or motel, a special facility such as a university dormitory, or private housing. To keep expenses lower, it is not uncommon for the players of teams from one community to house players from visiting cities. If you will have extensive housing requirements, assign someone to coordinate housing.

(continued)

A. Determine need and cost for participants, officials, and others.

The first step of course is to evaluate whether housing is needed, and if so for whom. If it is needed, what is the extent of the need and the best way to accommodate people? Keep expense and safety in mind.

Your response: _____

_____

_____

_____

B. Arrange for the accommodations.

Make reservations with hotels or motels, contract with other special housing units, or make sure you have commitments from the parents of players to house the visiting players. Try to negotiate special room rates at a hotel or motel. Obtain addresses and telephone numbers of the places where players will be housed so they can be easily contacted.

Your response: _____

_____

_____

_____

C. Communicate what will be offered.

Don't forget to inform those involved of the housing information well in advance of when it is needed so they can plan for their needs. Be sure to let people know the type of housing, the cost, and if they'll need to bring towels or other items.

Your response: _____

_____

_____

_____

D. Set up a housing registration system.

If you are coordinating housing for large numbers of participants coming to a site, you will need a system to register guests, assign the housing, and provide them with the information they need to find the place they are staying. Do as much as possible of this preparation prior to the visitors' arrival.

Your response: _____

_____

_____

_____

E. Set up a system to supervise housing.

If children are not supervised by their parents, you may need to supervise them when they are being housed, especially if they are staying in dormitory-type living quarters. Consider offering some special events for nonparticipating attendees.

Your response: _____

_____

_____

_____

14. PROMOTION PLAN

Promotion is the way you let your target audience know about the event and encourage them to participate. Below we present your tasks for developing your promotion plan.

A. Determine what you want to promote and to whom.

In youth sport programs you usually do one or more of the following:

- Promote the event to the children and youths for whom you have planned the event.
- Promote the event to parents who are asked to register their children in the event.
- Promote the event to coaches, officials, and other volunteers to help you conduct the event.
- Promote the event to potential spectators who you hope will come watch the event.
- Promote the event to potential sponsors.
- Promote the event in your community or many communities.
- Promote the event in one or more schools.

Your response: _____

_____

_____

_____

B. Determine how the event will be promoted to participants.

Select from the list below the methods you will use to promote the event to the audience you've chosen.

1. Advertising (promotions that cost you money to deliver the message)
   - Newspaper and newsletter advertising
   - Radio and television advertising
   - Magazine advertising
   - Brochures and flyers mailed directly to your audience, including all the previous year's participants
   - Billboards

(continued)

2. Publicity (basically free advertising)
   - Press or news releases for newspapers, radio, and television
   - Interviews on radio and television talk shows
   - Public service announcements in newspapers, radio, and television
   - A press briefing for the media immediately before the event
   - Flyers and brochures distributed door to door, through retail outlets, and to various public agencies
   - Posters placed in prominent locations in schools, retail outlets, and other public agencies
3. Personal contact
   - Speaking at places where the audience meets (such as schools, service clubs, or professional societies)
   - Direct telephone contact
   - Asking current participants to contact a certain number of people directly
4. Special methods
   - Piggybacking your message with advertising and promotion by others or mailings done for another purpose (for example, insert your message in the local cable TV monthly statements)
   - Promoting the event at local exhibits, fairs, and displays
   - Asking organizers of other events with the same target audience if you can stuff a flyer in their registration packets
   - Attending similar events and distributing information about your event by hand or on car windshields

Your response: _____

_____

_____

_____

_____

C. Prepare the promotional materials.

Whether the promotional material is an advertisement, press release, poster, or brochure, it should be prepared as professionally as possible for the budget available. A very poorly prepared promotional piece will have adverse effects on the image of your event and program. Form 6.4 is a sample press release promoting an event. Form 6.5 is a sample advertisement.

Your response: _____

_____

_____

_____

_____

D. Release the promotional materials.

The key is releasing the materials at the right time. You want to release neither too early nor too late. Timing is important, and you'll need to determine what is best for your event and the method of promotion you are using. Be sure to let the paper and radio know how long to promote your event.

Your response: _____

_____

_____

_____

E. Plan for responding to the inquiries generated by the promotion.

On occasion, youth sport administrators have promoted an event without preparing to respond to the inquiries generated by the promotion. Are people to respond by telephoning, mailing in a response, or coming in person? Does the director of the event need to finalize all registrations and their acceptance? Do you have sufficient staff to respond to the anticipated response? If the expected audience response is to register to participate in the program, you may have already planned for this in the registration plan described earlier (Part 6).

Your response: _____

_____

_____

_____

15. PUBLIC RELATIONS PLANS

Public relations is managing the image of your agency and the event you are conducting. It is especially important that you address public relations for ongoing events where you want the players, parents, coaches, and other volunteers to return on yet another day to participate in another event. The key to good public relations in youth sport programs is serving participant needs and interests well.

A. Plan your PR with parents.

An important aspect of PR with parents is communicating with them about their children's participation in your event. Let them know about the steps you'll take to ensure the safety of their children. If parents must register their children for the event, handling the registration process with friendly, efficient service will go a long way toward building PR with parents. Develop a system for responding promptly to and documenting complaints.

Your response: _____

_____

_____

_____

B. Plan your PR with coaches, officials, and other volunteer help.

The most important aspect of PR with coaches, officials, and other volunteers is keeping them informed about developments that affect them. Most people do not respond well when they are surprised to learn about changes in an event. When possible, it's also a good idea to give volunteers the opportunity to offer their input during meetings prior to the event.

(continued)

Your response: _____

_____

_____

_____

C. Plan your PR with the media.

Invite the media to a news briefing before the event, accommodate them at the event, and be sure to follow up by providing them with the results after the event. Also invite sponsors and / or community leaders to the event to talk to the media. Have a hospitality tent or room with refreshments where media and other VIPs can congregate.

Your response: _____

_____

_____

_____

D. Prepare your paid staff and volunteers to be good ambassadors for your event and agency by encouraging them to be courteous and helpful.

In your written and oral communications with your staff express your desire to make the event a positive experience for all involved. Describe how you would like them to handle problems and complaints so that participants feel satisfied. Role playing certain situations can be a good way to prepare staff for interaction with the public.

Your response: _____

_____

_____

_____

16. COMMUNICATION PLANS

So often we see technically well-organized events break down because of communication problems. In developing your event plans, don't forget the importance of good communication among yourself, your staff, your participants, and others.

A. Develop a communication system among you and your directors, and your directors and their staff.

Consider preevent, event, and postevent communication. How will you communicate among staff during the event, especially if you use multiple sites or multiple contests within a large site? How will changes and updates be announced? Will you have a message center? Will you need runners or phones?

Your response: _____

_____

_____

_____

B. Plan how to communicate with participants and coaches.

Keep all participants and coaches informed about contest times, location, opponents, contest results, accommodations, food, lockers, mailing, and other details.

Your response: _____

_____

_____

_____

C. Plan a system for communication with spectators.

If you expect many spectators or if you will charge admission to watch, you need to plan for introductions of players, officials, and coaches. Thus you may need a PA system, scoreboards, and signs. Decide if you need to publish an event program. If so, you'll need to determine what the content will be and how it will be produced, paid for, and distributed.

Your response: _____

_____

_____

_____

D. Plan a system for communicating with the media.

Delegate a person to keep the media informed prior to, during, and after the event. Sending out press releases before the event will prepare the media to schedule your event for coverage.

Your response: _____

_____

_____

_____

E. Plan for communicating results to the governing body of the sport.

If your event is sanctioned, the governing body needs to know the results of the event. Be certain you have the proper forms and know to whom and by when these results must be reported.

(continued)

Your response: _____

_____

_____

_____

17. EVENT EVALUATION PLAN

Once the event is over, it's still not quite over. A brief evaluation of the event will let you know what worked well and not so well so that you can improve on your next event. If you discover any items that we didn't think to include in this planner, add them to it and let us know so we can improve this tool for youth sport directors.

A. Determine the system for evaluation.

You can keep the evaluation informal, simply asking various people how well organized the event was and if they saw ways to improve it. Or you can be a little more formal and collect information systematically without turning it into a major project. We recommend the latter, using a brief questionnaire to assess how coaches, officials, parents, staff, and volunteer helpers viewed the event. Make the evaluation forms easy to complete and drop off.

Your response: _____

_____

_____

_____

B. Prepare the evaluation questionnaire.

You'll need to prepare your own questionnaire to suit your specific event, but here are some typical questions to ask:

- How well organized was the event?
- What aspects of the event could have been improved? How?
- What aspects of the event worked well?
- Was the event about the right length (or time, matches, games, and so on)?
- Were you kept adequately informed about the event? During the event?
- Were the facilities and equipment satisfactory?
- Will you plan to return next year? Why? Why not?

Your response: _____

_____

_____

_____

C. Have the evaluation forms completed by those selected to evaluate the event.

Distribute the evaluation forms near the end of the event, and if possible, request that they be returned before leaving the event (otherwise you'll likely get a low response rate).

Your response: _____

_____

_____

_____

D. Review and summarize the evaluation comments.

Collect the responses and review them with an open mind. Prepare a written critique of the event and share it with those who would benefit by reading it. Make note of what you believe are constructive criticisms and start thinking of ways to better manage that aspect of the event next time. Recognize that not all evaluations will contain constructive feedback but will be nitpicky idiosyncracies of a few individuals.

Your response: _____

_____

_____

_____

18. STAFFING PLANS

Here we'll present the tasks involved in planning your staffing needs. A common mistake of less experienced youth sport administrators is failing to staff adequately and being reluctant to ask others for help, leaving an inordinate workload for themselves. The consequence often is that they are so busy doing various functions that they neglect their major responsibility— the coordinating and supervising of the other staff. Also recognize that staffing is not only recruiting the right people but involves training, communicating, motivating, supervising, evaluating, paying, and recognizing those who work with you to conduct the event.

A. Determine the staff required to conduct the event.

If you followed our directions in completing the Sport Event Planner, you have indicated who is responsible for each of the tasks. This will make it much easier to determine all your staffing needs. Now review each category of steps and summarize your staffing needs using form 6.6.

Your response: _____

_____

_____

_____

(continued)

B. Hire the employees needed and recruit volunteers.

Even with superb planning, if you do not have good people to carry out the plans the event will be less than satisfactory. Review the procedures for recruiting and selecting coaches in chapter 2 and apply them to finding volunteers for your event. Use the same process but be even more thorough with the employees you hire. With large events, the extra help of "floaters" is essential.

Your response: _____

_____

_____

_____

C. Make assignments to all staff.

Appoint directors to head up the various committees you need such as finance, facilities, and promotion. Then, working with the director and select committee members, create for all personnel their schedules and timetables of work to be completed.

Your response: _____

_____

_____

_____

D. Provide orientation and training.

Determine who needs orientation and training and then provide it. Prepare written procedures for duties that are unknown to staff, difficult to remember, and important to do correctly.

Your response: _____

_____

_____

_____

E. Plan the communication system with staff.

Sustain a clear communication network before, during, and after the event; all involved should know whom to talk to about what. For large events, designate a continuously staffed headquarters to serve as the hub of the communication network.

Your response: _____

_____

_____

_____

F. Plan for supervision of staff.

A common mistake of inexperienced managers is to fail to supervise. Supervision is essential to ensuring that your plans are followed by those to whom you have delegated responsibilities. Supervision is overseeing, guiding, and directing others as they perform their duties. It is not looking for mistakes or problems to criticize staff but seeking ways to facilitate achieving the goal. Good supervision involves three steps:

1. Establishing clear expectations or standards of the duties assigned to a person
2. Evaluating the person's performance against these standards
3. Taking steps to correct performances that are not reaching these standards

Your response: _____

_____

_____

_____

G. Plan for the payment and/or recognition of your staff.

Pay temporary employees by the time you've agreed upon. Officials often expect to be given a check immediately before or after the event. As for volunteers, make plans to recognize them (publicly if possible) for their contributions. Some ways to recognize staff and volunteers are by giving them T-shirts or hats that show they are involved with the event, putting their names and photos in the program or on a bulletin board where the trophies are displayed, or having them step forward at an award ceremony. After the event, send thank-you notes to all involved.

Your response: _____

_____

_____

_____

Conducting the Event

Your event will now run perfectly because you have planned it perfectly, right? Don't count on it. Good planning is vital, but now you must see that your plans are carried out. First, you will find that not everything was planned as perfectly as you thought, and you will have to respond to problems, even crises, as they arise. That's normal when you are directing an event, so be prepared for it psychologically.

Once others join you in preparing for the event and helping you conduct it, your most important role is to provide leadership, directing and moving the team forward. You need to control events by monitoring and supervising others to be sure plans are carried out. You need to head up the communication system, making certain that everyone keeps informed. You need to be the inspiration and source of motivation for those who tire along the way. And as for those problems that are yours as director, prepare yourself to resolve them as they arise—because they will arise. Expect, for instance, that some people to whom you have assigned tasks will let you down. Or an official or timer may not show up. You may run into inclement weather, throwing off your entire schedule. You may encounter facility or equipment problems. You may need to resolve a dispute or conflict among people. And almost certainly communications will break down here and there and the situation will need your attention.

As you provide the leadership and supervision required, remember why you are doing this: to help young people enjoy sports and benefit from what sports have to offer. Don't lose sight of the fact that the event should be fun for the players, coaches, parents, volunteers, and you!

Form 6.1   Sample Registration Form

Fill in all appropriate spaces. Missing information will delay your registration. Photocopy this form for additional registrations or pick up a blank form at any registration office. The reverse side must be signed before your registration can be processed. Please include proof of residency with mail-in registration.

Family last name: _____

Street address: _____

City: _____ State: _____ Zip: _____

Work phone: _____ Home phone: _____

Class ID	Program title	Fee	First and last name	Gender/Height/Weight	Birthdate

Total payment $ _____ Do not send cash

Shirt size: _____

Does registrant require any special accommodations or assistance for enjoyment of the program? (circle)   Yes   No

If yes, please describe _____

Indicate choice of payment   Check _____ Money order _____

    Credit charge, circle: Visa   MasterCard

    Cardholder # _____

    Expiration date: _____ Signature: _____

Important Information

The ___(name of organization)___ is committed to conducting its recreation programs and activities in the safest manner possible and holds the safety of participants in the highest possible regard. Participants and parents registering their child in recreation programs must recognize, however, that there is an inherent risk of injury when choosing to participate in recreation activities. The ___(name of organization)___ continually strives to reduce such risks and insists that all participants follow safety rules and instructions designed to protect the participant's safety.

Please recognize that the ___(name of organization)___ does not carry medical accident insurance for injuries sustained in its programs the cost of which would make program fees prohibitive. Therefore, each person registering himself/herself or a family member for a recreation program/activity should review his/her own health insurance policy for coverage. It must be noted that the absence of health insurance coverage does not make the ___(name of organization)___ automatically responsible for the payment of medical expenses.

(continued)

Due to the difficulty and high cost of obtaining liability insurance, the agency providing liability coverage for the ___(name of organization)___ requires the execution of the following waiver and release. Your cooperation is greatly appreciated.

Waiver and Release of All Claims

Please read this form carefully and be aware in registering yourself or your minor child/ward for participation in the above program(s), you will be waiving and releasing all claims for injuries you or your minor child/ward might sustain arising out of the above program(s).

I recognize and acknowledge that there are certain risks of physical injury to participants in the above program(s) and agree to assume the full risk of any injuries, damages, or loss regardless of severity I or my minor child/ward may sustain as a result of participating in any and all activities connected with or associated with such program(s).

I agree to waive and relinquish all claims I or my minor child/ward may have as a result of participating in the program against the ___(name of organization)___ and its officers, agents, servants, and employees.

I do hereby fully release and discharge the ___(name of organization)___ and its officers, agents, servants, and employees from any and all claims from injuries, damage, or loss that I or my minor child/ward may have or that may accrue to me or my minor child/ward arising out of, connected with, or in any way associated with the activities of the program(s).

I further agree to indemnify and hold harmless and fend the ___(name of organization)___ and its officers, agents, servants, and employees from any and all claims resulting from injuries, damages, and losses sustained by me or my minor child/ward arising out of, connected with, or in any way associated with the activities of the program(s).

In the event of an emergency, I authorize ___(name of organization)___ officials to secure from any licensed hospital, physician, and/or medical personnel any treatment deemed necessary for me or any minor child/ward's immediate care and agree that I will be responsible for payment of all medical services rendered.

I have read and fully understand the above Program Details, Waiver and Release of All Claims, and Permission to Secure Treatment.

_____   _____
Participant(s) signature (or parent/guardian if under 18)   Date

Your suggestions for programs or parks: _____

_____

Rental Agreement

Your Logo

address   city   state   zip   phone

Rental agreement for _____

Name _____

Organization _____

Address _____

City/State/Zip _____

Day phone _____ Evening phone _____

Program description: _____

_____

_____

Special arrangements: _____

_____

_____

$_____ $_____ $_____
         Fee   Damage deposit   Payment due date
separate checks please

The undersigned agrees to use ___(name of organization)___ property with care. Any damage or loss during the specified rental time and attributed to the above group is the financial responsibility of the undersigned. Damage deposits are returned based on the postrental inspection cosigned by renter and building opener. Payment must be received by the date indicated above or reservation will be released. No refunds for cancellations within 2 business days of rental date. The undersigned and the above-named organization agree to accept and comply with all of the terms, conditions, and requirements set forth on the back of this rental agreement form.

_____   _____
                Renter's signature   Date

(continued)

Conditions of Rental Agreement

1. The Park District may require a cash deposit or an indemnifying bond, with acceptable sureties in the amount determined by the General Manager to cover any loss, damage, expense, or litigation sustained because of the permit holder's activity. Generally this requirement would be in effect for activities with intense use.

2. The Park Board or the General Manager may revoke any permit previously granted at any time if it is determined that the application for permit contained any misrepresentation or false statement, or that any condition set forth in the policies governing the permit requested is not being complied with, or that the safety of the participants in the activities of the applicant or other patrons of or visitors to the parks is endangered by the continuation of such activity.

3. The Park District will not be liable for any claims for injury or damages resulting from or arising out of the use of the District's facility or premises adjacent thereto and the renter agrees to indemnify the Park District and hold it harmless against any and all such claims, damages, losses, and expenses. If requested by the District, the renter shall carry insurance against such claims and furnish the District with a certificate of insurance evidencing same.

4. Alcoholic beverages are not allowed on Park District property.

5. Smoking is not allowed inside Park District buildings.

6. Requests for special equipment or assistance including electricity must be reviewed with Park District staff at time of use request. The cost of any special assistance or equipment will be charged to the user and paid in advance.

7. Buildings will be opened at the hour specified in the application and groups will vacate the building at the hour designated on the application.

8. Groups are responsible to see that all activities are properly controlled and supervised. Adequate adult chaperones must be provided if group members are under 21 years of age.

9. Due to space limitations, there are no provisions to store items in Park District facilities.

10. A park use permit is required for any group of 25 or more and permit holder agrees to comply with City of _____ Noise Ordinance.

11. Permit holder agrees to properly dispose of all trash that results from their activities.

Form 6.3A   Sample Inventory Form

Item	Description	1 Quantity in		2 Quantity out (issued)		3 Quantity deleted (poor condition)		4 Quantity ordered	Date ordered	Date received	New total (1 + 2 – 3 + 4)	Miscellaneous notes
		#	Date	#	Date	#	Date					
Soccer balls	Size 3 Mikasa	120	6/5	30	6/5	4	6/5	15	6/10	7/5	161	vendor info. P.O. # cost

Form 6.3B Sample Inventory Form

Item: _Soccer balls size 3_

	Date: January	Date: June	Date: January	Date: June
Description	Size 3 Mikasa			
Quantity in	120			
Quantity out	38			
Quantity deleted	4			
Quantity ordered	10			
Date ordered	3/1			
Quantity received	10			
Date received	3/30			
New total	164			
	Mikasas don't deflate quickly			
Notes	—use same brand for next season.			

Sample Press Release

Your Logo

June 17, 1994

White Pine Park District
706 Kenwood Road
Bloom Hills, IL 61821

Release date: For immediate release

Contact: Amy Hurd, Marketing/Special Event Coordinator, 523-2550

On Saturday, August 20, in Centennial Park, male and female athletes of all ages will be facing the challenge of the White Pine Park District's 12th Annual Mini-Triathlon.

The Mini-Triathlon is a physical and mental test of strength and endurance. The event consists of a 400-meter swim, a 6-mile bike ride, and 2-mile run. Men's and women's categories are divided according to age, with prizes awarded to the top three finishers in each division.

"We are excited to offer this athletic opportunity to our community," says Kevin Crump, White Pine Park District Sports Coordinator. "Our participants range in age from 5 to 80. You definitely don't have to be an ironman to compete in this triathlon."

Preregistration is required for the Mini-Triathlon. The $20 registration fee includes a Mini-Triathlon T-shirt. Registration is being accepted through Friday, August 12, at the Bresnan Meeting Center, 706 Kenwood Road, Bloom Hills.

For more information on the Mini-Triathlon or other White Pine Park District programs, call 523-2550.

10TH Annual
TWIN CITIES TWOSOME

May 19th, 2001 • 9AM
Crystal Lake Park • Urbana, IL

Fundraiser for A Woman's Fund
and the Transition Initiative and Men's
Emergency Services (T.I.M.E.S.) Center

2 x 5K Relay Run   **5K Open Run**
2 x 2.5K Relay Walk   **5K Open Walk**

Staff Planning Form

Review the list of positions and mark out those not needed for your event. Insert position titles for those needed in the space marked "Other." Then complete the information requested in the columns for each position as you review each task in your planner. In this form you enter only the manager's name for each planning category, not the names of the support staff. We assume you will have only one manager for each category. Often the same person will manage several categories. The Hours/Day column is to provide you with an estimate of how many hours the person will need to work to complete the task assigned.

Position	Hours/Day	# Needed
Event Director _____		
Event Planning Assistant	_____	_____
Clerical Assistant	_____	_____
Computer Assistant	_____	_____
Other	_____	_____
Other	_____	_____
Financial Manager _____		
Fund raisers	_____	_____
Other	_____	_____
Other	_____	_____
Rules and Officials Manager _____		
Officials (umpires, referees)	_____	_____
Scorekeepers	_____	_____
Timers	_____	_____
Judges	_____	_____
Announcers	_____	_____
Other	_____	_____
Other	_____	_____
Coaching Manager _____		
Coaches	_____	_____
Assistant Coaches	_____	_____
Team Statisticians	_____	_____
Other	_____	_____
Other	_____	_____

(continued)

Risk Manager _____

    Physicians   _____   _____

    Trainers   _____   _____

    Other

    Other

Registration Manager _____

    Registration Clerks

    Check-in Manager

    Other

    Other

Scheduling Manager _____

    Other

    Other

Facility Manager _____

    Facility Supervisor

    Facility Maintenance Workers

    Technical Assistants

    Ticket Takers

    Ushers

    Parking Assistants

    Other

    Other

Event Equipment Manager _____

    Site Equipment Manager

    Other

    Other

Awards Manager _____

    Awards Presenters

    Other

    Other

Food Manager _____

    Food Preparers   _____   _____

    Food Sellers   _____   _____

    Food Cleanup Workers   _____   _____

    Other   _____   _____

    Other   _____   _____

Transportation Manager _____

    Drivers   _____   _____

    Other   _____   _____

    Other   _____   _____

Housing Manager _____

    Other   _____   _____

    Other   _____   _____

Promotion Manager _____

    Merchandise Seller   _____   _____

    Other   _____   _____

    Other   _____   _____

Public Relations Manager _____

    Photographer   _____   _____

    Publications Assistant (programs, brochures)   _____   _____

    Other   _____   _____

    Other   _____   _____

Communications Manager _____

    Other   _____   _____

    Other   _____   _____

Staffing Manager _____

    Volunteer Help Manager   _____   _____

    Paid Help Manager   _____   _____

    Gate Help Manager   _____   _____

    Scorekeeper Manager   _____   _____

    Other   _____   _____

    Other   _____   _____

American Academy of Pediatrics List of Disqualifying Conditions

This table is designed to be understood by medical and nonmedical personnel. In the "Explanation" section below, "needs evaluation" means that a physician with appropriate knowledge and experience should assess the safety of a given sport for an athlete with the listed medical condition. Unless otherwise noted, this is because of the variability of the severity of the disease or of the risk of injury among the specific sports, or both.

Condition	May participate
Atlantoaxial instability* (instability of the joint between cervical vertebrae 1 and 2) Explanation: Athlete needs evaluation to assess risk of spinal cord injury during sports participation.	Qualified yes
Bleeding disorder* Explanation: Athlete needs evaluation.	Qualified yes
Cardiovascular diseases	
Carditis (inflammation of the heart) Explanation: Carditis may result in sudden death with exertion.	No
Hypertension (high blood pressure) Explanation: Those with significant essential (unexplained) hypertension should avoid weight and power lifting, body building, and strength training. Those with secondary hypertension (hypertension caused by previously identified disease) or severe essential hypertension need evaluation.	Qualified yes
Congenital heart disease (structural heart defects present at birth) Explanation: Those with mild forms may participate fully; those with moderate or severe forms or who have undergone surgery need evaluation.	Qualified yes
Dysrhythmia (irregular heart rhythm) Explanation: Athlete needs evaluation because some types require therapy or make certain sports dangerous, or both.	Qualified yes
Mitral valve prolapse (abnormal heart valve) Explanation: Those with symptoms (chest pain, symptoms of possible dysrhythmia) or evidence of mitral regurgitation (leaking) on physical examination need evaluation. All others may participate fully.	Qualified yes
Heart murmur Explanation: If the murmur is innocent (does not indicate heart disease), full participation is permitted. Otherwise, the athlete needs evaluation (see Congenital heart disease and Mitral valve prolapse above).	Qualified yes
Cerebral palsy* Explanation: Athlete needs evaluation.	Qualified yes

Condition	May participate
Diabetes mellitus* Explanation: All sports can be played with proper attention to diet, hydration, and insulin therapy. Particular attention is needed for activities that last 30 minutes or more.	Yes
Diarrhea Explanation: Unless disease is mild, no participation is permitted because diarrhea may increase the risk of dehydration and heat illness. See Fever below.	Qualified no
Eating disorders **Anorexia nervosa, Bulimia nervosa** Explanation: These patients need both medical and psychiatric assessment before participation.	Qualified yes
Eyes **Functionally one-eyed athlete, loss of an eye, detached retina, previous eye surgery, or serious eye injury** Explanation: A functionally one-eyed athlete has a best corrected visual acuity of < 20/40 in the worse eye. These athletes would suffer significant disability if the better eye was seriously injured as would those with loss of an eye. Some athletes who have previously undergone eye surgery or had a serious eye injury may have an increased risk of injury because of weakened eye tissue. Availability of eye guards approved by the American Society for Testing Materials (ASTM) and other protective equipment may allow participation in most sports, but this must be judged on an individual basis.	Qualified yes
Fever Explanation: Fever can increase cardiopulmonary effort, reduce maximum exercise capacity, make heat illness more likely, and increase orthostatic hypertension during exercise. Fever may rarely accompany myocarditis or other infections that may make exercise dangerous.	No
Heat illness, history of Explanation: Because of the increased likelihood of recurrence, the athlete needs individual assessment to determine the presence of predisposing conditions and to arrange a prevention strategy.	Qualified yes
HIV infection Explanation: Because of the apparent minimal risk to others, all sports may be played that the state of health allows. In all athletes, skin lesions should be properly covered, and athletic personnel should use universal precautions when handling blood or body fluids with visible blood.	Yes
Kidney, absence of one Explanation: Athlete needs individual assessment for contact/collision and limited contact sports.	Qualified yes
Liver, enlarged Explanation: If the liver is acutely enlarged, participation should be avoided because of risk of rupture. If the liver is chronically enlarged, individual assessment is needed before contact/collision or limited contact sports are played.	Qualified yes
Malignancy* Explanation: Athlete needs individual assessment.	Qualified yes

Condition	May participate
Musculoskeletal disorders Explanation: Athlete needs individual assessment.	Qualified yes
Neurologic **History of serious head or spine trauma, severe or repeated concussions, or craniotomy** Explanation: Athlete needs individual assessment for contact/collision and limited contact sports, and also for noncontact sports if there are deficits in judgment or cognition. Recent research supports a conservative approach to management of concussion.	Qualified yes
Convulsive disorder, well controlled Explanation: Risk of convulsion during participation is minimal.	Yes
Convulsive disorder, poorly controlled Explanation: Athlete needs individual assessment for contact/collision and limited contact sports. Avoid the following noncontact sports: archery, riflery, swimming, weight or power lifting, strength training, or sports involving heights. In these sports, occurrence of a convulsion may be a risk to self or others.	Qualified yes
Obesity Explanation: Because of the risk of heat illness, obese persons need careful acclimatization and hydration.	Qualified yes
Organ transplant recipient* Explanation: Athlete needs individual assessment.	Qualified yes
Ovary, absence of one Explanation: Risk of severe injury to the remaining ovary is minimal.	Yes
Respiratory **Pulmonary compromise including cystic fibrosis*** Explanation: Athlete needs individual assessment, but generally all sports may be played if oxygenation remains satisfactory during a graded exercise test. Patients with cystic fibrosis need acclimatization and good hydration to reduce the risk of heat illness.	Qualified yes
Asthma Explanation: With proper medication and education, only athletes with the most severe asthma will have to modify their participation.	Yes
Acute upper respiratory infection Explanation: Upper respiratory construction may affect pulmonary function. Athlete needs individual assessment for all but mild disease. See Fever above.	Qualified yes
Sickle cell disease Explanation: Athlete needs individual assessment. In general, if status of the illness permits, all but high-exertion, contact/collision sports may be played. Overheating, dehydration, and chilling must also be avoided.	Qualified yes
Sickle cell trait Explanation: It is unlikely that individuals with sickle cell trait (AS) have an increased risk of sudden death or other medical problems during athletic participation except under the most extreme conditions of heat, humidity, and possibly increased altitude. These individuals, like all athletes, should be carefully conditioned, acclimatized, and hydrated to reduce any possible risk.	Yes

Condition	May participate
Skin: boils, herpes simplex, impetigo, scabies, molluscum contagiosum Explanation: While the patient is contagious, participation in gymnastics with mats, martial arts, wrestling, or other contact/collision or limited contact sports is not allowed. Herpes simplex virus probably is not transmitted via mats.	Qualified yes
Spleen, enlarged Explanation: Patients with acutely enlarged spleens should avoid all contact sports because of risk of rupture. Those with chronically enlarged spleens need individual assessment before playing contact/collision or limited contact sports.	Qualified yes
Testicle, absent or undescended Explanation: Certain sports may require a protective cup.	Yes

*Not discussed in text of this monograph.

**Mild, moderate, and average congenital heart disease are defined in 26th Bethesda Conference: Recommendations for determining eligibility for competition in athletes with cardiovascular abnormalities. January 6-7, 1994. *Med Sci Sports Exerc* 1994: 26 (10 Suppl):S240-253.

Reprinted, with permission, from Committee on Sports Medicine and Fitness, 2001, Medical Conditions Affecting Sports Participation. *American Academy of Pediatrics* 105(5):1205-1209.

American Academy of Pediatrics Recommendations for Human Immunodeficiency Virus [Acquired Immunodeficiency Syndrome (AIDS) Virus] in the Athletic Setting

Because athletes may bleed following trauma, they represent a theoretical risk to others if they are infected with the human immunodeficiency virus [HIV, acquired immunodeficiency syndrome (AIDS) virus]. Two questions have concerned coaches, athletic trainers, and school administrators: Should an athlete known to be infected with HIV be allowed to participate in competitive sports, and should the universal precautions recommended for health care workers (1) be used when handling athletes' blood and body fluids? The risk of infection from skin exposure to the blood of a child or adolescent infected with HIV is unknown, but it is apparently minute and is much less than the risk of HIV infection by needlesticks from infected patients of approximately 1:250 (2). Although it is theoretically possible that transmission of HIV could occur in sports such as wrestling and football in which bleeding and skin abrasions are common, no such transmission has been reported in these sports. There is one report of possible transmission of HIV involving a collision between soccer players (3). However, this report from Italy remains undocumented.

If an HIV-infected athlete would choose to pursue another sport, this possible risk to others would be avoided; but, in the absence of any proven risk, involuntary restriction of an in-fected athlete is not justified. Informing others of the athlete's status would probably lead to his or her exclusion due to inappropriate fear and prejudice and therefore should also be avoided. This advice must be reconsidered if transmission of HIV is found to occur in the sports setting. Athletes should also be made aware of the hazards of needle sharing for illicit drug use, including steroids.

Universal precautions adapted for the athletic setting are provided in Recommendation 6 below. Risk of exposure to a variety of infectious diseases is greater for coaches and trainers because of their interaction with many athletes. Competitors have extraordinarily low exposure rates. Coaches and athletic trainers should use these precautions if they are exposed repetitively to athletes' blood because a rare athlete may have an HIV infection and because the athletic staff may not know this (as a result of the current practice of nondisclosure or because HIV-infected individuals may be asymptomatic and unaware of their infection).

The American Academy of Pediatrics recommends the following guidelines:

1. Athletes infected with HIV should be allowed to participate in all competitive sports. This advice must be reconsidered

if transmission of HIV is found to occur in the sports setting.

2. A physician counseling a known HIV-infected athlete in a sport involving blood exposure, such as wrestling or football, should inform him of the theoretical risk of contagion to others and strongly encourage him to consider another sport.

3. The physician should respect an HIV-infected athlete's right to confidentiality. This includes not disclosing the patient's status of infection to the participants or the staff of athletic programs.

4. All athletes should be made aware that the athletic program is operating under the policies in Recommendations 1 and 3.

5. Routine testing of athletes for HIV infection is not indicated.

6. The following precautions should be adopted:

    a. Skin exposed to blood or other body fluids visibly contaminated with blood should be cleaned as promptly as is practical, preferably with soap and warm water. Skin antiseptics (e.g., alcohol) or moist towelettes may be used if soap and water are not available.

    b. Even though good hand-washing is an adequate precaution (4), water-impervious gloves (latex, vinyl, etc.) should be available for staff to use if desired when handling blood or other body fluids visibly contaminated with blood. Gloves should be worn by individuals with nonintact skin. Hands should be washed after glove removal.

    c. If blood or other body fluids visibly contaminated with blood are present on a surface, the object should be cleaned with fresh household bleach solution made for immediate use as follows: 1 part bleach in 100 parts of water, or 1 tablespoon bleach to 1 quart water (hereafter called "fresh bleach solution"). For example, athletic equipment (e.g., wrestling mats) visibly contaminated with blood

should be wiped clean with fresh bleach solution and allowed to dry before reusing.

    d. Emergency care should not be delayed because gloves or other protective equipment are not available.

    e. If the caregiver wishes to wear gloves and none are readily available, a bulky towel may be used to cover the wound until an off-the-field location is reached where gloves can be used during more definitive treatment.

    f. Each coach and athletic trainer should receive training in first aid and emergency care and be provided with the necessary supplies to treat open wounds.

    g. In sports with direct body contact and other sports where bleeding may be expected to occur a skin lesion should be cleansed immediately with a suitable antiseptic and covered securely. If a bleeding wound occurs, the individual's participation should be interrupted until the bleeding has been stopped and the wound is both cleansed with antiseptic and covered securely or occluded (5).

    h. Saliva does not transmit HIV. However, because of potential fear on the part of those providing cardiopulmonary resuscitation, breathing (Ambu) bags and oral airways for use during cardiopulmonary resuscitation should be available in athletic settings for those who prefer not to give mouth-to-mouth resuscitation.

    i. Coaches and athletic trainers should receive training in prevention of HIV transmission in the athletic setting; they should then help implement the recommendations suggested above.

Committee on Sports Medicine and Fitness, 1990-1991

Michael A. Nelson, MD, Chairman
Barry Goldberg, MD

Sally S. Harris, MD

Gregory L. Landry, MD

David M. Orenstein, MD

William L. Risser, MD

Liaison Representatives

Kathryn Keely, MD, Canadian Paediatric Society

Richard Malacrea, National Athletic Trainers Association

Judith C. Young, PhD, National Association for Sport and Physical Education

AAP Section Liaison

Arthur M. Pappas, MD, Section on Orthopaedics

References

1. Centers for Disease Control. Update: recommendations for prevention of HIV transmission in health-care settings. MMWR. 1987; 36(Suppl. 1):1-18.

2. Henderson, D.K., Saah, A.J., Zak, B.J., et al. Risk of nosocomial infection with human T-cell lymphotropic virus type III/lymphadenopathy-associated virus in a large cohort of intensively exposed health care workers. *Ann. Intern. Med.* 1986; 104:644-647.

3. Torre, D., Sampietro, C., Ferraro, G., Zeroli C., & Speranza, F. Transmission of HIVI infection via sports injury. *Lancet.* 1990; 335:1105.

4. Task Force on Pediatric AIDS, American Academy of Pediatrics. Pediatric guidelines for infection control of human immunodeficiency virus (acquired immunodeficiency virus) in hospitals, medical offices, schools, and other settings. *Pediatrics.* 1988; 82:801-807.

5. World Health Organization in collaboration with the International Federation of Sports Medicine. Consensus Statement from Consultation on AIDS and Sports. Geneva, Switzerland: January 16, 1989.

National Sports Organizations

*These Web sites were available at the time of publication.

Archery

National Archery Association
1 Olympic Plaza
Colorado Springs, CO 80909
Phone: 719-578-4576
Fax: 719-632-4733
E-mail: info@USArchery.org
URL: www.USArchery.org

National Field Archery Association
31407 Outer I-10
Redlands, CA 92373
Phone: 909-794-2133
Fax: 909-794-8512
E-mail: wrueger@dotnet.com
URL: www.nfaa-archery.org

Baseball

American Amateur Baseball Congress
118 Redfield Plaza
P.O. Box 467
Marshall, MI 49068
Phone: 616-781-2002
E-mail: aabc@voyager.net
URL: www.voyager.net/aabc

American Legion Baseball
P.O. Box 1055
Indianapolis, IN 46206
Phone: 317-630-1213
E-mail: acy@legion.org
URL: www.legion.org/baseball/home.htm

Babe Ruth Baseball
P.O. Box 5000
Trenton, NJ 08638
Phone: 609-695-1434
URL: www.baberuthleague.org

Dixie Baseball
P.O. Box 877
Marshall, TX 75671
Phone: 903-927-2255
E-mail: boys@dixie.org
URL: www.dixie.org

**George Khoury Association
of Baseball Leagues**
5400 Meramec Bottom Road
St. Louis, MO 63128
Phone: 314-849-8900

Little League Baseball
P.O. Box 3485
Williamsport, PA 17701
Phone: 570-326-1921
URL: www.littleleague.org

**National Amateur Baseball
Federation**
P.O. Box 705
Bowie, MD 20718
Phone: 301-262-5005
E-mail: mabf1914@aol.com
URL: www.nabf.com

National Baseball Congress
P.O. Box 1420
Wichita, KS 67201
Phone: 316-267-3372

Pony Baseball/Softball
P.O. Box 225
Washington, PA 15301
Phone: 724-225-1060
E-mail: pony@pulsenet.org
URL: www.pony.org

USA Baseball
Hi Corbett Field
Tucson, AZ 85716
Phone: 520-327-9700
E-mail: usabaseball@aol.com
URL: www.usabaseball.com

Basketball

USA Basketball
5465 Mark Dabling Blvd.
Colorado Springs, CO 80918-3842
Phone: 719-590-4800
E-mail: fanmail@usabasketball.com
URL: www.usabasketball.com

Youth Basketball of America, Inc.
P.O. Box 3067
Orlando, FL 32802-3067
Phone: 407-363-9262
E-mail: yboahq@msn.com
URL: www.yboa.org

Little Dribblers Basketball, Inc.
911 Houston St.
Levelland, TX 79336
Phone: 806-894-1972
E-mail: littledribblers@door.net
URL: www.littledribbers.org

Bowling

USA Bowling
5301 S. 76th St.
Greendale, WI 53129-0500
Phone: 414-421-9000
E-mail: cpon@bowl.com
URL: www.bowl.com

Young American Bowling Alliance
5301 South 76th St.
Greendale, WI 53129
Phone: 414-421-4700
E-mail: jjocha@bowl.com
URL: www.bowl.com

Cycling

U.S. Cycling Federation
1 Olympic Plaza
Colorado Springs, CO 80909
Phone: 719-578-4581
E-mail: usac@usacycling.org
URL: www.usacycling.org

Diving

United States Diving
Pan American Plaza
Indianapolis, IN 46225
Phone: 317-237-5252
E-mail: usdiving@aol.com
URL: www.usdiving.org

Fencing

U.S. Fencing Association
1 Olympic Plaza
Colorado Springs, CO 80909-5744
Phone: 719-578-4511
E-mail: infor@usfencing.org
URL: www.usfencing.org

Field hockey

U.S. Field Hockey Association
1 Olympic Plaza
Colorado Springs, CO 80909-5744
Phone: 719-578-4567
E-mail: usfha@usfieldhockey.com
URL: www.usfieldhockey.com

Football

Pop Warner Football
586 Middletown Blvd, Suite C-100
Langhorne, PA 19047
Phone: 215-752-2691
E-mail: pwlsreg@aol.com

Golf

National Golf Foundation
1150 South US Highway 1, Suite 401
Jupiter, FL 33477
Phone: 561-744-6006
E-mail: ngf@ngf.org
URL: www.ngf.org

Gymnastics

U.S. Association of Independent Gymnastics Clubs
235 Pinehurst Rd.
Wilmington, DE 19803
Phone: 302-656-3706
E-mail: usaigc@delanet.com
URL: www.usaige.com

USA Gymnastics
201 S. Capitol, Suite 300
Indianapolis, IN 46225
Phone: 317-237-5050
E-mail: gg@usa-gymnastics.org
URL: www.usa-gymnastics.org

Ice hockey

USA Hockey
1775 Bob Johnson Dr.
Colorado Springs, CO 80906-4090
Phone: 719-576-8724
E-mail: usah@usahockey.org
URL: www.usahockey.com

Ice skating

Amateur Speedskating Union
651 Forest
Winfield, IL 60190
Phone: 630-784-8662
E-mail: ASUKostal@aol.com
URL: www.speedskating.org

Ice Skating Institute of America
17120 North Dallas Parkway, Suite 140
Dallas, TX 75248-1187
Phone: 972-735-8800
E-mail: ISI@SkateISI.com
URL: www.skateisi.ocm

U.S. Figure Skating Association
20 First St.
Colorado Springs, CO 80906-3697
Phone: 719-635-5200
E-mail: usfsal@aol.com
URL: www.usfsa.org

U.S. International Speedskating Association
P.O. Box 450639
Cleveland, OH 44145-0611
Phone: 440-899-0128
E-mail: usskate@ix.netcom.com
URL: www.usspeedskating.org

Judo

United States Judo Association
21 N. Union Blvd.
Colorado Springs, CO 80909
Phone: 719-633-7750
E-mail: usja@csprings.com
URL: www.csprings.com/usja/

United States Judo, Inc.
P.O. Box 10013
El Paso, TX 79912
Phone: 915-565-8754

Karate

USA Karate Federation
1300 Kenmore Blvd.
Akron, OH 44314
Phone: 216-753-3114
E-mail: usakf@raex.com
URL: www.usakarate.org

Roller skating

**U.S. Amateur Confederation
of Roller Skating**
4730 South St.
P.O. Box 6579
Lincoln, NE 68506
Phone: 402-483-7551
E-mail: usacrs@usacrs.com
URL: http://usarollerskating.com

Rowing

U.S. Rowing Association
Pan American Plaza
201 S. Capitol Ave., Suite 400
Indianapolis, IN 46225
Phone: 317-237-5656
E-mail: members@usrowing.org

Shooting

USA Shooting Team
1 Olympic Plaza
Colorado Springs, CO 80909
Phone: 719-578-4670
E-mail: Admin.Info@usashooting.com
URL: www.usashooting.com

Skiing

**Bill Koch Youth Ski League
(cross-country)**
P.O. Box 100
Park City, UT 84060-0100
Phone: 801-649-9090

U.S. Skiing
P.O. Box 100
Park City, UT 84060
Phone: 801-649-9090
E-mail: special2@ussa.org
URL: www.ussa.org

Soccer

American Youth Soccer Organization
12501 S. Isis
Hawthorne, CA 90250
Phone: 310-643-6455
E-mail: operations@ayso.org
URL: www.soccer.org

United States Soccer Federation
U.S. Soccer House
1801-1811 S. Prairie Ave.
Chicago, IL 60616
Phone: 312-808-1300
URL: www.us-soccer.com

Soccer Association for Youth
4050 Executive Park Dr., Suite 100
Cincinnati, OH 45241
Phone: 513-769-3800
E-mail: sayusa@saysoccer.org
URL: www.saysoccer.org

United States Youth Soccer
899 Presidential Dr., Suite 117
Richardson, TX 75081
Phone: 972-235-4499
E-mail: nationaloffice@youthsoccer.org
URL: www.usysa.org

Softball

Amateur Softball Association
2801 NE 50th St.
Oklahoma City, OK 73111-7203
Phone: 405-424-5266
URL: www.softball.org

**Cinderella Softball League, Inc.
Spruce St.**
P.O. Box 1411
Corning, NY 14830-1011
Phone: 607-937-5469
E-mail: croftjb@hotmail.com

Swimming

United States Swimming, Inc.
1 Olympic Plaza
Colorado Springs, CO 80909-5770
Phone: (719) 578-4578
URL: www.usa-swimming.org

Synchronized swimming

U.S. Synchronized Swimming, Inc.
Pan American Plaza
201 S. Capitol Ave., Suite 510
Indianapolis, IN 46225
Phone: 317-237-5700
E-mail: webmaster@usasynchro.org
URL: www.usasynchro.org

Taekwondo

United States Taekwondo Union
1 Olympic Plaza, Suite 405
Colorado Springs, CO 80909
Phone: 719-578-4632
E-mail: ustutkd1@aol.com
URL: www.ustu.com

Tennis

United States Tennis Association
70 West Red Oak Lane
White Plains, NY 10604
Phone: 914-696-7000
URL: www.usta.com

Track and field

USA Track and Field
One RCA Dome, Suite 140
Indianapolis, IN 46225
Phone: 317-261-0500
E-mail: usatfprogs@aol.com
URL: www.usatf.org

Volleyball

U.S. Volleyball Association
715 S. Circle Dr.
Colorado Springs, CO 80910-1740
Phone: 719-228-6800
URL: www.usavolleyball.org

Water polo

United States Water Polo, Inc.
865 W. United
Indianapolis, IN 46225
Phone: 317-237-5599
URL: www.usawaterpolo.com

Wrestling

USA Wrestling
6155 Lehman Drive
Colorado Springs, CO 80910
Phone: 719-598-8181
E-mail: admin@usawrestling.org
URL: www.usawrestling.org

Multisport Organizations

Amateur Athletic Union (AAU)
P.O. Box 10000
Lake Buena Vista, FL 32830-1000
Phone: 407-937-7200
E-mail: pam@aausports.org
URL: www.aausports.org

**American Alliance for Health,
Physical Education, Recreation and Dance
(AAHPERD)**
1900 Association Dr.
Reston, VA 22091
Phone: 703-476-3400
E-mail: evp@aahperd.org
URL: www.aahperd.org

Boys & Girls Clubs of America
1230 W. Peachtree St., N.W.
Atlanta, GA 30309
Phone: 404-815-5700
URL: www.bgca.org

Catholic Youth Organization (CYO)
580 E. Stevens St.
Indianapolis, IN 46203
Phone: 317-632-9311

Girl Scouts of the U.S.A.
420 5th Avenue
New York, NY 10018-2702
Phone: 212- 852-8000
E-mail: misc@gsusa.org
URL: www.girlscouts.org

Girls, Inc. National Headquarters
120 Wall St.
New York, NY 10005
Phone: 212-509-2000
E-mail: girlsincorporated@girlsinc.org
URL: www.girlsinc.org

**Jewish Community Centers
Association**
15 East 26th St.
New York, NY 10010-1579
Phone: 212-532-4949
E-mail: info@jcca.org
URL: www.jcca.org

National Council of Youth Sports
200 Castlewood Dr.
North Palm Beach, FL 33408
Phone: 407-844-1823

**National Exploring Division,
Boy Scouts of America**
1325 Walnut Hill Lane
P.O. Box 152079 (S210)
Irving, TX 75038-3096
Phone: 972-580-2000
URL: www.bsa.scouting.org

Police Athletic Leagues
200 Castlewood Drive, Suite 400
N. Palm Beach, FL 33408-5696
Phone: 407-844-1823

United States Armed Forces Sports
Hoffman Bldg. #1, Room 1456
2461 Eisenhower Ave.
Alexandria, VA 22331-0522
Phone: 703-325-8871

United States Olympic Committee
1 Olympic Plaza
Colorado Springs, CO 80909-5760
Phone: 719-632-5551
E-mail: weston@usoc.org
URL: www.olympic-usa.org

YMCA of the USA
101 N. Wacker Drive
Chicago, IL 60606
Phone: 312-977-0031
URL: www.ymca.net

YWCA of the USA
Empire State Building
New York, NY 10003
Phone: 212-273-7800
E-mail: jchestnutt@ywca.org
URL: www.ywca.org

Sport Organizations for Special Populations

American Athletic Association of the Deaf
3607 Washington Blvd., Suite 4
Ogden, UT 84403-1737
TDD: 801-393-7916
Voice: 801-546-2982
E-mail: homeoffice@usadsf.org
URL: www.usadsf.org

Dwarf Athletic Association of America
418 Willow Way
Lewisville, TX 75067
Phone: 972-317-8299
E-mail: Daaa@flash.net
URL: www.daaa.org

National Handicapped Sports
451 Hungerford Dr., Suite 100
Rockville, MD 20850
Phone: 301-217-0960

**National Wheelchair Athletic
Association**
3595 E. Fountain Blvd., Suite L-1
Colorado Springs, CO 80910
Phone: 719-365-9300

Special Olympics International, Inc.
1325 G St. N.W., Suite 500
Washington, DC 20005
Phone: 202-628-3630
URL: www.specialolympics.org

**United States Amputee Athletic
Association**
P.O. Box 210709
Nashville, TN 37221-0709
Phone: 615-662-2323

**United States Association
for Blind Athletes**

33 North Institute

Brown Hall, Suite 015

Colorado Springs, CO 80903

Phone: 719-630-0422

E-mail: usaba@usa.net

URL: http://usaba.org

**United Cerebral Palsy Athletic
Association**

25 W. Independence Way

Kingston, RI 02881-1124

Phone: 401-874-7465

E-mail: uscpaa@mail.bbsnet.com

URL: www.uscpaa.org

Winter Games for the Disabled

3701 Connecticut Ave., N.W., Suite 236

Washington, DC 20008-4556

Phone: 202-833-1251

Health and Medical Organizations Offering Recommendations on Youth Sport

Health and medical organizations offering recommendations on youth sports

American Academy of Family Physicians
11400 Tomahawk Creek Parkway
Leawood, KS 66211-2672
Phone: 913-906-600
E-mail: fp@aafp.org
URL: www.aafp.org

American Academy of Orthopaedic Surgeons
6300 N. River Rd.
Rosemont, IL 60018-4282
Phone: 847-823-7186
E-mail: webhelp@aaos.org
URL: www.aaos.org

American Academy of Pediatrics
141 Northwest Point Blvd.
Elk Grove Village, IL 60009-0927
Phone: 847-228-5005
E-mail: kidsdocs@aap.org
URL: www.aap.org

American Academy of Podiatric Sports Medicine
4414 Ives St.
Rockville, MD 20853
Phone: 800-438-3355
E-mail: info@aapsm.org

American College of Sports Medicine
401 W. Michigan St.
Indianapolis, In 46202-3233
Phone: 317-637-9200
URL: www.acsm.org

American Medical Soccer Association
350 Cheshire Dr.
Birmingham, AL 35242-3100
Phone: 205-991-6054
E-mail: jvpoa@juno.com

American Optometric Association
243 N. Lindburgh Blvd.
St. Louis, MO 63141
Phone: 314-991-4100
URL: www.aoanet.org

American Orthopaedic Society for Sports Medicine
6300 N. Rever Rd., Suite 200
Rosemont, IL 60018
Phone: 847-292-4900
URL: www.sportsmed.org

American Osteopathic Academy of Sports Medicine
7611 Elmwood Ave., Suite 201
Middleton, WI 53562
Phone: 608-831-4400
E-mail: aoasm@tmahq.com

American Running and Fitness Association
4405 East-West Highway, Suite 405
Bethesda, MD 20814
Phone: 301-913-9517
E-mail: run@americanrunning.org
URL: www.americanrunning.org

Canadian Academy of Sports Medicine
1010 Poytek St.
Glouchester, ON Canada K1J9H9
Phone: 613-748-5851
E-mail: jburke@casm-acms.org
URL: www.casm-acms.org

Canadian Association for Health, Physical Education and Recreation
1600 James Naismith Dr.
Glouchester, ON Canada K1B 5N4
Phone: 613-748-5622
E-mail: capherd@rtm.activeliving.ca
URL: www.cahperd.ca

National Athletic Trainers' Association, Inc.
2952 Stemmons Fwy., Suite 200
Dallas, TX 75247-6103
Phone: 214-637-6282
URL: www.nata.org

National Strength and Conditioning Association
1955 N. Union Blvd.
Colorado Springs, CO 80909-2229
Phone: 719-632-6722
E-mail: nsca@usa.net
URL: www.nsca-lift.org

National Collegiate Athletic Association
P.O. Box 6222
Indianapolis, IN 46206-6222
Phone: 317-917-6222
URL: www.ncaa.org

Sports and Cardiovascular Nutrition (SCAN) Dietic Practice Gro
216 W. Jackson Blvd.
Chicago, IL 60606-6995
Phone: 312-899-0040
E-mail: membrshp@eatright.org
URL: www.nutrifit.org

about the author

Rainer Martens has participated in sports all his life. He has coached at the youth, high school, and collegiate levels and has studied sport as a research scientist. The founder and president of Human Kinetics, he also started the American Sport Education Program, the largest coaching education program in the U.S. An internationally recognized sport psychologist, Martens is the author of more than 80 scholarly articles and 15 books, including *Successful Coaching*, the best-selling coaching book ever published, and *Joy and Sadness in Children's Sports*. He has also been a featured speaker at more than 100 conferences around the world and has conducted more than 150 workshops and clinics for coaches and athletes at all levels.

After receiving his PhD in Physical Education from the University of Illinois at Champaign-Urbana in 1968, Martens was a member of its faculty for 16 years. A past-president of the American Academy of Kinesiology and Physical Education, he has been recognized for his contribution to sport by the National Recreation and Park Association and by being inducted into the National Association of Sport and Physical Education Hall of Fame. He has received Distinguished Alumni awards from Emporia State University in Kansas (where he earned a bachelor's degree), the University of Montana (where he earned a master's degree), the University of Illinois, and Hutchinson High School.

Martens continues to enjoy sport today, especially senior softball. He was named a First Team All-American when his Daytona Beach team won the Senior National Championship in 2000.

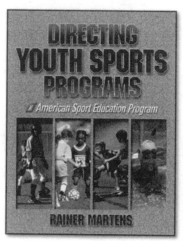
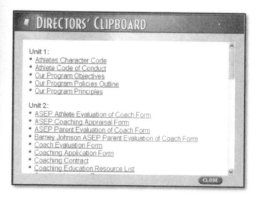